DAT ROSA MEL APIBUS

CLOCK SHAVINGS

By Tracy R. Twyman

O.:. L.:. E.:.

Clock Shavings

By Tracy R. Twyman

ISBN # 978-1-962312-20-2

Other Books by Tracy R. Twyman

Money Grows on the Tree of Knowledge

Solomon's Treasure: The Magic and Mystery of America's Money

The Merovingian Mythos and the Mystery of Rennes-le-Chateau

Mind-Controlled Sex Slaves and the CIA

The Arcadian Mystique: The Best of Dagobert's Revenge Magazine

Hocus Pocus: The Magical Power of St. Peter

The Judas Goat: The Substitution Theory of the Crucifixion

The Choice Vine: Mary Magdalene, the Sacred Whore, and the Benjamite Inheritance

The Cutting of the Orm: The Secret Calendar of the Priory of Sion

Dead But Dreaming: The Great Old Ones of Lovecraftian Legend Reinterpreted as Atlantean Kings

The Swedish witches had a special rite which was obviously intended to impress ignorant minds. They were given a little bag containing a few shavings of a clock to which a stone was tied; they threw this into the water, saying, 'As these shavings of the clock do never return to the clock from which they are taken, so may my soul never return to heaven.'

– Dr. Margaret Alice Murray, *The God of the Witches*

Contents

Preface

Anyone who asked me before about the Grail and took me to task for not telling him was very much in the wrong. Kyot asked me not to reveal this, for Adventure commanded him to give it no thought until she herself, Adventure, should invite the telling, and then one must speak of it, of course.

– Wolfram von Eschenbach, *Parzival*

The following is a true account of a series of deliberately invoked encounters with supernatural forces that took place from July 2001 until the present day. These events were experienced by both me, Tracy Twyman, and my husband, Brian Albert, along with other members of the occult group Ordo Lapsit Exillis, the secret order responsible for publishing *Dagobert's Revenge Magazine*. The details of the communications have been classified as *sub rosa* and *solis sacerdotibus* for many years now. Only recently, under influence from the spirit, has it been determined that it is proper now for a certain portion of this information to be shared with the general public.

Few people know the truth about the praeterhuman influences that operated behind the scenes of the OLE. Many people, including even me, have in public discussion referred to it as merely a group of friends associated with this particular publishing venture. It did indeed start out that way. However, once certain powers were tapped into, a chain of events was initiated that was impossible to stop: a chain of events that *initiated us* into the Western occult tradition. But unlike most students of the occult, we learned the mysteries of the Art directly from spirits.

Although I have alluded rather casually to these stories in several radio interviews I have conducted in recent years, the truth is that these are matters of utmost seriousness, and they deserve to be treated with respect. That is why I am presenting them with as much full context as I can with a delicate topic such as this, for the greatest understanding.

In the pages which follow are many transcripts of Ouija board sessions, as well as quotations from such sessions. The transcripts are mainly presented in script format. There are places within the scripts where it was necessary to provide comments or narration. For the most part, these are written in paragraph form, set within the transcript segments at the appropriate places.

In general, you will find that the words written by spirits have been put in all capital letters, especially in the transcript segments. Certain words or phrases that have been used by spirits when talking to us - the ones that are peculiar to these conversations - are also sometimes placed in all caps whenever they are repeated in the other segments of the book - at least in the first instance. Subsequent mentions are usually written in normal text format, depending on the context.

Lines in the transcripts do not have periods at the end unless there is more than one sentence in a particular line. Question marks are used when necessary. Normal punctuation is used, however, when the words of the spirit are presented in other places in this book beyond the transcripts.

In order to smooth the telling of the story, many portions of the transcripts are summarized or paraphrased in narrative form. I make it perfectly clear in the text when this is being done. It is obviously which parts are direct quotations, and which are summaries.

I have written these scripts so that it appears that I am the one mainly asking the questions. This, for the most part, was the case. However, there were many times in which the partners I was working with engaged in the discussion as well. I have tried, to the best of my memory and records, to attribute words to these other people as accurately as possible. But since I cannot be certain about each instance, I have by default attributed everything said on the human side of the conversation to myself, unless otherwise noted, to save everyone else the bother caused by having someone else's words put into their own mouths.

The word "we" generally refers to me and my late husband Brian Albert, although sometimes I use it more broadly to refer to the membership of the Ordo Lapsit Exillis, in particular the leadership. I made the assumption that most of the friends I worked with would not want their real names brought into this record, and therefore I have provided substitute names for these people. I have made an exception for those who are already public persons, as well as for Brian Albert.

As I write this, it has been almost two years since Brian's passing in March of 2012. It is in his memory that I dedicate this *revelatum*.

Also, I would like to give a special thanks to Chris Marchlewski for helping to make publication possible.

Tempora patet occulta Veritas.

Exordium: Ab Intio OLE

...No man can ever win the Grail unless he is known in heaven and called by name to the Grail ... Hear now how those who are called to the Grail are made known. On the Stone, round the edge, appear letters inscribed, giving the name and the lineage of each one, maid or boy, who is to make the blessed journey. No one needs to rub out the inscription, for once he has read the name, it fades before his very eyes.

- Wolfram von Eschenbach, Parzival

It all started one May morning, in Portland, Oregon. The year was 1996, and I was almost 18 years old. I was studying for my final exam in my Calculus class that I took at Portland Community College. I had dropped out of high school at age 14 and enrolled at the college instead. Now I was about to graduate with a high school equivalency diploma and an Associate's Degree simultaneously. As long as I passed all my finals, that is.

A few weeks earlier, a friend had lent me a copy of a nonfiction book called *Holy Blood, Holy Grail*, by Michael Baigent, Richard Leigh and Henry Lincoln. There I had learnt about the Holy Grail as a symbol of the divine essence of the universe - the hidden truth that organized religions try to hide from the masses. I learned that the secrets of the Grail rested with members of a particular bloodline, allegedly descended from Jesus and Mary Magdalene.

It appeared that the Catholic Church had attempted to exterminate this bloodline many times throughout history. But supposedly there was a secret society that had protected it, and the secrets of the Holy Grail, throughout the centuries: a group of mysterious Frenchmen called the Priory of Sion. This group was allegedly connected to a number of other secret societies with which I was already familiar, including the Freemasons, the Knights Templar, and the Rosicrucians.

This bloodline of Christ – this "Grail bloodline" – had allegedly resulted in the Merovingian kings of France, a medieval dynasty whose descendants could be found in almost every royal house in Europe. In the Priory's own literature it was strongly hinted that a king from this bloodline was destined to rule over a united European empire, and, perhaps, the world. This, the Priory's documents indicated, was the group's true agenda, in which many of the world's leading figures secretly conspired behind the scenes.

The Grail, in the view of these secret societies, seemed to symbolize the primordial occult power which was said to result from the union of opposite energies: particularly those of good and evil, male and female, fire and water.

In this way, it was similar to the Philosopher's Stone of the alchemists, and the "Kundalini power" of yoga.

Those of the Grail bloodline, it was implied, had that power inherently in their blood. The Holy Grail was written of in the Grail romances of medieval times as either a cup or a stone. As a cup, it had held the blood of Christ after he was crucified. As a stone, it was a magical jewel that had purportedly been chipped out of Lucifer's crown during his war with God's angels in Heaven. He who possessed the Grail had the power to rule the world.

Integral to all of this was a tiny village in the south of France called Rennes-le-Château. In the late nineteenth century the parish priest there at the Church of Saint Mary Magdalene, named Bérenger Saunière, had discovered some parchments underneath the altar of his church that were encoded with a hidden message. It was rumored that after having these parchments decoded, he had joined the Priory of Sion, and discovered a buried treasure somewhere in his environs that made him fabulously rich.

Supposedly, Saunière then used some of his money to redecorate his church in such a way as to communicate the secret of what he had discovered for future initiates of the Grail mysteries to decode. Or, at least, that's what authors on the subject had speculated was the reason for his decorations. Unraveling the enigma of Rennes-le-Château would be key for anyone seeking to understand the Holy Grail, the Grail bloodline, and the Priory of Sion. This was something stated in the Priory's own published literature.

I had been reading quite a lot of occult books in recent years about Freemasons, Aleister Crowley, conjuring spirits, Tantric sex magic, and the like. I found it all very fascinating. But this book about the Grail affected me like no other. I recall writing in my notebook that night that I felt "called to the service of the Grail."

According to the legends I had read, the Grail was sometimes depicted in medieval romances as a sacred stone which was possessed with a living intelligence. As the stories go, certain people are destined to serve the Grail, and when the time comes for them to be called to service, their names appear on the surface of the Grail stone. For some reason, I suddenly felt that I was one of the lucky few who had been chosen to fulfill that destiny. But I didn't know exactly what it would entail.

Later that morning, while studying for my final exam in Calculus, it came to me. It was like being struck on the head by lightning. I realized that I must create a magazine with the pretense of being published by the Priory of Sion. It would be called *Dagobert's Revenge*, after the last effective scion of the Merovingian kings of France, who was murdered in a coup orchestrated by the Catholic Church. I would fill the pages of *Dagobert's Revenge* with peculiar illustrations and curious sayings: occult shorthand meant to communicate to fellow initiates that I too knew the secret of the Grail.

I would try to catch the attention of the secret society underground I had read so much about, with the hopes of being initiated into one of the elite groups that held the ancient secrets of the Holy Grail, perhaps even the Priory of Sion itself. My tactic was to pretend like I was already one of them. I knew that someday soon, I would be reporting directly to the unknown superiors, serving the order in whatever way required. Perhaps they would want to use *Dagobert's Revenge* as an organ of propaganda. It could be a signpost pointing towards illumination for those who were earnestly seeking it. In this way, I might be able to serve the Grail, I thought.

So there I was at three o'clock in the morning, hunched over my notebook in bed, where I was supposed to be studying. But instead I was smoking cannabis and writing down ideas for this magazine I was going to create. I did not plan to make any money from it, nor did I have any idea how I would finance the publication of it.

I had a bit of experience with the process of publishing, thanks to my work at the school newspaper. But in this publication I did not intend to put any real information – only inferences. I would embed subliminal messages into the background, and leave everything in the foreground inscrutably cryptic. It would communicate something instantly recognizable to initiates, and instantly hypnotizing to those who were not.

As it got to be eight in the morning, I was still jotting down these thoughts. I knew that I had wasted my time and had not adequately studied. Now I had to get on the bus and head for school if I was going to make it in time for the test. But I was full of this pulsating energy. I could feel it burning like white light at the top of my head, then tingling through the rest of my body.

I had been struck by something powerful. I felt possessed. I continued to stay in that mental zone throughout the ninety-minute ride to school, including the change of buses at Fremont Avenue. The whole ride through I was writing out my plans for the magazine in my notebook, and did not turn my attention to Calculus until the moment I arrived at school.

Now here's the thing: I should have bombed that test. I hadn't studied, I hadn't gotten any sleep, and I was stoned out of my brain. But I still had that energy pulsating through my mind and body - the light of genius - and it was like the light took over for me so that I didn't have to think. I worked out the problems and wrote down the answers automatically, effortlessly, like I was folding laundry, or peeling a potato for dinner.

About twenty minutes later, as I set the completed test on the teacher's desk and walked out the door, leaving behind the nervous energy of my struggling classmates all sweating feverishly onto their scratch paper, I was strangely certain in the knowledge that I had gotten every answer right. The *hidden genius* that now possessed me had taken the test for me. Furthermore, I recall, somewhat with awe, that the entire time I had been taking the test my mind had been solely set on the magazine I was going to create.

The obsession with publishing *Dagobert's Revenge* continued as I finished off the school year. I learned that I did indeed pass the Calculus test with a score of 100%. At the school library I copied the pictures that I wanted to use from books, and I printed out the ones that I found on the internet (which was quite a different animal back in 1996). I also typed and printed out the key initiatory phrases I wanted to use throughout the document. Some of them were to be communicated subliminally, so I made pages onto which each phrase was printed in white, blurry text surrounded by a light gray fill. This made the words very difficult to read except at a certain distance. These pages then became the background on which the rest of the magazine's elements were to be laid.

I went to the art supply store and found a can of spray-on sticky stuff, which I applied liberally to the backs of the papers with the pictures and phrases I wanted to use. Then I cut out the words and pictures, arranging them on the background pages according to the directions I received from my hidden genius. When the document was complete, I knew it was done because it *shined*, just like the shining in my mind of the light that inspired me.

I went to Kinko's and had them print out one hundred copies of my publication. The guy behind the counter taught me how to arrange the pages I had (which were on 8 and 1/2" by 11" pages) into groups of four, each forming a double-sided 11" by 17" sheet. These would then be nested together and folded in the center with two staples going down the middle. While I was completing my layout, I noticed an elderly black lady and her five-year-old daughter leaning over, staring at my work. The lady had a flowery dress and the little girl's hair was braided with colorful animal-shaped barrettes.

"Are you a Freemason?" the lady asked, noticing Masonic symbols on one of the pages.

"No," I answered politely. "Only men are allowed to be Masons."

"That's not true", the lady replied. "I'm a Freemason. And I'm the Secretary." She reached into her purse and handed me a business card, identifying herself as the Secretary of a lodge of the Order of the Eastern Star, the Masonic ladies' auxiliary.

"Oh," I said. I didn't want to be rude and tell her that this wasn't as good as being a real Mason (or so I thought at the time). So I just smiled at her and put the card in my pocket. But I thought it was a strange coincidence that someone connected to the Masons in that way just happened to be standing next to me at Kinko's.

When my copies were done, they boxed them up, and I paid for them: one hundred copies for fifty dollars. That night when I got home, I folded the pages, collated them, and stapled them into booklets.

The next day I went out and delivered about half of them. I decided I would just disperse them for free wherever I could, and let divine providence lead the people to it. I left some in the section of Powell's Books where free literature was distributed, as well as Django Records, Ozone Records, and Rocco's Pizza. I left it upside-down on the tables of coffee shops. I left it at Panurge Emporium, the occult shop run by the local lodge of the Ordo Templi Orientis (the ritual magic group associated with Aleister Crowley). I slid it through the mail slot of several Masonic lodges. I left it at a place called Reading Frenzy that sold a lot of "'zines," as they were called, an underground industry that I was only vaguely aware of until I decided to create a 'zine myself.

When I revisited all of my distribution points a week later, there were no copies left anywhere. I used all but a handful of my last copies to restock these locations. The lady at Reading Frenzy - Chloe - told me that my 'zine had been very well-received by her customers. She said that I should do more issues, and that I should consider charging a cover price.

However, it took three more years before that initial effort was followed up by a new volume of *Dagobert's Revenge Magazine*. By that time, I was living in Union City, New Jersey, across the Hudson River from Manhattan, and preparing to study film at a local university. I was also in the mood to start some kind of business venture.

Luckily, my best friend Brian Albert from back home in Oregon came for a visit. We had known each other since we were twelve, in junior high, back in a little town called Sherwood. There we had attended a bit of high school together, before dropping out within a year of each other, and then starting together at the local community college instead.

Brian was tall, and heavy set, with dark hair. He usually wore black jeans and a black t-shirt every day. We both had gotten into Goth music around the same time as teenagers, and he was still into it. He was a bit shy when meeting new people, but a brilliant conversationalist once you got him going.

He had always been just about the smartest person I knew. In addition to his encyclopedic knowledge of plant biology, he also had a great deal of tangential information on file in his head about all sorts of things. He had great listening skills and a lengthy attention span too. Therefore, I frequently shared my ideas with him, as I valued his input.

I asked Brian if he was interested in starting some sort of business with me. Over the next few days, we passed a number of different ideas back and forth. We considered having a record company, and a band management company. It all seemed like too much work, and too risky. Finally, on the last day he was there, Brian convinced me that the most brilliant project I'd ever done was *Dagobert's Revenge*, and that I should do it again.

I had not thought about the 'zine at all since putting out that first issue. However, Brian thought that if we filled it with actual articles on the subjects of the Holy Grail and secret societies, it could gain a real following. If we included reviews and interviews of Goth bands that utilized occult themes in their works, we could probably get record stores to carry it, and record companies might be willing to advertise too.

To encourage me, he showed me a republished review of *Dagobert's Revenge* in a list of "'zine reviews" online from another 'zine called *Ben is Dead*. It seemed like the reviewer enjoyed it and found it rather enigmatic. That was all the ego stroking I needed.

Brian pressured me to set up a meeting with my friend Fred Berger, who published the famous Goth magazine Propaganda. A while back, I had sent Fred some poetry, and he had asked me to write some record reviews for him. He agreed to meet us at a Mexican restaurant in Manhattan, where he told us what he knew about independent magazine publishing.

Fred gave us invaluable information about getting advertisers and distributors. He also tried to discourage us from wasting our money on what he felt was a dying industry where only the big players could ever turn a profit. When he heard what type of magazine we wanted to publish, he thought we were utterly insane. "How many people on Earth would ever want to read a magazine about such an obscure topic?" he wondered.

I didn't blame him for his skepticism, but I wanted to venture forth anyway. He kindly offered me his best wishes, and a copy of a book called *Guardians of the Grail*, written by a Christian evangelist called J.R. Church. It was about how the author thought the "bloodline of the Holy Grail" was destined to bring forth the Anti-Christ.

That summer, Brian and I decided to reignite *Dagobert's Revenge* together, this time as a serious commercial effort. It took me six months to write articles and layout the next issue. Then, with some Christmas money from my parents and one hundred dollars kicked in by Brian, I printed it at a Lazerquick in Secaucus, New Jersey.

It ran over eighty pages this time, and included several articles written by me under pseudonyms. On Brian's advice, I included reviews of CDs and videos that had been sent to us upon request by various underground media companies. We started out distributing it ourselves. I walked on foot around Manhattan finding book stores, record stores, and occult shops that would take it on consignment. Brian did the same things back in Portland. The first one hundred copies sold out quickly. We printed another round, which sold even quicker.

At this point, we started selling advertising so that we could print another issue, mostly to record companies. We made a deal with the Small Publisher's Co-Op so that we could print a thousand copies of the next one. We even got three magazine distributors who placed *Dagobert's Revenge* in stores all over the country, as well as some places in Europe and Canada.

By the time the next issue came out, our website was getting several hundred hits a day. We were getting a continuous stream of gushing fan mail, as well as unsolicited guest submissions coming in from known occult authors. People reacted strongly to it because there was nothing else like it on Earth. Apparently the combination of subjects that we discussed appealed to an underserved segment of the reading public that had in fact been waiting for something just like this to come along.

I was being invited to do radio interviews constantly. There was even an internet TV show based in Manhattan which asked to have me on as a guest. It was "The Infinity Factory," hosted by up-and-coming young media mogul Richard Metzger of the Disinformation Company. It seemed like I had found my niche as a writer, quite unexpectedly.

Composing in-depth articles for the magazine really sped up the process of my initiation into the mysteries of Western occultism. I especially began to learn more about the topics of the Holy Grail, the Knights Templar, Freemasonry, the Priory of Sion, and the mystery of Rennes-le-Château. I started to notice patterns in the details of these subjects that few others seemed to be pointing out. In fact, almost all the authors ignored these things.

In my research I traced the imagery associated with the Grail symbol and bloodline beyond Jesus and Mary Magdalene (the standard stopping-point for most of the other writers at that time). Instead, I took it literally all the way back to the dawn of history. To me, it seemed to actually originate in the Garden of Eden, and with the god-kings of ancient Sumer, or even the lost kingdom of Atlantis.

From what I could tell, both the legendary Grail stone and the Grail bloodline were most definitely related to the myths of Satan, Lucifer, or the Devil. Specifically, it seemed that the bloodline could be traced back to an ancient deified king recorded in the chronicles of ancient Mesopotamia, whom some historians had once believed to be the inspiration for the biblical figure of Cain. My research concurred with this analysis. There were also Jewish fables stating that Cain had been spawned not by Adam, but by the serpent that tempted Eve in the Garden.

A related subject was the race of the Nephilim discussed briefly in *The Book of Genesis*, and more fully in apocryphal tomes like *The Book of Enoch* or *The Book of the Cave of Treasures*. As the story goes, in the beginning, angels defied God to come down from Heaven and mate with human females. The women then gave birth to a monstrous race of giants resulting from the hybridization of human and angelic blood. They were considered an abomination by God, who brought the Deluge upon the Earth to wipe them out, killing all mankind along with them. Then He punished the angels who had defied Him by imprisoning them beneath the Earth.

The bloodline of Cain, then, was the same as the so-called "Grail bloodline" in my eyes. Furthermore, it seemed to me that it was really a dynasty of human monarchs alleged to be descended from the fallen angels. As I studied different creation myths from around the world, I found that they all told a similar story about the origin of their first kings, who were also worshiped as incarnate gods.

These god-kings had civilized the Earth after the destruction of the Flood, teaching mankind how to farm, write, and build cities. They were remembered fondly because of it. But orthodox religions had apparently taken great pains to cover up these myths, perhaps because they did not want anyone to remember the royal bloodline that descended quite literally from the Devil himself.

What was the ultimate meaning of this? I had no idea, but I wanted to find out. For that, I would have to take my studies to the next level, to bring this field of research to a place it had never been before. To this end, Brian and I talked about forming a real secret order of our own.

In the very first issue of Dagobert's Revenge, I had identified myself as the "Exalted Grand Master." Of what, I did not specify. Now it seemed like we ought to come up with a structure to go with the title. The goal of this organization would be to further our esoteric studies into the mysteries of the Grail, and to disseminate this information via the magazine, as well as other organs.

Some of our research would be understandable only by occult initiates, and we knew that. But we also wanted to inject these ideas into popular culture, and various subcultures, in a way that had never been done: to explode a "Grail bomb" in the minds of the masses. We hoped that by launching this organization, we would be put into contact with initiates of other secret societies that might be able to help us in our work.

We called the group Ordo Lapsit Exillis, the incorrect Latin phrase used by the twelfth and thirteenth century German poet Wolfram von Eschenbach to refer to the Grail stone that "fell from Heaven." If the Latin were correct, it would translate to "the Stone of Exile." We decided to use the Cross of Lorraine, a symbol used by both the Knights Templar and the Grail-connected house of Lorraine, as our official insignia.

Our efforts did get the attention of several very strange people. In fact, virtually everyone who wrote to us was some kind of weirdo. We got more than our fair share of mail from prison: mostly people begging for free reading material, with some sending in money for subscriptions. Whenever we sent a magazine to someone in prison, we would always get it back a few weeks later with a note saying that it had been rejected by the censorship board.

Many of our fans wrote long, rambling, nonsensical letters about their ancestry, connecting themselves to the Grail bloodline. Many seemed to think that they were destined to fulfill some kind of grand purpose, and that we would somehow be able to help them with it. Some claimed to be members of various secret societies. Someone claiming to be the leader of the "American Priory of Sion" even contacted me and offered me membership.

I didn't take any of this stuff seriously. Every time I read one of these letters, my instinct told me to stay far away from these people. I knew that *Dagobert's Revenge* would eventually bring me into contact with initiates of the highest order, who would instruct me on how to fulfill my own destiny. So I waited patiently for my unknown superiors to show themselves to me.

But there was one crazy person with outrageous claims that I did pay attention to, because he really seemed to know what he was talking about. He was a man who called himself "Prince Nicholas de Vere von Drakenberg." Despite the noble title, he had a decidedly unglamorous life. He lived in London, but he was from Wales. He was on the dole, and he had been diagnosed with severe mental illness, for which he was taking medication. But despite his personal drawbacks, I found the man extremely interesting.

A good many of the conclusions that I had come to in my research were also found in the writings of Prince Nicholas de Vere, who claimed to be the head of a family descended from the Grail blood. He had written a book about his family history which he said could be traced back to Sumerian gods, and a super-human race that he termed "the Dragons." At one time, they had ruled the ancient world, and some day, he wrote, they would rule again.

He said the people of this race possessed magical powers, which is why, in olden times, they were seen as the natural leaders of human societies. The stories of fairies, pixies, elves, vampires and witches from medieval times were really based on memories of this illustrious Dragon race. They had been largely exterminated, and viciously persecuted, by humans who had overthrown their kingdoms. Those that remained had retreated into hiding, in forests, mountaintops, and underground, leading to the rumors of fantastic creatures inhabiting these places.

But the good news was that some of them had survived, and continued their royal bloodlines, with their own secret royal courts and witchcraft covens. The one he belonged to was called "the Dragon Court," and he of course was the head of it. More than that, he actually proclaimed himself heir to the title "King of the Dragons," and a lot of other, more mundane titles as well. To back this up he had hundreds of pages of genealogies, which he has compiled, along with a family history, into a voluminous text called *From Transylvania to Tunbridge Wells.*

Unfortunately, he said that a former associate of his named Laurence Gardner, who had been helping him gather the material, turned on him all of the sudden. The man then published De Vere's work as his own, robbing him of all credit and royalties. This was all the more painful because this associate's book had gone on to become an international bestseller, netting hundreds of thousands of dollars.

I was familiar with the book, as I had already read it years before Nicholas contacted me. When I checked the book on my shelf, I found that it was dedicated to Mr. De Vere, and that Gardner thanked him in the acknowledgements for providing him with "privileged access to his household archives."

De Vere claimed to possess a right recognized by the British government that permitted him to create a sovereign nation over which he could rule. If he could afford to buy a private island, in theory, he could proclaim it the kingdom of Drakenberg, and the Queen of England would recognize it. Then he and his friends could live by their own rules there. It was this right of sovereignty which, he now believed, others were trying to steal from him.

A couple of years earlier, his Dragon Court had many more members, and had been operating out of London. But when Laurence Gardner left, many went with him, and formed their own Dragon Court, which had since then schismed even further. There were now no less than four "Dragon Courts" headed by former members of his own organization, all soliciting new recruits on the internet. They were also conferring royal titles within the principality of Drakenberg. This seemed to make him angrier than anything else they had done to him, for he said that he alone had the right to give these titles.

But for whatever reason, De Vere had decided not to fight them on any of it. He frequently called Laurence Gardner a plagiarist and a liar on internet chat groups, but would never move against him legally. He never challenged the rival Dragon Courts legally either. He just asked one of his few remaining loyal friends to put the text of his book up on the internet for him, and then retreated to lick his wounds.

Then *Dagobert's Revenge* magazine came around, and in one of our issues we published an interview I had done with representatives of a revived Scottish royal house. They were attempting to spearhead a pro-monarchist, secessionist movement. After running the interview, I had been bombarded with mail from people telling me that the interviewee, "Prince Michael Stewart of Albany," was making a false claim to the throne of Scotland. His genealogy and the organization that supported him were fake, these people all said. One of the letters was from De Vere.

He said that Prince Michael's revived "House of Stewart" was the bastard son of his own Dragon Court, operating without permission. Prince Michael's royal titles had all been conferred by De Vere. But they were not meant to bolster a claim to the Scottish throne. They had been titles in the principality of Drakenberg. They had been rescinded when Michael left the Dragon Court, but he was continuing to use them anyway.

This was how my relationship with De Vere had begun. We started exchanging emails, and he called me frequently on the phone. We found that our ideas on the subject of the Grail and Grail bloodline were almost identical: I, theorizing based on my research, and he, allegedly speaking from experience as the head of a prominent Grail family. We also found that we had a similar sense of humor and irreverent attitude towards societal norms.

We spent hours on the phone lambasting culture. He would sometimes get drunk on his end, and become a foulmouthed sailor, spewing profanities.

These insults he usually aimed at members of the modern Wicca movement, former Dragon Court members, or Tony Blair. His Queen's English morphed into a thick Welsh brogue that slurred more and more with every shot of whiskey. His writing was also in this voice, with the same type of humor, and that was part of why I liked it.

I had De Vere write a few articles for *Dagobert's Revenge*. He told me I was the only person who truly understood his writing. He offered to let me have the rights to his book if I could find a proper publisher for it. He made me a "member" of the Dragon Court, and also conferred, without my ever asking for it, a royal title upon me: Baroness Renee von Drakenberg. He did these things through the mail and over the phone even though we had never met in person.

I found it a bit embarrassing, because I didn't yet believe his wild claims were true. I also knew that he had always eschewed selling titles, because titles shouldn't be based on anything except ancestry, in his opinion. Was giving away a title to someone you like any better? He had asked me for a genealogy, to see if he could find proof of my "Dragon ancestry."

In response, I told him I didn't even know the name of my great-grandfather, but that I was descended from European and American peasant stock. As far as I knew, I had no royal genes. Still, he asked for a sample of my blood, claiming that there was a college in England that was studying the Dragon DNA and knew how to test for it. I found the claim and the request so absurd that I chose to ignore it.

Even though I had not spoken at all about these things in public, somehow the members of the rival Dragon Courts knew about my friendship with Nicholas De Vere. They also knew about the Baroness title and my membership in Court. I started receiving harassing emails from these various people.

One woman, using the screen name “Star of the Sea,” implored me to stop talking to Nicholas because he was "a fraud," and implied some kind of physical harm could come to me if I didn't. When I told this woman to screw off, I was suddenly dropped from a Priory of Sion-related email list where she was apparently influential. Another person - a man - threatened to sue my magazine into the ground because we had apparently printed without permission a few lines of his translation of a famous French poem. He would drop the suit, he claimed, if I disassociated myself with De Vere. In addition, other people lambasted me on internet chat groups for accepting a "fake" royal title, and implied that I had paid cash for it, or that De Vere and I were having sex.

I told Brian about my experiences with De Vere. He agreed that he was a weirdo and thought that I should be cautious in dealing with him. But he also thought that De Vere's writing was interesting, and his claims about the history of the Grail bloodline matched up precisely the ideas we were promoting in the magazine. So in the end it was decided that I would try to keep my relationship with him low-key, and would not involve myself any further in the Dragon Court. But I would continue to be friendly with De Vere, just in case he became useful somehow later on. Besides, I liked him anyway, even if he was a crazy drunk with delusions of grandeur.

It was around this point, sometime between the third and fourth issue of *Dagobert's Revenge*, that I became acquainted with another narcissistic alcoholic with severe mental problems. But this one's intentions were far more sinister. My decision to become involved with him was a fateful one.

The third issue of the magazine included an interview with Douglas Pierce of the dark folk band Death in June, which had been a favorite with me and Brian for many years. To us it seemed that they rarely did interviews, and they rarely toured America. How amazing it was, then, when I wrote them a letter asking them to do an interview for the small magazine I had started, and received a personal, hand-typed letter in reply from Mr. Pierce. Not only would he do the interview, but he said my magazine was one of the most interesting things he had ever seen!

Sometime shortly afterward I received a fan letter from a writer named Kevin Coogan. Within a couple of days of that, I coincidentally ran into a music 'zine at one of the stores that carried *Dagobert's Revenge*, containing an article by none other than Kevin Coogan! The article was about what he perceived as fascism and white power ideology in underground music. It traced the personal connections between a variety of musicians, artists, writers and publishers. It was almost a conspiracy theory. I began to research each individual mentioned in the article.

One of those discussed was a sort of avant-garde "noise" artist named Boyd Rice. As it turned out, Rice had appeared as a guest on several albums by Death in June. I don't even think Death in June had been mentioned in Coogan's article at all.

I was thunderstruck. I had never noticed Mr. Rice's name in the liner notes of the records before, but then again, I was just listening to the music. I wasn't, until then, someone who followed the details of who was in the band. So I just found it amazing that one of the people in Coogan's article was, coincidentally, connected to my favorite band. I wrote Mr. Rice a letter requesting an interview for *Dagobert's Revenge*.

But then a funny thing happened. I very quickly received a letter from him in reply, saying that when my letter to him had arrived, he was already at the Post Office to send a letter to me. He was interested in the Grail and someone had recommended our magazine to him. It seemed like an extraordinary coincidence. We talked on the phone, and became fast friends.

At this time, Brian and I decided to let him in on the secret of the Ordo Lapsit Exillis. He was very enthusiastic to become a member, and began mentioning his involvement with the Order in interviews he did with other magazines. He had previously been a High Priest of the Church of Satan, and one of their official spokesmen, as well as a close personal friend of Anton LaVey until his death.

Boyd told me that, after joining the OLE, he had written a letter of resignation from the Church and dated it December 23, which was St. Dagobert's Day and a date important to the mystery of the Grail bloodline. He said that he had a reputation as a Satanist as well as a Nazi sympathizer (due to elements in his music and public persona), which he wanted to change. He openly told me that he wanted build a new image based on his involvement with the OLE and *Dagobert's Revenge*. He thought that then he would be taken more seriously and be able to move beyond underground music into a career as a writer.

Boyd began calling me frequently, and conversing with me for long periods. In fact, I often had to avoid his calls just so that I could get my work done each day! He also sent me lots of letters and gifts in the mail. I was still living with my parents at the time, and I would frequently tell my mother to ignore the phone if the caller ID showed Boyd's number. Otherwise I would have had their phone line tied up all day.

I told him I was planning on writing a book about the Holy Grail. I had some experience writing a full-length nonfiction book a couple of years earlier (although it remains unpublished to this day). Therefore I felt that I had the self-discipline and organizational skills necessary to complete such a task. He suggested that he and I should write the book together. He had submitted an article to me about his Plantagenet ancestry (connected to the Grail blood), which wasn't bad. I figured his following of loyal fans might help with the marketing of the book, so I agreed.

A short while later, I received an email from the producers of a new Fox TV series that was in the works. It was going to be a revival of Leonard Nimoy's In Search of…, and they were going to do a segment on the mystery of Rennes-le-Château. They wanted to know if I would fly there with them to do an on-location interview about the subject. Of course I agreed. I also suggested they bring Boyd along, as he was going to be the co-author of my new book.

So this was how I got to see Rennes-le-Château, the center of the world as far as my research was concerned, with my very own eyes without spending a dime. As the production crew's rented van pulled up into the village, right up next to Bérenger Saunière's famous church, I felt the weight of my destiny come upon me. I was aware once again that something - some outer entity - had tapped me to do a job pertaining to the Grail mystery.

My being there at that moment was integral to the plan. I felt as if all of the details of my life since I'd started publishing *Dagobert's Revenge* had been arranged for me by someone unseen. It was all leading me to an unknown - but, I felt, important - destination. As I soaked up the details of the landmark for the first time with all of my senses awake, I knew that this was a mystery of historic proportions, and that somehow, I was a part of it.

Chapter 1: Testament of Cocteau

I remain with you.

- Epitaph of Jean Cocteau at the Chapel of St. Blaise

Within less than a year, Brian and I had moved in together in an apartment in Denver, Colorado, about three blocks from where Boyd Rice lived. It had been Boyd's suggestion, since he knew that I wanted to move in with Brian somewhere anyway, and he argued that it would help facilitate our book project. We had all been working on the research into the Grail mystery for a while now, sharing our discoveries and theories with each other. We knew that we were somehow involved in something important and even Boyd had reported that he had felt himself being guided in his research by an unseen hand since joining our mission.

For me personally, I was on fire intellectually. Whenever I decided to follow a particular line of inquiry, the information I needed would almost instantly come to me through no effort of my own. A book not considered to be relevant to the question at hand would fall off of a shelf and open to a particular page that contained just the clue I needed for what I was studying. A chance internet search about an unrelated topic could lead me there as well. I even discovered a key piece of information once in a magazine I found at the dentist's office.

Those spiritual influences were felt acutely when the Ordo Lapsit Exillis held its first ritual shortly after we moved to Denver. Looking back, I realize that this was the OLE's first step to becoming something more than just an occult research and publishing society. The newest member of our order was Boyd's friend Vadge Moore (drummer for the punk band the Dwarves). He decided to get married to his new bride in the apartment that Brian and I shared, right there in my office. We made it an official OLE event.

Boyd performed the service, since he had experience as a priest in the Church of Satan. He wore black pants, and a black shirt with a white priest's collar. We painted my office black for the occasion. Boyd brought over some decorations: a giant Cross of Lorraine, perhaps four feet tall, made out of five wooden planks spray-painted black; an antique sewing machine, folded up into a table that was used as an altar; a black alter cloth, a plastic silver-colored goblet with a real human skull resting inside of it; black candles; and a ceramic head of Bacchus, painted black and looking menacing, which was mounted to the closet door in my office.

Our apartment was made from the basement of a house, and there were water pipes hanging from the ceiling throughout the whole place. So with the black walls and all of these other additions, the result was very foreboding. When the guests arrived (some of them known musicians) we made them wait on the patio outside, where drinks were served. When the ceremony was about to begin, we put on a Hildegard von Bingen CD, placed black hoods (dyed pillow cases) on the heads of the guests, and led them down, hoodwinked, into the ritual chamber. The room was charged with a certain spiritual energy, obvious to anyone with the eyes to see it, and the guests certainly picked up on it.

Perhaps it was because we already thought ourselves subject to supernatural influence in our work that we felt inclined to seek even more. Therefore, Brian and I decided to use the Ouija board to contact one of the most misunderstood French artists of the 20th century: Jean Cocteau, who had died in 1963. He was alleged to have been a Grand Master of the Priory of Sion.

We hoped that he could illuminate some of the mysteries we were trying to solve about the Holy Grail. I had gotten the idea of using the Ouija board to contact him after reading about some of the table-rapping séances that Cocteau and his friends had famously performed. Perhaps, I thought, if he had talked to the dead while he was alive, he would be willing to talk to us now that he was dead.

I had never been successful with the Ouija board before. The few times I had used it in high school with other teenage girls, it had just been stupid. Everybody asked about who they were going to marry and things like that. When the answers came you could tell someone was pushing the planchette. But this time I had a good feeling about it.

So there I was with Brian, sitting in a blackened dungeon in Denver on a hot summer night in July 2001, choking on the smoke of incense, spooky music playing faintly in the background, with a Ouija board, a candle, and an empty jar of cumin on the table in front of us. We both took a deep breath and placed our hands on the jar. I cleared my throat and opened the séance:

"Jean Cocteau, are you there?"

Instantly, and much to our surprise, the bottle began to move. I could feel not only the bottle itself moving, but what seemed like a current of energy that pushed it in the direction it wanted to go. Because of its shape, the bottle wobbled awkwardly, but it did so quickly and purposefully. It stumbled directly up to the top of the board where the words "Ouija Board, by William Fuld" were written, and circled the first three letters, "OUI" The bottle circled these letters three times while Brian and I stared at each other, shocked. Then it wobbled over to the word "YES" written in the upper left-hand corner of the board, and stopped there.

"Wow," said Brian. "I really felt it moving!" I was astonished too. It was unlike any previous Ouija board experience I had ever had. There was no question of whether the other person was pushing it. You could *feel* the force that was doing the pushing, and it definitely wasn't coming from either one of us. I was filled with wonder and amazement, but no fear. The air seemed to be full of electricity.

"Well," I said, pulling myself together. "It seems to be working. I guess I should ask him some questions."

We still had our hands on the bottle, and as soon as I said that, it wobbled back over to the first three letters in "Ouija." We laughed. He seemed to be agreeing with us, and speaking in French! I fumbled for the notebook where I had written down the planned questions, which was sitting on the floor next to the coffee table. Then we put our hands back on the bottle.

"OK, Mr. Cocteau. Were you the Grand Master of…." Before I even finished the question, the bottle moved to the letter P. Then it went over to the number 0, the letter S, and the word YES. So he was able to anticipate my questions before I even spoke them!

"POS - Priory of Sion. Yes," I said. "That's what I was about to ask. So what is the meaning of …." Then he did it again. The bottle began moving before I finished speaking. It wrote:

"681681681681."

I had been about to ask him about the meaning of the enigmatic code number 681, mentioned in the mysterious parchments Father Bérenger Saunière had discovered at Rennes-le-Château.

"Yes, 681. That's right. What does it mean?" His reply came swiftly:

"DDDDDDDDD."

Here was yet another strange code, this one specifically related to Cocteau's work.

"Are you referring to the way you signed your painting of the Crucifixion at Leicester Square?" I asked. "With the initials DDD'?"

His answer was very odd: "666NWO."

We both took our hands off of the bottle.

"That was weird" said Brian. "What do you think that meant?"

I wrote the letters of his answer down in my notebook. Then I examined them carefully.

"Well, NWO could stand for 'New World Order,' and '666' for the Anti-Christ. But I don't know why he would be talking about that." Brian shrugged, and we put our hands back on the bottle.

"Jean, what can you tell us about the secrets of the Priory of Sion? What should we be looking for?"

A minute passed, and the bottle didn't budge. So I rephrased the question.

"What are the secrets of the Holy Grail?" I asked. Finally, the bottle wobbled slowly onto the letter C. Then it went to the sun symbol in the upper left-hand side of the board. It repeated this motion several times, moving in-between the C and the sun. I wasn't sure what this meant, so I asked for clarification:

"Jean, are you actually saying the letter 'C' and the Sun? What does that mean?"

He repeated it again several more times.

"Are you saying 'See the sun,' like with your eyes?" I asked. He confirmed.

"YES DO." He paused, and then continued, spelling out the words "LOOK C." Then he went to the sun again.

"Are you talking about the sun in the sky?" I asked. "Or is it the Black Sun?"

With the latter option, I was referring to the myth of the fiery dark orb that allegedly resides in the center of the Earth, according to the beliefs of certain German and Eastern mystics.

"Or," I continued, "are you talking about a picture of the Sun in one of your drawings or paintings?"

I thought of this last possibility, especially, because in more than one instance, Cocteau's work included pictures of people staring at the Sun with their eyeballs seemingly popping out of their heads. But he didn't answer. I repeatedly asked "What does 'See the sun' mean?" But all he could do was repeat that very phrase.

Then the bottle jerked its way over to the bottom left and right corners of the board. In each corner there was an identical drawing of two people playing with a Ouija board, and a tiny spirit hovering over them in the air. The bottle went back and forth between these two corners several times, each time centering itself upon the depiction of the hovering spirit. Then it began wildly wobbling onto different letters and numbers with no apparent meaning.

"ONACGSLNADNH316U8W9X9W82423UI3TOUHUD6UIWDKAW787STU VWXYZATUVRURURUNOQSUV756461723481748485748172381264848362381737823671278236756D," he wrote.

Afterwards the bottle returned to the center of the board. By the end of that spurt, our arms were aching.

"What was the meaning of that?" I asked.

"IAMBLCK04U," Cocteau replied. The bottle then seemed to actually slide rather than wobble down to the word "goodbye" at the bottom. It only stayed there for a second, where it appeared to levitate underneath our fingertips. Then it literally flew off to the left, zipping past the candle and falling onto the carpet. As it flew past, the flame on the candle suddenly became much brighter, and a sound like the zap of static electricity echoed through the air.

"Jesus, did you see what just happened to the candle?" Brian shouted. "And the bottle just flew right off the board!"

I was in a state of shock too. Throughout the entire event we had both maintained an eerie calm, not frightened in any way by our apparent encounter with the supernatural. I had always thought that I would flip out if I ever really saw a ghost or anything like that. But talking to the dead had put me in a state of wonder without fear. However, when the bottle flew off the board, I felt an electric surge up my spine, and my hair stood on end.

"Should we try to talk to him again?" I asked.

"I think he's done for now," Brian replied. "Let's try again when we can get a real planchette. I think he was pissed about the bottle."

"Yeah," I said. "I think that's why he kept going to the little spirit hovering in the corner: to indicate that he was having a hard time communicating. And in the end I think he was trying to say 'I am blocked for you.'"

"I wonder what 'see the sun' means," said Brian.

At three o'clock the morning after that first Cocteau séance, as I sat at my desk, staring at the sewing machine and the wooden cross (which were still there where Boyd had left them), I reflected on what had taken place in that very room a few weeks earlier. A (supposedly former) High Priest in the Church of Satan had performed a wedding right there, attended by well-known figures in the underground music scene, under the auspices of an organization that I Brian and I had created! Now, I realized, in the very same house, we had successfully contacted a famous dead artist, one of the former Grand Masters of the Priory of Sion. I must not be easily spooked, because I could definitely feel a presence in the room, but it didn't scare me one bit. It actually made me feel less alone. But the Bacchus head on the wall, with its terrifying, demonic facial expression, did creep me out a little bit, so I tried not to look at it.

I flipped through the notebook with the transcript of the séance. I couldn't believe it had really happened. We hadn't gotten any useful information, but Cocteau had definitely been trying to communicate. What did he really mean by "See the sun"? What about "666 NWO"? The term "New World Order" didn't become a buzz word for conspiracy theorists, and associated with the reign of the Anti-Christ, until well after Cocteau's time.

I decided we would have to work it out in a later séance. I told Boyd about what we had done, which seemed to excite him. He said he had a Ouija board planchette we could borrow, and promised to bring it by the next day. We agreed that the three of us would try to contact Cocteau together.

When he arrived the next day, I was sitting out on the patio by the table, on one of the white plastic chairs, sipping vodka and grape Kool-Aid. He was dressed as usual in black pants, a black Death in June t-shirt, and black slip-on shoes he had gotten out of the dollar bin at Walgreens. There were no socks. He was holding a plastic grocery bag with some stuff in it and he seemed to be in a good mood. He took a chair next to me and sat down.

"I tried contacting Cocteau last night," he said, taking the planchette out of the bag and placing it on the table.

"Oh, you mean you tried the Ouija board by yourself?" I asked.

"Yeah, I sat there for a long time with my hands on the thingy, and it never moved," he said. "But I felt like he was trying to contact me. So I laid down on the couch and tried to relax so he could contact me through my mind. I went to sleep and had this fabulous dream that I was a student in a classroom all by myself. Cocteau was the professor. And he was teaching me all of the secrets of the cosmos." I recognized the dream as being inspired by a scene from Cocteau's film *Testament of Orpheus*, which we had all watched together at our apartment the week before.

"Then when I woke up, I started flipping through this book about Cocteau again." He pulled a hard-bound book out of his bag that he had shown me many times before. He opened it to a bookmarked page that showed detail on

Cocteau's mural *St. Peter Walking on Water* at the Chapel of Saint Peter in Villefranche-sur-Mer, France. Then he pulled out a stack of papers from his bag, all of which showed a copy of that very same page in the book.

On each copy he had drawn various geometric figures, by connecting dots and intersecting lines in the mural. There was a pentagram on one page, a hexagram on another, a square and compass on still another. He thought he had made a new discovery of another secret code embedded in Cocteau's artwork, just as Grail researcher Henry Lincoln had famously discovered a pentagram "encoded" into Cocteau's mural at Leicester Square in London.

"Hmm," I said, not knowing what to make of it. I couldn't decide if it was meaningful, or if he was just projecting patterns onto a splatter of dots. It was interesting, but without an interpretation of a particular meaning for the code, I had no real use for it. I picked up the planchette. "Shall we begin?"

We went inside and set everything up as we had before, with the candles and incense. We didn't play any music, though. I decided to get my video camera out to record the session. We strapped it to one of the pipes on the ceiling and pointed it down on the board. Then we all sat down and placed our hands on the planchette. Because there were three of us, there wasn't enough room for each set of hands, so we just put our two fingers on instead. When it seemed like everyone was ready, I started:

"Jean Cocteau, are you there?"

With a bit of hesitation this time, the planchette started to move. It slid over to the word "YES." But I could tell that the weight of all six hands was making it difficult. So I asked Brian to take his hands off, and take notes in the notebook instead. We resumed the session.

"Boyd says you were visiting him in his dreams last night," I said. "Is that true, Mr. Cocteau?"

The planchette started to move again, but as it did, the board itself started pivoting on its axis, until it turned all the way around. We straightened it out and repeated the question, but it happened again. It was strange, because we hadn't had this problem at all with the first séance. Finally, Brian got a towel and placed it underneath the board so that it wouldn't move anymore. Then we started again.

"Jean, what secrets have you embedded into the mural of St. Peter Walking on Water?"

This time, the planchette glided rather easily across the board. Boyd's eyes widened. You could tell he was shocked that it was actually working. He was feeling for the first time the sensation of the planchette being moved by an invisible force, with his hands just being dragged along. It zipped through the entire alphabet, from the ends to the middle, in this fashion:

"AZBYCXDWEVFUGTHSIRJQKPLOMN."

"What does that mean?" I asked.

"C SUN C SUN C SUN," was the swift reply.

"I think the 'sun' may be a reference to Cain," I said, alluding to the biblical figure that I had theorized was a king of the ancient world and progenitor of the Grail bloodline. I had also theorized that the myth of the Black Sun might be symbolic of Cain in the underworld. Furthermore, Jean Cocteau had placed an image of the Black Sun in his Crucifixion mural at Notre Dame de France in London (portraying when the sun went dark as Christ died). So I decided to go ahead and ask.

"Cocteau, when you say 'c the sun,' are you referring to Cain?"

"YES," Cocteau replied. "C SUN C SUN C SUN."

"Is he the same as the Black Sun," I asked. The reply was the same:

"YES. C SUN C SUN C SUN. AZBYCXDWEVFUGTHSIRJQKPLOMN."

"What is that all about?" I questioned. "Are you trying to get us to look at the alphabet for some sort of clue?" All he said in reply was a repeat of the inverted alphabet sequence. He gave the same answer to the next few questions as well. Then he went into a long stream of seemingly random numbers and letters.

Finally Boyd took his hands off the planchette, and reached into his pocket for the can of snuff he always carried with him. He dumped some of the brown powder onto his hand between his thumb and forefinger, then snorted it up his nose, making a loud snuckering noise as he did. He seemed frustrated.

"Is everything OK?" I asked.

"This whole thing just seems like bullshit," he said. "I've never been able to get the Ouija board to work."

"But it's working now," I said.

"He's not saying anything that makes any sense! 'See the sun'? What are we supposed to do with that information?"

I didn't know how to react. The messages seemed at least as meaningful to me as the pictures Boyd had drawn on the copies of Cocteau's mural. Also, it's not every day that a dead French artist talks to you, even if you're not sure what he's saying. But I could tell that Boyd was choosing not to believe that the communication was real. Did he think that I was pushing the planchette? If so, why would I have made up answers like that?

"I've got an idea," said Boyd, placing his hands back on the indicator. "Can I ask a question?"

"Go ahead," I said, putting my hands back on as well.

"Does your consciousness tell you what people are thinking?" he asked. Cocteau replied in the affirmative.

"Then what letter am I thinking of."

I couldn't believe it. Boyd actually had the audacity to test Jean Cocteau in this manner! How rude! I was totally embarrassed. But the planchette immediately moved to the letter E. Boyd laughed.

"So why are you wrong?" he asked.

He was being a total ass. Cocteau responded again with the letter E. Boyd pushed the planchette away and got up in disgust.

"All right," he said. "You can keep the thingy. I'm going home." He picked up his book and his copies of the mural, excused himself swiftly. I locked the door behind him. I was surprised that things had gone so badly.

"Sorry about that," I said to Cocteau. "We'll try this again later, and we won't bring him next time."

I stopped the video camera and took the VHS-C tape out so that I could make sure it had recorded. I placed the tape in the converter case, which allowed it to be played on a regular VCR, then rewound it, and pushed play. I noticed something really interesting.

"Look at this," I said to Brian. "The shot is upside-down. It was upside-down the entire time."

"We'll have to remember to turn the board around the other way next time," he said.

"But that's not what's significant," I said. I pointed to the video. It was the beginning of the séance, before we put the towel down, when the board kept turning around.

"He was trying to turn the board around for us. He knew that the shot would be upside-down, and he was trying to fix it." We stared at each other for a moment in wonder and disbelief.

"Well, he is a filmmaker," Brian said. "He wanted us to get a good shot."

Cocteau's emphasis on the inverted alphabet sequence got me thinking about the fact that there were 26 letters in the modern alphabet, which was a factor of 13. I knew that there was a book called *Alphabet of the Sun*, written by a French journalist named Jean-Luc Chaumeil, who was known for his work on the subject of the Priory of Sion. Also, the Priory had published papers pertaining to the subject of a zodiac with thirteen houses, including the insertion of "Ophiuchus, the Serpent Holder" to the traditional twelve. Their writings indicated that they held some secret significance to this.

I reread *Holy Blood, Holy Grail* and *The Messianic Legacy* by Baigent, Leigh and Lincoln looking for clues about these ideas. I came across information that the Priory had published about the structure of their order. Specifically it was about how many members there were in each grade, which was a set amount.

There was one structure that existed, allegedly, prior to Jean Cocteau's Grand Mastership of the order. Then there was another set of numbers for the new structure after he "reformed" the Priory. I noticed patterns forming in both sets of numbers, particularly factors of 13. Of those, I noticed particularly the number 364, the total amount of members after the reforms.

What I found out, which I was totally unaware of before, was that 364 is the number of days in a lunar calendar year, with thirteen months per year. Also, if, theoretically, you were able to measure the solar year with such a calendar (in other words, if the year was just a little more than a day shorter), then each month would have 28 days exactly. Each month would start out on the same day of the week. This led me to intuitive leaps of understanding about a possible hidden 13-based time measurement system that might have been encoded in these numbers found within the Priory of Sion's structure.

I even realized that the same sets of numbers could be found in a traditional deck of playing cards. Originally this game had been used for divination, and it was the progenitor of Tarot cards. Was the calendar encoded in the playing cards too, maybe put there by occult initiates?

Perhaps also, I thought, the 26-letter modern alphabet was a repository of cabalistic secrets, as the Hebrew alphabet is seen to be. Maybe groups like the Priory of Sion were aware of this. Given the title of Jean-Luc Chaumeil's book, Alphabet of the Sun, I wondered about possible solar and lunar calendrical connections to the alphabet as well. I wanted to ask Jean Cocteau about this, and decided to pressure Brian for another séance.

Chapter 2: See the Sun

...It is desirable to note the distinction between good and evil Magic, between the Sanctuary of the Sons of Seth and the profanation of the science by the descendants of Cain.

- Eliphas Levi, *Magic: A History of Its Rites, Rituals, and Mysteries*

It wasn't until the end of October that we finally got around to using the Ouija board again. But then something happened that got our attention. We received in the mail what appeared to be a magazine almost identical in style and content to our own. The main difference was that it was in the German language, with *Wolfzeit* as the title.

They had articles about the Priory of Sion, Rennes-le-Château, the Knights Templar, and the Holy Grail. There was a Gothic look to the design, and it contained interviews with the same kinds of bands that we were reviewing in *Dagobert's Revenge*. It even had the Cross of Lorraine as a logo, just like we did, and "Mythos, Mystik, Minnesang" as a subtitle, very similar to our own "Musick, Magick, Monarchism."

Included in the package was a letter from the Editor, Peter Felsch. It stated that he had started his magazine a few months earlier (and thus much later than *Dagobert's Revenge* had started in 1996). But he was unaware of our existence until someone told him that his own magazine looked like "a German version of *Dagobert's Revenge*." He had researched the name and, sure enough, there was already an American publication very similar to his.

Brian and I found this a shocking coincidence, since our magazine was indeed so very unique. So shortly after receiving the package, on October 31, we invoked the spirit of Jean Cocteau on the Ouija board. We asked him if he could explain why there was another magazine so similar to our own.

In response, he repeatedly used the planchette to indicate the picture of people playing Ouija in the corner of the board, with the spirit hovering above. We took this to be a reference to mediumistic influence. Cocteau was saying that Peter Felsch was channeling the same muse that we were.

I thought back to that night several years earlier, when I had come up with the idea for Dagobert's Revenge while studying calculus, under the influence of something other than myself. Had Felsch been charged with the same mission that I had been given? If so, were we meant to compete with each other, or would our efforts each complement those of the other? Were there others out there who were being similarly influenced? If so, by whom? Was it the spirit of Jean Cocteau who had been leading me all this time?

I decided to ask this of Cocteau directly. What I got in reply was "C THE SUN." I wanted to know if "the sun" was Cain. He said "YES. OUI," and also repeatedly used the letters "BS." We inquired as to whether or not this stood for "Black Sun," and he answered in the affirmative. So we asked if this meant that we should try to talk to Cain on the Ouija board, and put our questions to him instead of Cocteau. We were given an emphatic "YES." We proceeded.

"Cain," I said. "Are you there?"

The response that we got was strong and swift, much more so than when we were talking to Cocteau. It was an incredible sensation. I felt this spirit very powerfully, and it immediately spelled out an ominous phrase.

"YRUBIDDING."

We were shocked, and a little bit scared. Why are you bidding? He seemed to be acting somewhat threatening and standoffish. The exchange that followed went thusly:

Tracy: Are you asking us why we're calling upon you?

Cain: YES

Tracy: Because we want to figure out the mystery of the Holy Grail. Are we asking questions we shouldn't be asking?

Cain: YES

Tracy: Do you want us to stop asking you questions?

Cain: NO

Tracy: Is someone else mad at us for asking these questions?

Cain: YES

Tracy: Who?

Cain: BOPHOMET (sic)

So there it was: the name of the demonic idol Baphomet, worshipped by the Templars, slightly misspelled.

Now, you've got to understand: I was aware of the topic of Baphomet at this time, but just slightly. I had written an article on the subject for the magazine years earlier, but it was brief, and short on details. I knew that the Templars had worshipped a severed head or skull by that name (at least, according to their confessions when they were accused of blasphemy). At the time, the tortured Templars claimed that the head had spoken to them, protected them on the battlefield during the Crusades, and helped their organization to become fabulously wealthy.

I knew that later occultists had glommed onto the idea of Baphomet. Somehow it became, in occult iconography, an androgynous human with a goat's head. I knew the modern depiction of Satan enthroned was based on this image. I knew that conspiracy theorists thought that the Freemasons worshipped Baphomet. Beyond this through, I hadn't really thought about it much. However, the goaty Baphomet figure had been shown on one of the covers of *Wolfzeit Magazine*.

Why on Earth was Cain telling us that Baphomet didn't want us to ask him questions about the Holy Grail? I asked for clarification.

Tracy: Baphomet?

Baphomet is mad at us?

Cain: YES

Tracy: Is it Baphomet who has been trying to influence us in this work all along? Is that who has been guiding my research this whole time?

Cain: YES

I thought about all of the supernatural help I seemed to have gotten with my work. However, I also thought about all the money problems we'd been having along the way. Bad financial luck that had repeatedly prevented us for being able to publish the magazine on time. It was also making it difficult for me to find time to research and write, as I was doing a lot of odd jobs now to try to get by. I wondered if maybe we weren't also being cursed for some reason, in addition to being influenced mentally. So I asked.

Tracy: Is there a curse causing all of these money problems we're having?

Cain: YES

Tracy: Who has cursed us?

Cain: BAPHOMET

Tracy: What can we do so that Baphomet isn't angry at us anymore?

Above: Eliphas Levi's depiction of Baphomet.
Right: A "sigil of Baphomet" based on a design from Stanislas de Guaita.

**Above: Seal of the Ordo Lapsit Exillis. Below:
The sun turns black at the Crucifixion, from Cocteau's mural at Notre Dame de France, London.
(Photo Tracy R. Twyman, 2005.)**

Above: Wedding of Tracy R. Twyman and Brian Albert, 2002. Below, clockwise: Douglas Pierce, Brian Albert, Tracy R. Twyman, Boyd Rice.

Bookplate used by Berenger Sauniere

Cain: AKNOWLEGE (sic)

Tracy: Acknowledge what?

Cain: BAPHOMET

Tracy: How can we acknowledge Baphomet?

Cain: PUBLISH A BOOK

Was he talking about the book I was writing with Boyd? Or another book project I was also working on at the time? Or was it yet another one that hadn't been started yet? I didn't know, so I asked "Which book?" The response I got was totally unexpected. He answered:

"DE VERE."

I hadn't even thought about Nicholas De Vere in months. I had completely blown off the work he wanted me to do, finding a publisher for his work *From Transylvania to Tunbridge Wells*. But apparently, Baphomet wanted me to live up to my promise to Nick for some reason.

Tracy: How should we publish De Vere's book?

Cain: 1000

Tracy: A thousand copies?

Cain: YES

Tracy: How are we going to get the money to publish it?

Cain: A PUBLISHER

Tracy: Which publisher?

Cain: OLE

Another wave of shock came over me. Cain, as a spokesman for Baphomet, appeared to be endorsing the crazy but beautiful work of Nicholas de Vere (so much so that Baphomet was apparently punishing me for failing to help Nick publish it). Moreover, it seemed that he was explicitly endorsing our creation, the Ordo Lapsit Exillis, as a secret society, and wanted it to be publicly connected to the Dragon Court through the publishing of this book.

Now, *Dagobert's Revenge* was officially listed as the organ of the OLE. But it was registered with the government as a for-profit partnership with Brian and me as owners. We used advertising and subscription revenue to come up with the money to publish each issue. I had no idea at that time how to raise money to publish a book.

However, we had received a few unsolicited donations for *Dagobert's Revenge*, as well as letters from people who said they wanted to invest large money in the venture (but never followed through). We had thought about creating a website to receive donations for the OLE. So we asked about that.

Tracy: Is someone going to donate the money we need for this book to the OLE?

Cain: YES.

Tracy: Who?

Cain: BS

Tracy: What does BS stand for?

Cain: BAPHOMET SUN

Earlier, it had been affirmed by Cocteau that "BS" meant "Black Sun," and that this was a reference to Cain himself. Now Cain was saying that it meant "Baphomet Sun." But understanding the nature of esoteric symbols, I knew they could have several meanings. Those multiple meanings were often connected to each other as well.

He could have been saying that "Baphomet," "the Black Sun" and "Cain" were all somehow the same entity, or different aspects of some larger concept. In this specific context this evening, "Baphomet Sun" could even be a human being acting as an avatar or incarnation of this larger entity. How else would "Baphomet Sun" be able to donate money to us? I resumed the interrogation.

Tracy: Is this a live person?

Cain: YES

Tracy: Is "Baphomet Sun" his real name?

Cain: YES

Tracy: Is this his given name?

Cain: NO

Tracy: What's his given name?

Cain: AKIDMAN

A. Kidman? I thought. Or "*A Kid-Man*," like a *man-child*? *Or maybe even a goat-man*? I continued questioning.

Tracy: Does he live in Europe?

Cain: YES

Tracy: Does he live in France?

Cain: NO

Tracy: Does he live in Britain?

Cain: YES

Tracy: Is he rich?

Cain: YES

Tracy: Is he a businessman?

Cain: YES

Tracy: What line of business is he in?

Cain: ART

Tracy: Is he an artist?

Cain: YES

Tracy: Is he a famous artist?

Cain: NO. LAWER (sic).

Tracy: Is he a famous lawyer?

Cain: YES

Tracy: Does he donate money to artists?

Cain: YES

Tracy: How much will he donate to the OLE?

Cain: 100000

We asked if all we needed to do was set up the apparatus on the internet for the OLE to take donations in order to receive something from this "A Kidman." Cain said "YES." So we asked if there was anything, such as a code word, that we needed to put on the OLE web page in order to ensure that it captured A. Kidman's attention. That's when it got really weird. Cain answered:

"BUY NEW ON SALE CD NON AVAILABLE NOW."

"Non" was the name of Boyd's ongoing "noise art" project. It was represented on Mute Records, and he put out a new record about once a year, usually with an accompanying tour of small venues in the US and Europe. I wasn't really that much of a fan. So what was this Cain was saying about Boyd's new CD? I inquired.

Tracy: Are you saying we need to advertise Boyd's CD in order to get a donation?

Cain: YES

Tracy: Are there any alternative words we could use instead of "BUY NEW ON SALECD NON AVAILABLE NOW"?

Cain: NEW NON TRACK

Tracy: Why is advertising Boyd's CD important to getting the donation?

Cain: LOVE NON

Tracy: Is Mr. Kidman a fan of Boyd?

Cain: YES

Tracy: So in order to get the donation we need tc publicize Non?

Cain: YES

Tracy: But we do publicize Non

Cain: NOT ENOUGH

Tracy: Why is Baphomet interested in the success of Non?

Cain: ANTON

Tracy: Anton LaVey?

Cain: YES

Boyd had been friends with Anton LaVey, and a spokesman for the Church of Satan. The "Sigil of Baphomet," which featured the Goat-head of Baphomet inside of a pentagram, was used by the Church of Satan as its official insignia (although the symbol existed long before that). So, as Baphomet seemed to be a patron of the Church of Satan, I thought that maybe his loyalty to Anton was spilling over onto Boyd. I asked for more details.

Tracy: This CD we're supposed to advertise: is it his current CD?

Cain: NO

Tracy: Is it the next Non album?

Cain: YES

Tracy: When will it come out?

Cain: JANUARY

Tracy: What will it be called?

Cain: BLACKSUN RISING

Boyd did indeed put out a record with this title, years after I showed him this prophecy.

Tracy: Are we going to somehow be involved in the making of this CD?

Cain: NO

Tracy: Will this CD be put out by Mute?

Cain: NO

Tracy: Will it be put out by Tesco?

This was an Australian label that was being used by Death in June at the time.

Cain: YES

Tracy: Is Boyd's contract with Mute about to end?

Cain: YES

Tracy: Why is Boyd's contract going to end?

Cain: BIOGRAPHY OF BOYD

Tracy: Is Mute going to cancel Boyd's contract because of something in Boyd's biography?

At the time, there were no films or books about Boyd's life, but I have heard that such material was published years later.

Cain: YES

Tracy: Why?

Cain: BOYD IS NOT ON THE COUNSEL (sic) OF 9

The "Council of Nine" is the name for the group of elders that runs the Church of Satan. Boyd used to always brag about being on the Council in interviews.

Tracy: Does this have something to do with internal Church of Satan politics?

Cain: YES

Tracy: Is the Church of Satan somehow connected to Mute records?

Cain: YES

Tracy: So is Boyd's contract going to end because of something he said about the Church of Satan?

Cain: BIOGRAPHY OF BOYD GOING TO END MUTE. SOY NO VIVE.

Tracy: Why did you just say that in Spanish?

Cain: BECAUSEOF BRIAN

Brian had taken a couple of years of Spanish in High School. He said that these last words translated to "I am not alive." Was Cain reminding us that he was a ghost, no longer living? Or was he speaking of someone else's death? This frightened me a little bit, and brought me back on point.

Tracy: Why is Baphomet interested in publishing De Vere's book?

Cain: BECAUSESHE IS RELATED

The word "she" reminded me that Baphomet was androgynous, having both a penis (wrapped with snakes) and paps (for nursing her kids, as she was called "the Goat with a Thousand Young.") I was also reminded that Nicholas traced his royal lineage back to figures that were god-kings or demi-gods of the ancient world: entities that were said to be more than human. Cain was one of his ancestors, he claimed, and in my research I had identified Cain as one of the first of these deified kings. It occurred to me that perhaps Cain was saying that Baphomet was such a being as well, and literally De Vere's blood ancestor. So I asked about that.

Tracy: Is Baphomet related to De Vere?

Cain: YES. AUDE IS NOW DE VERE.

Aude is the department in France where Rennes-le-Château is located.

Tracy: You mean that the region of Aude somehow belongs to De Vere now?

Cain: YES

Tracy: Who gave it to him?

Cain: PLANTARD

Pierre Plantard was one of the most recent Grand Masters of the Priory of Sion, and owned land in the Chapter Rennes-le-Château area. He also claimed to be the rightful King of France. So in some sense, I suppose, some might think that the whole region was "his," or that there was a title one could inherit from Plantard bestowing rulership over the realm.

Tracy: Does De Vere know about it yet?

Cain: NO

Tracy: How will he find out?

Cain: BOOK. ARC IS NOW DR.

"Arques," pronounced just like "arc," is the name of the commune in the Aude department that includes the Languedoc-Roussillon region, within which Rennes-le-Château is found. Also, "Arc" could be a reference to the Ark of the Covenant or Noah's Ark. It could even denote Arcadia, the region of Greece that features in the Greek myths of Hermes, patron of Western occultism.

"Arcadian" has come to symbolize, to Rosicrucians and other initiates of the esoteric, the source of the hidden wisdom associated with Hermes. The syllable "ark" or "arc," in so many different languages, indicates a vessel of some sort, usually a box, such as a coffin. In the realm of the occult, a repository of secret knowledge could be called an "Ark," and the word "arcane" is related to this idea. In Nicolas Poussin's famous painting *The Shepherds of Arcadia* (which many believe contains clues pertaining to the enigma of Rennes-le-Château), four shepherds are seen pointing at a tomb engraved with the words "Et in Arcadia Ego" ("I am in Arcadia").

So what was Cain saying here? First he told us that Nicholas de Vere was somehow going to inherit ownership or control of the department of Aude from Pierre Plantard. Then he appeared to say that "Arc," whatever that was, somehow belonged to "DR," which, he affirmed, stood for *Dagobert's Revenge*.

We didn't know what to make of this, but several things had become clear that evening. For one thing, our divination efforts had just made a fantastic leap when we decided to contact Cain, a god-king of the ancient world, instead of Jean Cocteau, a mere dead human. Instead of meaningless codes, we were getting real answers spelled out in real words, even if they were still very cryptic at times.

Furthermore, Cain and his accomplice Baphomet appeared to be taking an acute interest in me, the OLE, Nicholas de Vere, and even Boyd Rice. Also, Cain seemed to be admitting that Baphomet was using a system of punishment and reward, through curses and blessings, to try to get me to do what he wanted. Some of the blessings that were being promised now included six-figure donations and possible property inheritance in France.

As Brian and I discussed these matters, our mental clarity began to fade, and we noticed a strange amnesia falling over us. The more we talked, the more we found that we couldn't remember the details of what had just happened to us. Luckily we had recorded it all and taken notes. With foggy brains, we both went to bed and drifted off into oblivion.

Chapter 3: The Second Square

The rules of the game are fixed, the pieces arranged by file and by rank: 8 lines, 8x 8 squares, solidly framed on aboard and set on a table. The way each piece may be moved is approved by traditions already obscure in the East for 1000 years before the game began to be played in the West.

And yet if everything which is fixed must sometime or other start moving, then should the humble be patient forever, never shake up his position, shake off his occupation? Shake the pieces. Shake them for a new game, to bring into play your own imagination, to transform into human beings the wooden knights and queens.

- Hans Richter, *8 X 8: A Chess Sonata*

After talking to Cain, I experienced what seemed like a quantum leap in consciousness, greater than I had ever experienced before. I felt that I had tapped into a higher intelligence, really communicated with it directly, and connected with it much more deeply than I had previously to anything else. My research, my intuition and my reasoning expanded exponentially, quite all of the sudden.

I shared the transcript of the latest Ouija session with Boyd. Even before he read it, he looked very perturbed when I handed him the document. He repeated his assertion that the Ouija board was "stupid" and "didn't work." I tried to assure him that it was working very well for us now.

He seemed, frankly, mad that we were doing this without him, but didn't express any interest in doing it with us either. It seemed like jealousy to me. I think he didn't like the fact that we had relationships with both Jean Cocteau and Cain that he wasn't a part of. He said the prediction about something in his biography ruining his record contract made no sense. I decided to no longer tell him anything a tall about our séances, and I never mentioned it to him again.

Meditating on the mystery of Rennes-le-Château once again, I became intrigued by the prevalence of chess references and symbolism in the story. A chessboard had been embedded on the floor of Saunière's church in Rennes-le-Château, and there were several nearby landmarks with chess-related names, such as "Pas de la Roque" ("the Pass of the Rook.") Also, the coded parchments found by Saunière in his church, which may have led him to discover the alleged treasure, had been written in a cipher that was made using a Knight's Tour on a chessboard. Furthermore, there were several chess references in *Le Serpent Rouge*, the poem published by the Priory of Sion that was supposedly full of clues to the riddle of Rennes-le-Château. As well, I remembered that a chequered floor was considered the standard in a Masonic lodge, and the Knights Templar also made prominent use of the pattern in their heraldry.

One night Brian and I called up Cain again on the Ouija board. Mainly we wanted to ask him once more about the curse Baphomet had placed on us, and how it affected our finances. I thought that by repeating questions from the previous session, maybe I would get a clearer answer. So I asked him once again if we were cursed, which he affirmed. When I asked, again, why, he said:

"BECAUSE OF YOUR GOAT MONEY."

Well, I took the goat reference to mean "Baphomet," but I still didn't understand what he meant. So I switched gears and asked him about the origins of chess, something I had not yet researched on my own. The exchange that followed was absolutely fascinating.

Tracy: Who invented Chess?

Cain: ARYANS

He used the old, now politically incorrect term to denote the noble race that some historians believe civilized the ancient world.

Tracy: Where on a modern map was it invented?

Cain: AFGHANISTAN

Tracy: What was it called?

Cain: AGEIO

Tracy: Is that pronounced 'Ah-Gee-Oh,' like the Agean Sea?

Cain: YES

Tracy: Are those two words related?

Cain: YES

Tracy: Were the pieces the same?

Cain: YES

Tracy: Did they move in the same way?

Cain: YES

Tracy: What are the pieces called?

Cain: TENATS

Tracy: How do you play?

Cain: ON DIFFERENT POINTS, PUT DIFFERENT BUCKS

Tracy: What are bucks?

Cain: AGEI. GOAT MONEY.

Tracy: What do the Agei represent?

Cain: BUCKS

Tracy: Are bucks like tokens?

Cain: YES

Tracy: What are they tokens for?

Cain: SANGREAL

"Sangreal" was the original French word used in the Grail romances that has been translated as "Holy Grail." The Grail is thought by many esoteric researchers to be a symbol synonymous with that of the Philosopher's Stone. This object, in the system of alchemy, has the power to transform lead into gold, or anyone thing into any other thing. It is the transformative power of magic, and in the romances the Grail is said to possess a similar power. So I began to understand what Cain was saying here. The "tokens" used in the game of "Ageio," which Cain said was the origin of chess, represent the Holy Grail or the Philosopher's Stone. He also called them "bucks" and "goat money," indicating that they possess the power to produce wealth, to make gold out of dross.

Somehow this had something to do with Baphomet the Goat. As it later occurred to me, Baphomet is associated in the occult with alchemical transmutation. He is thought to embody the concept of the power of transmutation, which is why occultist Eliphas Levi famously depicted him seated upon the Cubic Stone of the alchemists with the words "solve" (Latin for "dissolve") and "coagula" ("coagulate") written on either side of him. This alluded to the idea that practitioners of magic were meant to somehow utilize Baphomet to dissolve a thing (or a situation) down to its most basic constituents, and then rebuild them into the object of desire.

I also learned later that the root syllable, "Ag," meant "goat" in Greek and in other languages too. This is why the Aegean Sea, and the culture associated with it, was so named, as that civilization was largely based on goat husbandry. Also, there is a word in English, "agio," that to this day actually refers to the profit made from currency exchange, such as the wealth gained by the money changers who famously traded at the temple in Jerusalem (to the ire of Jesus).

Even the word "buck" originally indicated specifically a male goat, and the syllable "buc" can still be found in goat-related words in several languages. As I later determined, "buck" ended up as a slang term for money because goat skins were at one time used for currency. It seemed to me Cain was saying that the original game of chess, Ageio, could be used for magic and alchemy, even to make yourself rich, somehow. So I asked:

Tracy: What's the object of the game?

Cain: GAIN THE AGEI

Tracy: How do you gain the Agei?

Cain: GAIN THE AGEI BY SURROUNDING THE SECOND SQUARE ON THE AGEI

Tracy: Does gaining the Agei allow you to change reality?

Cain: YES

Tracy: What do you have to do to win?

Cain: ACCEPT DEFEAT

Tracy: Why is it important to accept defeat?

Cain: IF YOU ACCEPT DEFEAT, REALITY CANNOT WIN

Now I was getting awfully excited. I had to know exactly how this original game worked. I didn't know much about chess, but Brian did, having been a chess champion as a school boy. He helped me interpret Cain's answers. Since we knew that the rules of the game were largely the same as modern chess, we asked what exactly needed to happen differently in a game of Ageio in order to make it work.

He answered "KXK." That meant, as Brian told me, that one king captures the other king. Well that made sense, and - at least I thought initially - was no different than normal chess (but I was wrong). We asked if there were more special rules, and were given several.

The next answer was "QXB": the Queen takes the Bishop. So in Ageio, before the checkmate, the Queen on the victor's side must take one of the loser's bishops. Furthermore, he said that pawns could take each other "HORIZONTALLY." When we asked if the knight's moved in the same way as modern chess, he said:

"YES. KNIGHT'S MOVE IS SACRED.ROOKS ALL DIE. CASTLES FALL. KILL KING WHEN LOWER SCORE."

As we sat dumbfounded, wondering how you "keep score" in chess, Cain sudden announced:

"REAL POWER IS IN THE SECOND SQUARE:"

Now this was the second time he had mentioned the "Second Square." We asked which one of the 64 squares on the board was the "Second Square," and he replied:

"TELL ME THE CODE OF THE SQUARE:"

We had no idea what he meant, but we did have a chessboard available. It occurred to us that Cain could just show us directly how to play, which he agreed to do. We brought out the board, placed the planchette on top of it, and asked Cain to show us the second square. He immediately used it to mark out the corners of the 36 inner squares on the board. This was the "Second Square": the square within the larger square!

Then we asked what these agei tokens looked like. He said they were coins that were black on one side and red on the other. We asked if we could use pennies to represent the agei, since the binary "heads or tails" system could apply just as easily as a black and white system. Cain replied:

"YES. I-CHING."

Of course! The Chinese system of I-Ching involved a binary heads-or-tails coin toss. Cain told us to take 36pennies and place them on top of the "second square," with one in each of the little squares. In I-Ching, each possible arrangement of six "heads or tails" coins corresponds to a glyph with a particular divinatory meaning. Here, in Ageio, it was explained that each possible arrangement of the 36 agei tokens represents a "FORTUNE," which defined the spell that you were trying to cast, the specific type of transformation that you were trying to make through magic. This was the "CODE OF THE SQUARE."

We asked what kind of fortune we should cast for our very first trial. He suggested that we make a "LEARNING" spell, to help us learn Ageio. For this, he said, the "AGEI NEED TO BE SETUP IN A PATIERN OPPOSITE THE COLOR."

We set up 36 coins, declaring that heads represented red, and tails indicated black. We put them in a simple head-tail-head-tail pattern, with each coin on an opposite-colored square among the 36 squares of the Second Square. For our purposes, we considered the white squares on the board to be "red," which I assume was the proper color on the original game board. Then Cain used chess shorthand to tell Brian which moves to make for both sides. When a piece had to stand on a square that had an agei tokens on it, we just placed the piece directly on top of the coin. They went through the whole game together, and when the white king checkmated the black king, Brian assumed that the game was over.

But it wasn't. Cain insisted that Brian go through the motions, remove the black king from the board, and place the black king on the vacated square, victorious. That's when it occurred to us: *This isn't a competitive game. It's a ritual.* The pieces were like voodoo dolls. It was a ritual sacrifice of regicide. The sacrifice was what powered the ritual, enabling the desired outcome, encoded in the agei fortune, to become reality.

After the black king died, Brian and I both started getting sleepy. That same amnesia from last time was creeping upon us again. So we went to bed, mesmerized by the wondrous display of supernatural power that had just occurred in our own living room.

Chapter 4: The Dohir Kings

...Amongst these titles for him in the Edda is _Gunn_ *or* _Kon_, *corresponding to his Sumerian title of* _Gun_, _Gin_ *or* _Gan_, *which is thus disclosed as the source of the Hebrew 'Cain' ...It is also seen to be the source of 'Gawain' of the Arthur legend, and akin to his Egyptian title of* _Khonsu_. *His more common titles in the Edda, as we shall see, are Aegis (the Azag of the Sumerians)* _Bauqe_ *(the* _Bakuz_ *of Sumerians or Bacchus, and especially applied to him in Babylonian records as King or Erech or Enoch (the city founded by 'Cain') ....*

- L.A. Waddell, *The British Edda*

So now we had been told about the origins of chess. I did some research, and sure enough, although the exact origins were unknown, Northern Afghanistan was in fact one of the places where the earliest versions of the game have been discovered. Furthermore, it was thought to have been developed from an Indian game called "Chaturanga." This same game was, amazingly, also the origin of playing cards, since the Indian game included cards made of goat skin which featured four suits very similar to those of the modern card deck.

Cain told us that the pieces were originally called "tenats," which may be related to the English word "tenacity" and the Latin "tenacitus" ("a firm holding"). The word basically seems to indicate something that you grip or hold with your hand. Also, in the oldest forms of chess, the pieces did move on the lines instead of the squares, just as Cain had said.

The actual earliest game found so far that is thought to be a direct ancestor to chess was the Chinese game of Xianqi. The pieces stand where the grid lines intersect, instead of the squares, just like in Ageio. These crossroads, as I just discovered now while editing this book, are actually called "points," just like Cain said they were in his game.

Instead of statuettes, the pieces in this game are coins with symbols on them representing the characters. They are red on one side and black on the other, just as Cain described the agei tokens. The rooks or "castles" of modern chess are said to be "chariots" in Xianqi, as they are in Chaturanga. In early chess boards the rooks, as upright-standing figurines, still retained the imagery of a siege tower. Even today, the piece is called a tower in many European languages. It's called a "tour" in French, but it is also sometimes called a "roque."

In Chaturanga, the "bishops" are ships, which may be an echo of something from the original proto-chess game. Considering that Cain said the events commemorated in Ageio include the Deluge and Fall of Atlantis, it would be fitting for there to have been boats on the board. In Xianqi there is a "river" running through the center of the board. When a pawn crosses it, he acquires the power to capture other pawns by moving horizontally. This is significant considering that Cain told us "PAWNS CAN TAKE EACH OTHER HORIZONTALLY" in Ageio.

Another interesting detail that I learned is that the I-Ching system involves exactly 64 of those binary six-part glyphs, or "hexagrams" as they were called. The whole system had come to Fu Hsi, one of the fabled ancestors of the ancient Chinese, in a vision he had of a dragon emerging from a river with these hieroglyphs imprinted on the creature's back. Also worthy of note is that ancient China was also host to some of the earliest versions of playing cards as well, in which each suit was a different type of monetary coin.

Consider also that the name of God in Hebrew, "YHVH," adds up to 64 in the Jewish numerology system of Gematria. Meanwhile, if you add the numbers 1-36 altogether (36 being the number of squares in the "Second Square" on the Ageio board), the sum is 666!

While researching chess, I learned that it was thought to be one of the oldest board games ever. It was also presumed to be related to the oldest known board game. This is the Royal Game of Ur, from ancient Sumer, which is also related to backgammon. In general, from what I was reading, most of these original board games and card games were used mainly for purposes of divination and gambling. These two things were apparently not mutually exclusive. Many of these old games also had various calendar systems encoded into them, and some modern researchers have connected chess to the lunar calendar as well.

Perhaps most provocatively, I learned several historians had theorized that the Knights Templar had been largely responsible for spreading the popularity of chess in the West during the Crusades, because of their extensive contacts with Arab traders who played it all the time. They may have even used chessboards somehow in the keeping of their financial accounts for the banking system that they were running throughout Europe (the first in history). This is interesting considering that the "agei tokens" in Ageio are said to represent "GOAT MONEY" and the alchemical power to make gold.

The Templar system relied on the use of "chits" (coded parchments that functioned like modern checks). Interestingly, the words "check" or "cheque" and "chequer" come from the English "exchequer" (a state revenue manager). This is because in medieval times the royal treasury used an abacus made out of a chessboard and tally tokens to square the various accounts. So the chessboard may have a connection, via the Templars, to the evolution of today's credit-based monetary system as well. Note that this is even more significant when you consider the aforementioned financial term "agio."

Also, I have just now, while editing this book, discovered two more possible clues about the etymological influence of the word "Ageio." Apparently, in the Greek language, "agios" means "sacred," "holy," or "saint." (It is more often written "hagios.") Interestingly, there is supposedly a ceremonial magic grimoire called *The Book of Soyga* that famous magician Dr. John Dee purportedly owned at one point. It was allegedly dictated to Adam by angels while still in the Garden of Eden, and requires an invocation of the archangel Michael to interpret. The meaning of the book's title has been interpreted to be a backwards rendering of "agyos," yet another alternate spelling of the Greek word.

"Ageio" also may be related to another word from the Greek language as well: "ageiro," which means "to extract." This, when combined with the Greek word "spao" ("to collect"), was the inspiration for the term "spagyric," coined by alchemist and physician Paracelcus to refer to medical remedies prepared alchemically. "Spagyric" is thus equivalent to "solve et coagula" (dissolve and coagulate), the alchemical phrase associated with Baphomet.

So everything that Cain had told us about the origins of chess seemed to fall in line with, and even explain certain mysterious aspects of, the known history on the subject. *But what about the history of Cain himself*, I wondered.

Cain was, according to my research, one of the oldest kings of the ancient world. The controversial Orientalist L.A.Waddell, whose work I took very seriously, had written several books theorizing that the myth of the rivalry between Cain and Abel in the Bible represented the historic reality of an ongoing military feud between this ancient king and a kingdom ruled by one of his brothers. In fact, he thought it was a war between two federations, or an empire against its satellites that were trying to break away. This, he believed, all happened in pre-diluvian times, before the flood of Noah.

We decided to call up Cain again, to ask him more about himself. First we asked about his relationship with Baphomet, and he indicated that they were somehow two opposing halves of the same being. However, he implied that this had not always been the case.

Then we asked, since he had identified himself as the "Black Sun" of mythology, if he was in fact speaking to us from the center of the Earth (where the Black Sun purportedly resided). He answered "YES," and the most depressing feeling came over me all of the sudden. When asked why he was there, he answered "JAIL."

So Cain was in Hell. He was imprisoned in the center of the Earth, just as the fallen angels, the Watchers, and their descendants, the Nephilim, were said to have been jailed by God beneath the Earth after the Flood. We then asked him why he was being punished. The exchange went as follows:

Tracy: Why are you in jail?

Cain: WRATH OF CAIN

Tracy: Who was your father?

Cain: ADAM

Tracy: Who are your descendants on Earth?

Cain: ALL WEST

Tracy: Are your descendants cursed?

Cain: YES

Tracy: Why?

Cain: WRATH OF CAIN

Tracy: What is the origin of civilization?

Cain: EDEN

Tracy: Was there a war between you and your brother, as L.A. Waddell suggests?

Cain: YES

Tracy: What was that about?

Cain: THRONE OF ADAM

Tracy: Why are you called the Black Sun?

Cain: PRISM

Tracy: Are you within a prism?

Cain: YES

Tracy: Is there a connection between the word "prison" and "prism"?

This suggestion was Brian's idea.

Cain: YES

Tracy: Do you radiate energy through the prism? Is that why they call you the Black Sun?

Cain: YES

Tracy: Tell us about the war with your brother.

Cain: FALL OF ATLANTIS. I WANTED YOUTH. TRIED TO SAVE EVE. LIVE WATER.

Tracy: Is this the same as the Flood of *Genesis*?

Cain: YES

Tracy: Was there an Ark?

Cain: YES. ADAM IN ARK.

Tracy: Adam was on board the Ark?

Cain: BODY

Tracy: His dead body was carried on the Ark?

Cain: YES

Tracy: So who were your enemies in the war?

Cain: DOHIR KINGS. KINGS OF THE FALLEN LAND EDEN. LAST KINGS OF EDEN.

Tracy: Who were they the descendants of?

Cain: CAIN

Tracy: So they were your own children? On your brother's side?

Cain: YES

We asked about the connection with the Ageio board. He said it represented the "BATTLE," and that there were special spots on the board that marked where each of the "DOHIR KINGS" fell in the battle. He indicated that the game was somehow meant to recreate this battle, and what he kept calling the "WRATH OF CAIN." We asked "Who defeated the Kings of Eden?" and we were told "KINGS OF NOD MEET WITH ALL."

Nod, of course, was the name of the land that Cain was exiled to after killing his brother in the biblical version of the story. It was said to be to the It east of Eden," and that Cain "built a city" there, naming it after his son Enoch. This son had the same name as one of his brother Seth's descendants also. It was Seth's Enoch who is credited with writing the famous *Book of Enoch* about the sex crimes of the Watchers and the Flood that resulted. The conversation continued:

Tracy: So were the kings of Eden rebellious against your authority?

Cain: YES

Tracy: Where on a modern map was Eden?

Cain: AFGHANISTAN, PAKISTAN, INDIA, IRAN, UZBEKISTAN, WATER.

Tracy: Does that mean that a portion of Eden is now underwater?

Cain: YES

Tracy: What is the connection between playing cards and Ageio?

Cain: DIVINATION

Tracy: What is the analog of playing cards in the original game of Ageio?

Cain: MINOR ARCANA

Tracy: Are you referring to the red and black bucks?

Cain: YES

Tracy: So does the Aegean Sea have anything to do with this?

Cain: YES. NOD.

Tracy: That's where Nod used to be?

Cain: YES

Tracy: Where is Eden now? I mean the parts that sunk underwater? Is it under the Persian Gulf?

Cain: YES

Tracy: So the battle was over who would rule Eden?

Cain: YES. MOLOCH.

Tracy: Is that the position of Emperor over the Dohir Kings?

Cain: YES

Tracy: How many Dohir Kings were there?

Cain: 10

Tracy: Were there multiple kings in Nod as well?

Cain: YES. 70.

Tracy: What kinds of weapons were used?

Cain: SWORDS, AXES

Tracy: You mean it was hand-to-hand combat?

Cain: YES

Tracy: So why did the lands of Eden and Nod both sink underwater?

Cain: WRATH OF CAIN

In response to a series of questions that we were inspired to formulate, Cain affirmed that what he kept calling "WRATH OF CAIN" was an anger-driven magical operation that he performed against his enemies, which tragically resulted in the Flood somehow. We asked for more details.

Tracy: Was Dohir under the control of the land of Nod before the war?

Cain: YES. 12 RACES OF ATLANTIS.

Tracy: Is this what the twelve tribes of Israel symbolize?

Cain: YES

Tracy: Do all of these races still exist?

Cain: NO

Tracy: How many still exist?

Cain: 3

Tracy: Which are they?

Cain: ARYAN, FAERY, UNDERGROUND

Tracy: Were the giants one of the races?

Cain: YES

Tracy: Are they still around?

Cain: NO

Tracy: Were they killed in the Flood?

Cain: YES

Tracy: Are there such things as gods?

Cain: YES

Tracy: How does one become a god?

Cain: DIVINE AUTHORITY

Tracy: Who gives divine authority?

Cain: BLOOD

Tracy: Are there entrances to the Hollow Earth where we can travel to where you are now?

Cain: YES

Tracy: What's the nearest one to where we are?

Cain: HOTEL BIAZA

Tracy: Where's that?

Cain: ASPEN

Tracy: Aspen, Colorado?

Cain: YES

Tracy: One more thing before we leave off. Where can we look to understand more about the origin of playing cards and their relationship to Ageio?

Cain: BOTT TAROT AND PAY DAGOBERT AND SION

Tracy: What do you mean by that?

Cain: BUG BOTTICELLI

Tracy: You mean the painter?

Cain: ASK TAROT. BEELZEBUB. KANE. BOOB.

Tracy: That doesn't make any sense.

Cain: HOW DO YOU NOW (sic)

We asked if Cain could explain to us more about the relationship between the story he had just told us and the game of Ageio. He just repeated the same inverted alphabet sequence that Cocteau had been giving us, and then told us to "ASK BAPHOMET."

Certain aspects of what was said that night became clearer later on after further research. As it turned out, Botticelli the painter and his mentor Montegna are both credited with producing tarot decks that were thought to have been some of the earliest. Botticelli was also one of illustrious historical figures on the Priory of Sion's list of alleged Grand Masters. So Cain was telling us to "BUG BOTTICELLI" - that is, to conjure the painter to ask about the relationship between tarot, playing cards, and the divination connection with Ageio.

Moloch is a Semitic root word that means "king." It was also the name of a god worshipped by the Ammonites, Canaanites and Phoenicians, to whom human babies were given as burnt offerings. Moloch worship is strictly prohibited in the Old Testament of the Bible.

The word "Dohir," identified by Cain as a name for the "KINGS OF THE FALLEN LAND EDEN," is not found in any known language. However, "Dohat," is an Arabic word for "bay" or "gulf," and Cain did say that part of Eden is now under the Persian Gulf. On the shores of the Persian Gulf, we find the city of Doha in Qatar.

The origin of the name is unknown and scholars simply speculate that the word might come from "dohat." Another theory is that it stems from "Ad Dawha" ("the Big Tree"), a reference to a landmark that used to be there. But is it possible that both "dohat" and "Doha" connect somehow to an ancient memory of a "fallen land" that one day, ages ago, sank beneath the waves where we now find the Persian Gulf?

To this point, there is another Arabic word found in a passage in The Koran (Surah 7 - "Al-A'raf" - verses 10-20) that turns out to be very relevant. It is "dahhar," which means "banished," or "put away and outside of a particular enclosure." The word also specifically has a connotation implying the bringing down and casting out of an enemy.

The surah in question describes the angel Iblis (Lucifer) refusing to bow down before Adam when ordered by God to do so. He is then cast down into Hell, as the Koranic version of the story goes. The story of Adam and Eve's temptation by the serpent and expulsion from Eden is then related as well. The entire passage is worth quoting. I have highlighted line 18, which contains the word "dahhar," and underlined the word - "banished" - that was translated from it.

And We created you, then fashioned you, then told the angels: Fall ye prostrate before Adam I And they fell prostrate, all save Iblis, who was not of those who make prostration. He said: What hindered thee that thou didst not fall prostrate when I bade thee? (Iblis) said: I am better than him. Thou createdst me of fire while him Thou didst create of mud....

He said: Go forth from hence, degraded, banished. As for such of them as follow thee, surely I will fill hell with all of you.

This is very important, as will become obvious later on when this Koran passage comes up again in another séance. However, it is still unclear whether the phrase "DOHIR KINGS OF THE FALLEN LAND EDEN" refers to Adam and his lineage falling from Paradise, or Iblis and his companions being cast down to Hell, or the angels loyal to God dutifully falling down prostrate in worship before Adam.

It has occurred to me, recently, that the line "KINGS OF NOD MEET WITH ALL" might connect to the end of line 18 in this surah: " ... surely I will fill hell with all of you." Of note is the fact that the Greeks perceived Hades, the lord of the underworld named after him, as being the "all-receiver." He was the god with the largest territory and subjects in his kingdom, because it was the ultimate destination of every living soul (Elysium, the "paradise" section, being a mere chamber within this underground realm). This concept is still reflected in the symbol for the planet Pluto, named after the Roman equivalent of Hades. That sign features a figure with arms outstretched in the shape of a cup, receiving a circle that descends from above, representing the souls of the dead.

The phrase "Wrath of Cain" brings to mind *The Wrath of Khan*, the second *Star Trek* film from 1982. In this film there is something called the "Genesis Device" which reorganize smatter for the purpose of terraforming planets. The title character, Khan, attempts to utilize it as a weapon of mass destruction to wipe out everything in an entire nebula of space. We don't know what the "Wrath of Cain" was that purportedly caused the sinking of Eden/Atlantis and Nod, but Cain may have been trying to indicate that it was something like this. *Wrath of Cain* is also the title of a prison-themed film that came out in 2010 - nine years after this séance occurred.

Chapter 5: I Reap All the Wealth

The Templars were Jesuits who failed. Their principle was to become rich in order to purchase the world ....

- Eliphas Levi, *Magic: A History of Its Rites, Rituals, and Mysteries*

The next day, I woke up late and found that Brian was in the office, already doing something on the computer. He said that he had felt inspired to create a new Ouija board. He told me that the details of the design had been coming to him spontaneously since he'd woken up.

The alphabet was arranged in the inverted manner shown to us by the spirits. The letters were placed in a circle surrounding a thirteen-pointed black star with a twenty-six pointed white star inside of it. Surrounding the letters were the symbols of the thirteen houses of the Priory of Sion's zodiac. The pillars of Jachin and Boaz from Solomon's temple were on the right and left sides. For some reason, on inspiration, he put the planetary symbols of Jupiter and Venus on either side of the wheel in the center, as well as a pentagram and a hexagram.

Above, there was a banner decorated with crosses of Lorraine running across it, as well as a fleur-de-lys (a symbol of royalty) in the left and right corners. On the bottom there were waves of water representing the infernal Abyss covering the unseen realms of the underworld below, instead of the typical "Goodbye." The Sun and the Moon at the top of the board (standard on all Ouija boards as well as Masonic tracing boards) were still featured, but the sun was colored black and had twenty-six points as well.

In the bottom left corner, there was a Golden Dawn style rose-cross on top of a black triskaidecagon. On the bottom right, there was a chessboard surmounting a black nonagon. It was also decorated with fleur-de-lys in each of the four corners, and it was topped with a crown. Also, the four corners of the inner 36 squares, the "Second Square" of the Ageio game, were marked with equilateral Templar crosses. The result of the design was utterly astounding.

We went to Kinko's and had them print out the design in poster size. The clerk at the counter gave us a very strange look as he handed it to us. We took it home and placed it inside of a poster frame that Brian already had. This way the planchette could slide across the surface easily.

YES
NO
A B C D E F G H I J K L M N O P Q R S T U V W X Y Z
1 2 3 4 5 6 7 8 9 0

That night we tried out the board for the first time. We also conjured Baphomet himself for the first time. Once again, I could feel the influence of the spirit, and it was qualitatively different than what I had felt from Cain. It was perhaps stronger, as well as swifter and more dynamic.

The first thing he did was quickly explore every letter on the wheel and every element on the board, with quick, jerky movements. He went through the alphabet in inverse order. This caused our hands to form zigzag patterns as the planchette moved from letter to letter. Then he went around the board visiting all of the other elements, very methodically.

We opened by asking what else Baphomet could add to what Cain had already told us about Ageio. His reply was "FAERY QUEEN OF BOAZ." Well, I knew that Sir Edmund Spenser had written a book called *The Faerie Queene*, and that Boaz was one of the pillars on the Ouija board. But I didn't know what he meant. Then I asked, "What is the aim of the game?" He replied:

"MAKE REAL AGEI. SENGREAL (sic)."

He then used the planchette to point out the "Second Square" on the chessboard that Brian had placed in the corner of the Ouija board. "REAL POWER IS IN THIS BOARD," he added, just as Cain had emphasized.

We then asked if he could tell us the names of the ten Dohir Kings that had fallen in the battle Cain had talked about. The planchette began spelling out bizarre names, giving each one a corresponding number as well. The list started off like this:

30 TENJI

56 SEOING

29 GOADD

4 BINOM

27 PEOD

We were then given a name - "LAUDPA" - without a corresponding number given first. Rather, the next number came after "Laudpa" was spelled. It was the number 2. It was quickly followed by yet another name: "FEARY." But this time, it seemed that the planchette had been taken over by the Dohir king in question. It was not Baphomet speaking to us anymore. It was FEARY. It is unknown if this character is the same as the "FAERY QUEEN OF BOAZ" mentioned earlier, but the name was spelled "Feary" consistently from there on out. He introduced himself, and made a strange proclamation:

"FEARY IS HERE.I REAPALL THE WEALTH."

The transition occurred seamlessly, and the message was spelled out so quickly, we didn't have time to analyze it before the rest of the Dohir Kings started taking over and introducing themselves as well:

"SEOING IS HERE. I REAP ALL THE WEATLH."

"BINOM IS HERE. I REAP ALL THE WEALTH."

"MAYA IS HERE. I REAP ALL THE WEALTH."

"TITIN IS HERE. I REAP ALL THE WEALTH."

"MY NAME IS DASHOD. I REAP ALL THE WEALTH."

"TEZETECEL IS HERE."

"TITIN IS HERE."

"SOEING IS HERE, AND ON THE END OF THE GAME BOARD."

"PEOD IS HERE AND MY HOUSE IS UNDER THE ROOK."

The Dohir Kings seemed to be fighting for control of the planchette so that they could state their names and their personal declarations. They were all whipped up into a frenzy and moving at a fevered pace. This phrase "I REAP ALL THE WEALTH" sent a shiver through me. It seemed to stir up an ancient ancestral memory within me that I couldn't quite put my finger on. We called for Baphomet to restore order.

At our beckoning, Baphomet returned and reclaimed control of the planchette. But like the others, he was now in an agitated state, and his answers were hard to pin down. He became very uncooperative, giving us strings of apparently random numbers and letters in reply to each query. When we asked what this meant, he said it was "CODE." Frustrated by the unclear answers and a bit frightened at seeming to lose control of the conversation, we retired for the night.

Only just now, in July 2014, while doing the final edit for this book, have I come to understand many of the clues about Ageio that the spirits gave us. As I said, Brian was inspired, while designing the Ageio board that sits at the corner of the Ouija board he created, to mark off the 9 x 9 field of the "Second Square" inside of it with four small Templar crosses. As it turns out, in the

Chinese game of Xianqi, the starting points of soldiers and cannons are marked on the board with small crosses.

Also, in Xianqi the king and queens on each side reside in areas on the board called "palaces" or "forbidden cities" which they are not permitted to leave. This is based upon the truth about the Imperial Palace of the Ming and Qing dynasties in Beijing, where the emperors, as well as their wives, concubines, children and staff, were not allowed to leave without official escorts watching their every move. This carries an eerie echo of the testimony of Cain, allegedly locked in a subterranean prison, presumably along with all of those who fought with him and lost the war for Eden.

Furthermore, the reference to a "FEARY QUEEN" makes much more sense to me now, as I have just read that the piece now known in chess as a "queen" was originally a "vizier." The name was "farzin" in Persian," "firz" in Arabic, "alferza" in Spanish, and "fierce" or "fierge" in French. In Russia they still call it the "ferz." Writer Marylin Yalom has theorized that the piece morphed over time because of the influence of powerful European queens like Blanche of Castile, and the growing reverence for the Virgin Mary, the "Queen of Heaven."

Formerly, the ferz could only move one square diagonally per turn, but now the queen is the most powerful piece on the board, able to move any number of squares in any direction. At one point in history, according to author H.J.R. Murray, she could even move at right angles like a knight. Yalom argues that this change took place after 1300as it took on aspects of the "Fierce Dieu," an image of the Virgin Mary as a powerful chess queen that was referenced in medieval poetry.

Also interesting in this regard are some other figures from Greek mythology mentioned by Robert Graves in his book The White Goddess: King Phoroneus, founder of Argos; his mother Argeia (whom Graves equates with Hera Argeia), and Fearineus, the God of Spring. He writes:

Pausanias ... [disregards] the Prometheus legend ... [by] making Phoroneus the inventor of fire. Hyginus gives his mother's name as Argeia ('dazzling white'), who is the White Goddess again. So Phoroneus ... was borne by, married to, and finally laid out by, the White Goddess: his layer-out was the Death-goddess Hero Argeia to whom he is said to have first offered sacrifices. Phoroneus, then, is Fearineus, the God of Spring to whom annual sacrifices were offered on the Cronian Mount at Olympia at the Spring equinox. His singing head recalls that of Orpheus ....

As for the possible connection with Edmund Spenser's *Faerie Queene*, I will discuss that in the final chapter of this book. As I learned just recently, it does, in fact, tell a story about a war in Eden.

Chapter 6: The Curse of the Nemes

God, who had decreed the issue, reserved Judas for the cross, in order that he might suffer that horrible death to which he had sold another. He did not suffer Judas to die under the scourges, notwithstanding that the soldiers scourged him so grievously that his body rained blood.

- The Gospel of Barnabas, Chapter 217

After that last séance, I remember reflecting on it for days. I was fascinated by how the different entities expressed themselves on the board. In particular, I was amazed at how Baphomet and Cain did seem to be inverted mirror opposites of one another, yet somehow connected together, just as Cain had said they were.

I noticed that Baphomet chose to move from one side of the wheel to another, so that when spelling out words, he would always, in-between letters, jerk it to the other side quickly. He would do this even if he didn't need to use one of the letters there, and even if the letter he needed next was right beside the one he had just used.

Cain, on the other hand, preferred to move in circles. Even if two letters that he was using to spell something were right next to each other on the wheel, he would circle around to the other side to get the next letter. I thought maybe this had to do with the fact that Cain, the Black Sun, was a solar entity, while Baphomet was lunar (according to Eliphas Levi, at least) and an embodiment of opposing polarities.

I also discovered that the inverted alphabet sequence which all of the entities we spoke with were emphasizing, was in fact something known as the "Atbash cipher." The writers of *Holy Blood, Holy Grail* had mentioned that the Atbash cipher was used by the Knights Templar! Incredibly, if you apply the same rearrangement to the Hebrew alphabet, then when you take the word "Sophia" (the name for the divine wisdom of God) using the Aramaic spelling (the Hebrew-Greek mix language used at the time of Christ) and run it through the cipher, you get "Baphomet." This is especially interesting because another theory about Baphomet's name, put forward by nineteenth-century Viennese Orientalist Joseph von Hammer-Purgstall, is that it comes from "Bapho Metis," Greek words for "Baptism of Wisdom." He speculated that this might be the title of an Ophite Gnostic rite secretly observed by the Templars.

The possible connection between Baphomet's name and a rite of baptism is potentially important as well. The first mention of baptism in the Bible is in Matthew 3:10-12, when John the Baptist immerses Jesus in the river Jordan. Of course, the patron saint of the Knights Templar was John (as he is for the Freemasons as well).

When the Templars were accused of heresy and blasphemy, one of the specific charges was of practicing Johannism. This was an underground cult that venerated John as the real Christ, viewing Jesus as a false prophet. It is still practiced today in Iraq, as part of a sect called the "Mandeans."

The Baphomet idol that the Templars were accused of worshipping has been speculated by some writers to have actually been the skull of John. As you will of course recall, John was famously beheaded at the request of Salome, according to the Gospels. Certain historians actually think that the Knights may have discovered the real skull of John some time during their occupation of the Holy Land. In the Gnostic text *The Apocryphon of St James*, John's head is referred to as the "Head of Prophecy." The tortured Templars confessed to their inquisitors that the Baphomet head "prophesied" for them as well.

With ideas like these running through our heads, Brian and I decided to conjure up Baphomet again for a thorough interrogation on just who or what he was. We wanted to know what, if anything, he had to do with John the Baptist, severed heads, or wisdom. The conversation that followed was long, very revealing and quite hair-raising at times. It will make your blood run cold.

Tracy: Why is Baphomet associated with a head?

Baphomet: JOHN

Tracy: John the Baptist?

Baphomet: YES

Tracy: Why is John the Baptist important?

Baphomet: JESUS

Tracy: Did John think that he was the Messiah instead of Jesus?

Baphomet: NO

Tracy: Did Jesus and John hate each other?

Baphomet: YES

Tracy: Why?

Baphomet: RABBINICAL LAW

Tracy: They had a disagreement over rabbinical law?

Baphomet: YES

Tracy: Did the disagreement involve marriage?

Baphomet: YES

Tracy: Did it have to do with Jesus marrying Mary Magdalene?

Baphomet: YES

Tracy: What was the problem?

Baphomet: LEVI

Tracy: Was Magdalene from the tribe of Levi?

Baphomet: YES

Tracy: But the tribe of Levi is the priestly line, isn't it?

Baphomet: YES

Tracy: So what's the problem with Jesus marrying into the tribe of Levi?

Baphomet: END OF ILM

Tracy: What does "ILM" mean?

Baphomet: RACE

Tracy: Marrying into the line of Levi meant the end of Jesus' race?

Baphomet: YES

Tracy: What line was Jesus from?

Baphomet: DAVID

Tracy: Why can't the line of David marry into the line of Levi?

Baphomet: WORLD LAW

Baphomet then visited the rose-cross symbol in the lower left-hand corner of the board.

Tracy: Why didn't John want Jesus to marry into the line of Levi?

Baphomet: PROPHECY

Tracy: What was the prophecy?

Baphomet: CURSE

Tracy: What do you mean?

Baphomet: PROPHECY OF DANIEL 5:5

At this point, we had a brief intermission in the discussion so that we could take the King James Bible from the bookshelf to look up the reference that Baphomet was giving us. As it turned out, Daniel 5:5 is the famous line describing how Belshazzar, King of Babylon (and son of Nebuchadnezzar) witnessed a disembodied hand writing mysterious words on the wall:

In the same hour came forth fingers of a man's hand, and wrote over against the candlestick upon the plaister of the wall of the king's palace: and the king saw the part of the hand that wrote.

The words written - "MENE MENE TEKEL UPHARSIN" - are interpreted to prophecy the king's imminent demise and that of his kingdom as well. At the time, I didn't get what this passage had to do with the story of Jesus and John that he was telling me. So I came up with an interpretation about how it might be metaphorically relevant, and asked Baphomet if I was right.

Tracy: Did John see writing on the wall similar to that in Daniel 5:5 about his own demise?

Baphomet: YES

Tracy: Whose hand did the writing?

Baphomet: ME

Tracy: Is Levi the line that the king needs to marry into?

Baphomet: YES

Tracy: Is it that John did not want Jesus to marry Mary Magdalene because it would be an announcement of his intention to be the King of Israel, and John knew that would cause both John and Jesus to be persecuted by Herod and Pilate?

Baphomet: YES

Tracy: Did Jesus disbelieve that the threat was real?

Baphomet: YES

Tracy: And he went ahead with the marriage anyway?

Baphomet: YES

Tracy: Is that why the bloodline of Jesus was cursed?

Baphomet: YES

Tracy: Who cursed them?

Baphomet: ME

Tracy: What was the curse?

Baphomet: QUARREL

Tracy: Can the curse be broken?

Baphomet: YES

Tracy: How?

Baphomet: NOT FOR YOU

Tracy: Did Jesus die on the cross?

Baphomet: NO

Tracy: Did someone else die in his place?

Baphomet: YES

Tracy: Was he a willing sacrifice?

Baphomet: NO

Tracy: Who was it?

Baphomet: JUDAS

Tracy: He was the sacrificial goat?

Baphomet: YES

Tracy: Did anyone else know about it?

Baphomet: SARAH

Tracy: Who arranged for this to happen?

Baphomet: ME

Tracy: Were you alive at the time?

Baphomet: NO

Tracy: How did you accomplish this?

Baphomet: TRICKS

Tracy: So the head of John the Baptist was the Baphomet relic that the Templars had?

Baphomet: YES. 58

Tracy: Head 58?

"Caput 58M" was a designation found written on one of the gold-plated heads that were discovered at Templar preceptories after their arrest by French police in 1307.

Baphomet: YES

Tracy: What does 58 mean?

Baphomet: MM

Tracy: Does that stand for Mary Magdalene?

Baphomet: YES

Tracy: Why would the head of John the Baptist have a reference to Mary Magdalene on it, if John didn't want the marriage to take place?

Baphomet: HATE

Tracy: Did the Templars hate Mary Magdalene?

Baphomet: YES

Tracy: Was she a prostitute?

Baphomet: NO

Tracy: Did they call her a whore because her marriage to Jesus cursed their bloodline?

Baphomet: YES

Tracy: Was that the Church's viewpoint as well?

Baphomet: YES

Tracy: Is that why they cut her out of the Bible?

Baphomet: YES

Tracy: Did you create the Templars as a hate cult against Mary Magdalene?

Baphomet: YES

Tracy: Did the Priory of Sion know this?

Baphomet: NO

Tracy: Is this what caused the "Cutting of the Elm"?

Baphomet: YES

The "Cutting of the Elm" is the name given by the Priory of Sion's literature for the division that allegedly occurred in 1188 between the Priory of Sion and the Knights Templar. The Priory claims that both orders were at one time part of the same group.

Tracy: Who has the head now?

Baphomet: SION

Tracy: Why do the Priory of Sion call their Grand Masters "John"?

Baphomet: SIX JS

Tracy: What are the six Js?

Baphomet: JACOB, JESUS, JOHN, JOSHUA, JEAN, JOB

Tracy: Is the head of John the Baptist the relic with which the curse is associated?

Baphomet: YES

Tracy: Do you need the head to break the curse?

Baphomet: YES

Tracy: Is the head the Holy Grail?

Baphomet: NO

Tracy: Is this what the Templars found in Jerusalem?

Baphomet: NO

Tracy: What did they find?

Baphomet: ARK

Tracy: Why did the Templars want to capture Jerusalem?

Baphomet: DESTINY

Tracy: Is the head the treasure of Rennes-le-Château?

Baphomet: YES

Tracy: Is it the only thing you need to break the curse?

Baphomet: NO

Tracy: What else?

Baphomet: 4 PARCHMENTS

Tracy: The parchments that Saunière found?

Baphomet: YES

Tracy: Are the ones that have been published correct?

Baphomet: YES

Tracy: Are the genealogies a part of it?

Baphomet: YES

Tracy: Are the parchments a ritual to break the curse?

Baphomet: YES

Tracy: Are the genealogies important because they name the people who have been affected by the curse?

Baphomet: YES

Tracy: Can you tell us the meaning of the parchments?

Baphomet: YES

At this point, we went line by line through the coded message found on the second of the four mysterious parchments found by Bérenger Saunière in his church in Rennes-le-Château. The message goes:

SHEPHERDESS NO TEMPTATION THAT POUSSIN TENIERS HOLD THE KEY PAX 681 BY THE CROSS AND THIS HORSE OF GOD I DESTROY THIS DAEMON GUARDIAN AT MIDDAY BLUE APPLES.

So we asked Baphomet about it:

Tracy: Is "shepherdess" a reference to the Poussin painting *The Shepherds of Arcadia*?

Baphomet: YES

Tracy: Do you need the painting to undo the curse as well?

Baphomet: YES

Tracy: Which David Teniers painting is the message referring to?

Baphomet: TEMPTATION OF CHRIST

There is no known painting by David Teniers called "The Temptation of Christ." There is however, one called *The Temptation of Saint Anthony*.

Tracy: Was the temptation of Christ the temptation to marry Magdalene and seize the crown?

Baphomet: YES

Tracy: By whom as he tempted?

Baphomet: YIAY

Tracy: Who's that?

Baphomet: A FRIEND

Tracy: Is this what the film *The Last Temptation of Christ* is about?

Baphomet: YES

Tracy: Who was responsible for that film?

Baphomet: ME

Tracy: What does "PAX 681" mean?

Baphomet: QUARREL

Tracy: How does PAX 681 mean "quarrel"?

Baphomet: CODE

Tracy: Which code?

Baphomet: MINE

Tracy: What does "by the cross" mean?

Baphomet: JESUS

Tracy: What does "horse of God" mean?

Baphomet: JUDAS

Tracy: Does "I destroy the demon guardian" mean "destroy the curse"?

Baphomet: YES

Tracy: What does "at noon" mean?

Baphomet: AT NOON

Tracy: You mean the ritual has to be done at noon?

Baphomet: YES

Tracy: What does "blue apples" mean?

Baphomet: BLOOD SACRIFICE

Tracy: Does someone have to be sacrificed in the place of Jesus in the ritual?

Baphomet: YES

Tracy: Is it a real-life game of Ageio, where you kill the king?

Baphomet: YES

Tracy: Is that what was going on with Jesus and John as well?

Baphomet: YES

Tracy: Did they know it?

Baphomet: NO

Tracy: Do you hate Mary Magdalene because you did you not want her to marry Jesus?

Baphomet: YES

Tracy: Why?

Baphomet: LEVITES ARE HERETICAL

Tracy: Why are they heretical?

Baphomet: NEMES

Tracy: What is "NEMES"?

Baphomet: CITY

Tracy: Where is the city of Nemes?

Baphomet: BABYLON

Tracy: Did Nemes have another name?

Baphomet: UR

Tracy: So what's the significance of Nemes?

Baphomet: RIVAL BLOODLINE

Tracy: Rival to what?

Baphomet: DAVID

Tracy: Did Magdalene have the blood of Nemes in her?

Baphomet: YES

Tracy: Did the Levites intermarry with the Nemes?

Baphomet: YES

Tracy: Did they do that during the Babylonian captivity?

Baphomet: YES

Tracy: Is that why the Levites are heretical?

Baphomet: YES

Tracy: Is there another name for the Nemes?

Baphomet: YES

Tracy: What is it?

Baphomet: NEBUCHADNEZZAR

Tracy: What do you think of the Nemes?

Baphomet: SLAVES

Tracy: Are the Nemes and the line of David originally of the same stock?

Baphomet: YES

Tracy: At what point did the two lines separate?

Baphomet: ABRAHAM

Tracy: Is this the story of Ishmael and Isaac?

Baphomet: YES

Tracy: Are the Nemes cursed?

Baphomet: YES

Tracy: Who cursed them?

Baphomet: BS

Tracy: The Black Sun?

Baphomet: YES. SEPTAGUINT (sic) ABRAHAM

The Septuagint is a Greek translation of the Hebrew Bible, although I did not know this at the time. The Septuagint has a different chronology from other versions of the texts.

Tracy: Baphomet, do you appear as one of the characters in the Bible?

Baphomet: YES. MANY.

Tracy: Tell us what some of them are.

Baphomet: DANIEL 5:5

Tracy: You were the hand that wrote on the wall in *The Book of Daniel*?

Baphomet: YES

Tracy: What else?

Baphomet: WEDDING CANA

Tracy: You were at the wedding at Cana?

Baphomet: YES

Tracy: Which character were you?

Baphomet: 7

Tracy: You were seven characters at the same time?

Baphomet: YES

Tracy: Name some of your presences there.

At this point, Baphomet abruptly moved the planchette down to the Abyss at the bottom of the board (which I will from this point on refer to as "WATER" in the transcripts), then spelled out the word "WINE."

Tracy: You're saying that you're the one who changed the water into wine?

Baphomet: YES

Tracy: What's another character from the Gospels that was actually you?

Baphomet: JUDAS

Tracy: Why is Mary Magdalene associated with Venus?

Baphomet: FEMALE. WATER.

Tracy: Because she's female and she's associated with water?

Baphomet: YES

Tracy: Does Magdalene represent a lesser aspect of the female side of Baphomet?

Baphomet: YES

Tracy: Do you curse that part of yourself that Magdalene represents?

Baphomet: YES

Tracy: Why?

Baphomet: NAÏVE

Tracy: She's naive?

Baphomet: YES

Tracy: Does the Black Sun excuse naiveté?

This was a question that Brian wanted to ask.

Baphomet: YES

Tracy: Does that bother you?

Baphomet: YES

Tracy: Does the Black Sun love you?

Baphomet: YES

Tracy: Is the Black Sun naive?

Baphomet: YES

Tracy: Is anyone who loves you naive?

Baphomet: NO

Tracy: Do you hate anyone who loves you?

Baphomet: YES

Tracy: Why?

Baphomet: DUALITY

Tracy: Do you hate us?

Baphomet: NO

Tracy: Do you curse everything that the Black Sun blesses?

Baphomet: YES

Tracy: Did the Black Sun tempt Jesus?

Baphomet: YES

Tracy: Did you curse the Nemes?

Baphomet: YES

Tracy: How many curses?

Baphomet: 7

Tracy: What are they?

Baphomet: FEAR

Tracy: Fear of what?

Baphomet: ME

Tracy: What else did you curse them with?

Baphomet: POVERTY, DISEASE, DROUGHT, GREED, TREACHERY, CONFUSION

Tracy: Did they receive any blessings?

Baphomet: YES

Tracy: From who?

Baphomet: BS

Tracy: How many?

Baphomet: 6

Tracy: What were they?

Baphomet: CULTURE, WILL, VIGILANCE, FERTILITY, LOYALTY, MEMORY

Tracy: Why did the Black Sun bless them?

Baphomet: PITY

Tracy: How do you feel about John the Baptist?

Baphomet: HATE

Tracy: Why?

Baphomet: NEMES

Tracy: Was he of the blood of Nemes?

Baphomet: YES

Tracy: Did you have a deal with John the Baptist?

Baphomet: YES

Tracy: What was the deal?

Baphomet: NO MARRIAGE

Tracy: You made a deal with him to stop the marriage?

Baphomet: YES

Tracy: What would he get in exchange?

Baphomet: LIFE

Tracy: You would let him live if he stopped the marriage?

Baphomet: YES

Tracy: But he didn't so you had his head chopped off?

Baphomet: YES

Tracy: Why did the Templars keep the head of John the Baptist?

Baphomet: HATE

Tracy: Did the Templars hate John the Baptist too?

Baphomet: YES

Tracy: Did they forget that as time went on?

Baphomet: YES

Tracy: Why did the Priory of Sion want the head?

Baphomet: CURSE

Tracy: Did they want to break the curse?

Baphomet: NO

Tracy: Is it that whoever has the head is immune from the curse?

Baphomet: YES

Tracy: Is that the reason for the Cutting of the Elm? The Priory and the Templars split up because of a fight over possession of the head?

Baphomet: YES

Tracy: Is that the reason why the Templars were disbanded by the Church?

Baphomet: YES

Tracy: Did some renegade Templars give the head back to the Priory?

Baphomet: YES

Tracy: Do the Templars exist anymore?

Baphomet: NO

Tracy: Did the hate cult of John the Baptist continue on in Freemasonry?

Baphomet: YES

Tracy: Are the Freemasons fighting against the Priory of Sion as a continuation of feud that the Templars had with them?

Baphomet: NO

Tracy: Are they all part of the same organization now?

Baphomet: YES

Tracy: The Elm is back together again?

Baphomet: YES

Tracy: Do they have any enemies anymore?

Baphomet: YES

Tracy: Who?

Baphomet: NEMES

Tracy: Where did the Baphomet head go?

Baphomet: KADISH

Tracy: Is it still there?

Baphomet: NO

Tracy: So where is it now?

Baphomet: ISTANBUL

Tracy: Where is the spirit of Baphomet?

In reply, he visited the little black star by the crescent moon in the upper right corner. Then he went down to the watery abyss at the bottom of the board, and, we presume, to the real Abyss below as well. Thus ended what was, up until that point, the most productive, amazing, and frightening session we had ever experienced on the Ouija board.

At the time, we had no idea what "KADISH" was. When we looked it up the next day, all that was found was "Kadesh," a city in the ancient Levant and now in modern Syria. More recently, I have discovered that there is a village in Iran named "Kadish," currently populated by fifteen people from four families. But since the Knights Templar controlled territories in Syria, I think this is a much more likely location for the Baphomet head to have landed.

The word "kadesh" or "kadosh" means "holy," and this is the meaning behind name of the thirtieth degree of Scottish Rite Freemasonry, "Knight Kadosh." Although the accusation appears unfounded, the 1918 version of the *Catholic Encyclopedia* stated that there was a version of the Knight Kadosh initiation ritual written by influential Mason Albert Pike, which allegedly included the trampling of something representing the papal tiara. This was imagined by the *Encyclopedia's* authors to be an homage to the rite purportedly practiced by the Templars in which they were supposed to have desecrated a crucifix in such a manner.

Istanbul is an excellent candidate for the hiding place of the Baphomet skull, although I only learned more about this possibility years later. Of course, this city was once called "Constantinople," and was the capitol of the Byzantine Empire. The Christians who lived there spoke Greek and followed the Eastern Church, which had schismed from Rome in 1054.

In 1204 (16 years after the "Cutting of the Elm"), a crusader army (including the Templars) was redirected by the Doge of Venice to attack Constantinople (instead of the Saracen enemy) in order to eliminate the Venetians' chief international trade competition. The knights sacked the city, and even destroyed the Hagia Sophia, the ancient "Church of the Holy Wisdom."

But they didn't just sack it. In the style of the alleged blasphemous secret rites of the Templars, they performed a Satanic "Black Mass" of sorts there. Upon the very throne where the Bishop sat, they crowned and enthroned a woman who was both a witch and a prostitute, then had her perform a lewd song and dance routine.

In 2005 I published my book *Solomon's Treasure,* which contained a couple of chapters about possible connections between the head, the Templars, and

Hagia Sophia. One noteworthy fact is the purported link between "Sophia" and "Baphomet" via the Atbash cipher. More directly, Constantinople, and a place just outside of it called "Hebdomon," were host to not one, but two claimed heads of John the Baptist, one of which came into the possession of the Knights of Saint John (an order that merged with the remnants of the Templars after they were disbanded).

These relics were considered to possess magical protective powers. They were said to have played an important role not only in the history of Constantinople, but of Byzantium as a whole. One of the heads was stolen by the Crusaders during the sack of the city, and is now on display in the Amiens Cathedral in France. Another is still on display in Topkapi Palace in Istanbul. The Hagia Sophia stands rebuilt, and now rededicated as a mosque, in Istanbul today.

The story that Baphomet told us about Jesus being substituted on the cross by Judas is actually the plotline of something called *The Gospel of Barnabas*, dismissed by most scholars as a medieval forgery and Muslim propaganda. We knew nothing about this text during the séance, but later discovered that many details of Baphomet's tale, including using "tricks" to make people believe it was Jesus being crucified, are to be found *Barnabas*.

This is a much more elaborate version of something mentioned briefly in *The Koran*. There it merely says that Jesus allowed somebody to die in his place, and let people think it was him. So although we could tell that Baphomet was giving us a heretical version of the gospel story, and putting himself forth as one of the main characters, we didn't realize at the time that he was giving us specifically Islamic-based heresies.

Regarding Baphomet's claim that the marriage of Jesus and Mary Magdalene resulted in the "END OF ILM," let us look at what that might mean. "Elohim" was a plural noun used to refer to God in the Bible. It was also the name the Canaanites gave for their pantheon of gods.

The Canaanites had a myth about 70 "sons of Elohim" who each bred with humans to found different nations of people. This seems to link up to *Genesis* chapter 6, where the same term, "sons of Elohim" (rendered in English as "sons of God") bred with human females to produce the giants.

At any rate, it seems that one way or another, Jesus was considered a direct inheritor of the DNA of God. There are three ways to think about this: (1) conceived by the Holy Ghost (Christian view); (2) his possible descent from the Nephilim, or (3) his unpolluted descent from Adam through the line of David by both Joseph and Mary. Either way, maybe the marriage with the

Magdalene would have somehow desecrated that lineage, in Baphomet's view.

However, it would take years before I became aware of most of the hidden meaning in this particular séance, which came to be known between Brian and me as "the Gospel According to Baphomet." In the meantime, I filed this transcript away with the others, only bringing it out occasionally to show certain friends, for entertainment purposes. We both became involved in other business, as real life problems and personal dramas sucked us in again.

Chapter 7: Learning to Know

Now I having replied that I was a Brother of the Red- Rosy Cross, he both wondered and seemed to rejoice at it, and then proceeded thus: 'My brother, have you nothing about you with which to purchase a token?' I answered that my ability was small, but if he saw anything about me he had a mind to, it was at his service.

- *The Chymical Wedding of Christian Rosenkreutz*, Johann Valentin Andrae

Over the next few months, we struggled to come up with the money to publish the next issue of our magazine. Finally, it occurred to us that we had not acted on the advice we'd been given from Cain. He had told us that Baphomet had cursed us with money problems, and that the only way to break this curse would be to help Nicholas de Vere publish his book. But I just found it hard to believe that Baphomet could take seriously something as seemingly silly as the Dragon Court. So we called up Baphomet in person again to ask him about it.

Tracy: Is the Dragon Court a "real" organization

Baphomet: YES

Tracy: What is the meaning of De Vere's title?

I was asking about "Prince of Drakenberg." However, the reply I received was about a different title altogether.

Baphomet: DE VERE STUDENT

Tracy: What? Student of what?

Baphomet: STUDENT 37

Tracy: What do you mean by that?

Baphomet: RANK

Tracy: What kind of rank?

Baphomet: DRAGON COURT

Tracy: Are you talking about ranks in the Dragon Court?

Baphomet: YES

Tracy: How many ranks are there in the Dragon Court?

Baphomet: 4008

Tracy: Is "Prince of Drakenberg" a rank?

Baphomet: NO

Tracy: So what is Nick's rank?

Baphomet: STUDENT 37

Tracy: OK ... So what's my rank then?

Baphomet: TWYMAN HEAD

Tracy: My rank is "head"?

Baphomet: YES

Tracy: And De Vere's rank is "student"?

Baphomet: YES.STUDENT 37

This made no sense to me at all. But I persisted with my questions.

Tracy: So what is Brian's rank then?

Baphomet: STUDENT 128

Tracy: OK. Does Boyd have a rank?

Baphomet: 230

Tracy: How do you go up in rank?

Baphomet: LEARNING TO KNOW

I now understand that in chess, "ranks" are the horizontal rows of squares, which one tries to progress one's pieces through to reach the other side of the board. Pawns, when they reach the eighth and final rank, can be transmuted into queens. All of this was totally meaningless to us at the time, however, so we decided to change subjects. We switched to the more personal topic of what curses we each were carrying.

Tracy: What is the most major curse in my life?

Baphomet: MONEY. TRUST GOD.

Tracy: What can we do to improve our luck with money?

Baphomet: BE AT HOME MORE

Tracy: Does Brian have any curses?

Baphomet: YES

Tracy: What's the biggest one?

Baphomet: LETHARGY

Tracy: Does Boyd have any curses?

Baphomet: YES

Tracy: What's the main one?

Baphomet: DRINK

Tracy: What can he do to break the curse?

Baphomet: SELL MORE RECORDS

Tracy: Is there anything else you want to talk about?

Baphomet: MONEY

Tracy: What about money?

Baphomet: LETTER FROM DE VERE

Tracy: I haven't received one lately. Are you telling me there's one coming?

Baphomet: YES. IN THE MAIL.

Tracy: You mean it's already been sent?

Baphomet: YES

Tracy: What's it about?

Baphomet: BOOK

Tracy: Did you want to ask us how we're going to get the money to publish the book?

Baphomet: NO

Tracy: Are you telling us?

Baphomet: YES

Tracy: How?

Baphomet: SELL WINE

Tracy: Sell wine?

Baphomet: WATER. WINE. WATER. WINE. WATER. WINE.

Tracy: You want us to turn water into wine?

Baphomet: YES

Tracy: Like you say you did at the wedding at Cana?

Baphomet: YES

Tracy: How many guests were at the wedding?

Baphomet: 4680

Tracy: Who were they?

Baphomet: DIME

Tracy: What does "dime" mean?

Baphomet: 10 CENTS

Tracy: Did the guests pay 10 cents to get in?

Baphomet: YES

Tracy: Why?

Baphomet: DONATION

Tracy: You're telling me that the wedding guests donated money to Jesus' ministry in exchange for admission to the wedding?

Baphomet: YES

At that moment I remembered that Cain had encouraged us to start a website for the Ordo Lapsit Exillis to raise money to publish Nick's book. Was Baphomet trying to draw an allegorical connection between our fund raising needs, and this strange tale about taking donations at the wedding at Cana? He had also suggested we turn water into wine, as he claimed he had at the wedding, and then sell it. What did this mean, and what was the parallel in our own lives?

Brian and I talked about it for a moment, reasoning it out. The transformation of water into wine was like alchemy. To sell it would be to make money out of nothing, or at least, to take something that isn't worth anything and transform it into something very valuable.

The "wedding" could be a metaphor for the "marriage" of polarities, as in the Rosicrucian alchemical allegory *The Chymical Wedding of Christian Rosenkreutz.* I learned later from re-reading the *Rosenkreutz* text that guests at this wedding did in fact have to be invited, and did have to render payment in the form of a certain coin in order to be admitted. This Rosicrucian connection seemed a fitting one to make, for when discussing the dispute between Jesus and John over the wedding with Mary Magdalene, Baphomet had visited the rose-cross symbol in the corner of the board.

So what we had here, in the story, were guests paying money to be admitted to a wedding, perhaps a secret one (as a controversial one like that between Jesus and Mary might have been). Furthermore, the payment was considered a "donation." The use of the word "dime" (meaning "a tenth") might imply the payment of a tithe (the payment of a tenth of one's earnings to the church).

While there, they were privileged to witness an alchemical union (the wedding itself) and transformation (the water turned to wine). They were even allowed to take communion and consume the magical wine, which they had purchased with their donation. By being invited and paying to attend this secret function, they were signaling their membership in an elite, underground and closed society.

It occurred to us that this was what Baphomet was telling us to do with the OLE. We should turn it into a proper school of alchemy, magic, and the Western occult tradition. We should charge membership fees and solicit donations to fund various works, such as the publishing of De Vere's book. Perhaps Baphomet was telling us that this was the proper way to raise money for such things, and that following this process was, in its own way, a form of alchemy.

I then thought about the sudden riches that Bérenger Saunière came into, supposedly after finding coded parchments hidden in his church. "Debunkers" who believed that the story had a mundane explanation would always point out that Saunière was practicing simony, and was even forbidden by the Church from holding services because of it. He was "selling masses" to both his parishioners and the general public. You could pay him to perform a mass for you for almost anything. He would even advertise these services in local newspapers. It was like paying a voodoo witchdoctor to do a ceremony to help you gain love or win money at gambling.

I realized that Saunière could have gotten rich from donations as well. Furthermore, the parallels with what Baphomet was telling us about the wedding at Cana were direct. Saunière's parishioners there at Rennes-le-Château (a village that still has less than 100 people) were very loyal to him. They believed he possessed supernatural powers, which is why, when he died, the townspeople collected tassels from his robe, as magical talismans. It was as though they were members of a secret society, with Saunière performing magical operations on their behalf, in exchange for tithes and donations. Word got around about Saunière's abilities, and people even came from far away to pay him for masses.

We decided to ask Baphomet for more details on this subject.

Tracy: How did Saunière gain his wealth?

Baphomet: AGEIO

Tracy: Did you teach him how to do this?

Baphomet: YES

Tracy: How?

Baphomet: PRAYER

Tracy: He prayed to you and you talked to him?

Baphomet: YES

Tracy: What is the meaning hidden in the Stations of the Cross that Saunière placed in his church?

Baphomet: DAGOBERT

Tracy: What about Dagobert?

Baphomet: HE IS HERE DEAD

In the first of the parchments found by Saunière, the coded message declares "TO DAGOBERT II KING AND TO SION BELONG THIS TREASURE AND HE IS THERE DEAD."

Tracy: So Dagobert is buried beneath the church?

Baphomet: YES

Tracy: And the Stations of the Cross depict his burial?

Baphomet: YES

This was interesting, because authors on the subject usually speculated that it was Jesus who was buried beneath the church, and that the Stations of the Cross actually depicted his body being removed alive from the tomb in Jerusalem by his secret cohorts. The theory is that he faked his death and ran away with his bride Mary to Southern France, where they both later died and were buried in secret, after spawning children whose descendants would become the Merovingian kings. But Baphomet was merely saying that King Dagobert II was buried there.

I decided to ask about the painting made by Saunière himself, which he placed right at the front of the altar. It depicted Mary Magdalene in a cave, contemplating a skull. Some authors had seen, in the visible landscape outside of the cave, certain similarities to landmarks at Rennes-le-Château. In *Dagobert's Revenge Magazine* we had written about the geometry of a pentagram that appeared to be encoded within the painting also. I wanted to know if that was the Baphomet skull she was looking at.

Tracy: What is the meaning of Saunière's painting of Mary Magdalene?

Baphomet: WEALTH

Tracy: Does it contain the secret of how he gained his wealth?

Baphomet: YES

Tracy: How did Saunière become wealthy?

Baphomet: HE REAPED ALL THE WEALTH

Tracy: Through Ageio?

Baphomet: YES

Tracy: By what agency did he cause his wealth to materialize?

Baphomet: GOD

Tracy: What part of the painting reveals the message?

Baphomet: 5

Baphomet then visited the pentagram symbol on the board.

Tracy: The pentagram?

Baphomet: YES

Tracy: Does the pentagram somehow contain the power to materialize wealth?

Baphomet: YES

We then decided to ask about the so-called "Blanchefort Tombstone." This was a document that had been discussed in all of the books about Rennes-le-Château for decades. It purported to be a rubbing from a tombstone that used to be located in the environs of the church, marking the remains of Marie de Blanchefort, a local noblewoman and heir to the Merovingian blood.

The "tombstone" rubbing contained several strange words and symbols, including an octopus or spider depicted at the bottom of it. Saunière had supposedly made the rubbing before destroying the stone itself, just after finding the parchments and right before the first signs of his wealth emerged. I asked Baphomet about it:

Tracy: What is the hidden message in the Blanchefort tombstone?

Baphomet: FEAR OF GOD

Tracy: What is the meaning of the octopus?

Baphomet: 8 X 8

Tracy: The Ageio board?

Baphomet: YES

Tracy: Did Saunière gain his wealth by transforming base metals into gold?

Baphomet: YES

Tracy: How did he do this?

Baphomet: GOD

I didn't know what to make of all of this stuff about God, but I was curious about the purported "power" of the pentagram. Henry Lincoln was one of the original *Holy Blood, Holy Grail* authors who helped bring the mystery of Rennes-le-Château to the attention of the English-speaking world in the late 1970s. He wrote two books on his own about what he claims is a perfectly mathematically symmetrical pentagram that can be found by connecting the tops of the five mountains which surround the village on a topographical map.

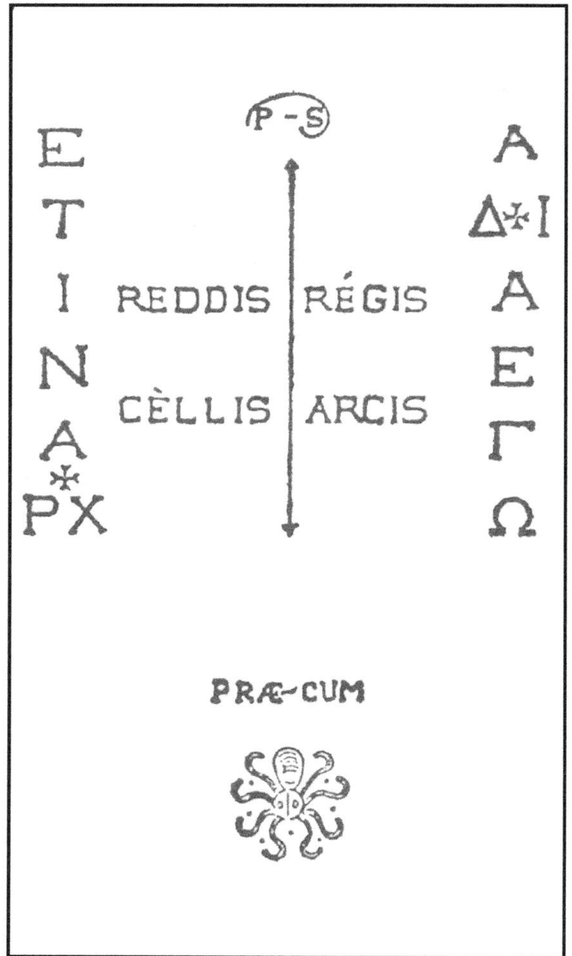

The Blanchefort Tombstone

I had recently interviewed Mr. Lincoln for the magazine, and he had reiterated his theory that this was both 1) a highly unlikely occurrence, and 2) completely natural. He believed that, because this area was the location of a very rare, spontaneous manifestation of an ancient sacred symbol, Rennes-le-Château had become a place of reverence to members of secret societies who were aware of the formation's existence. In his mind, the pentacle of mountains constituted a "natural temple" to the divine, visible to those with eyes to see.

However, because for years I had been writing about the subject of giant super-human antediluvian god-kings in connection to Rennes-le-Château, and because those entities were rumored to exist now in an underground realm, I was considering a different possibility. Throughout the annals of archeology, there are stories of ancient temples and even entire cities being unearthed from places where the only indication of something underground (often beneath layers of dirt, rock and overgrowth formed over thousands of years) is the presence of something that appears artificially symmetrical. I had just recently heard of someone in Bosnia discovering ancient pyramids within some of the mountains there.

Therefore I wondered: *Is it possible that the mountains are really the mark of something artificially made? Could it be that someday, somebody will find underneath them a vast pentagonal temple complex made by giants to venerate some ancient god-king or queen? Is it possible that initiates in the Priory of Sion have known all along that the temple was there? Might there even be hidden tunnels in Rennes-le-Château that allow access to the temple to this day? Could it be that the chosen few still perform ceremonies there?* I had to know the answers, so I asked Baphomet.

In response, he affirmed that it was there, and also indicated that it was the site of a very important tomb from prediluvian times. When we asked who built the complex, he answered: "DAGON." This was the name of a Philistine god always depicted as half-humanoid from the waist up, with a fish tail from the waist down.

Dagon was adored by many ancient societies, as, according to legend, he had come from the sea to teach mankind the most important arts of civilization, just like the Anunnaki fish-gods of the Sumerians. I had written articles speculating that he was one of the god-kings related to Cain, connecting him with the Watchers and the Nephilim. I had also speculated that the name "Dagobert," used by several of the Merovingian kings, might hearken back to Dagon. Indeed, the legend of the Merovingians said that they were descended from a union between a princess and a sea creature, which could have been an echo of a memory of Dagon as their literal ancestor.

Excited about the idea of an ancient underground temple being buried beneath Rennes-le-Château, we got out one of the maps of the area that I had purchased when I visited the village for the Fox TV interview. We took the glass door off of the entertainment center there in the living room, placed the map on the card table that we were using for the Ouija board, and covered it with the glass door to give the map a smooth surface. We then put the planchette on top of the glass and the map. I asked Baphomet to show us where the temple was.

What followed was a good 90-minute segment in which the spirit made the same spiral shape over and over again, always focusing it on the same spot right there at the altar of the church. He would start the spiral from the outside, work his way in, and then methodically spiral out again. He also used the planchette to mark out several important spots on the map, to which he assigned numbers. We had to move the planchette back and forth between the map and the Ouija board constantly so that he could number the locations. He instructed us to write it all down in a list.

At the end of this session, we were utterly exhausted. Our arms ached so much! We didn't analyze it until the next day, when Brian got out a protractor and a ruler. He measured the distance and the angles between the points, then plotted them on a graph. At first it seemed meaningless. Then I realized that it matched up with something I had seen before in a book about sacred geometry by Michael S. Schneider called *The Beginner's Guide to Constructing the Universe.*

This book was about different geometrical patterns that can be found both in nature and in artificial works. In the chapter about the pentagram, Schneider demonstrated how, as the leaves of a plant grow along the stem, they always conform to the shape of a pentagonal Fibonacci spiral. By forming this pattern with certain points on the map, each corresponding to particular (mostly man-made) landmarks in the area, Baphomet seemed to be telling us that the locals there had commemorated this pattern with the locations in which they chose to place certain buildings. Or, perhaps they had been guided subconsciously by a higher intelligence.

It was only a few weeks later that I discovered for the first time translations of the magazines *C.I.R.C.U.I.T.* and *Vaincre,* both published by Pierre Plantard of the Priory of Sion. Before this, I had only seen excerpts from these publications quoted in the books *Holy Blood, Holy Grail* and *The Messianic Legacy* by Baigent, et. al. In it, the authors wrote about an underground temple beneath Rennes-le-Château, accessible somehow via a tunnel near the Blanchefort tomb, which contains thirteen stone seats and a giant image of a sun. The spiral shape was not mentioned, but I wondered if that was the shape of the tunnels leading down to it, perhaps passing through all five mountains along the way. *Maybe,* I thought, *there are even chambers in these tunnels corresponding to the numbered spots marked by Baphomet on the map.*

The revelation from the Priory's publication, and the close correspondence there with what Baphomet was telling us, convinced me more than ever that he was giving us real information. I was even more impressed when, a few days after that last séance, I received a letter out of the blue from Nicholas de Vere, whom I had not talked to in many months. In it he made two amazing requests: (1) That I accept ownership of the copyright for his book *From Transylvania to Tunbridge Wells,* and seek to have it published right away, and (2) That I accept, at least temporarily, the title of "Grand Master" of the Dragon Court. He would retain ultimate control by elevating himself to a different title: "Sovereign Head." But I would be the official leader of record.

All of this made no sense because, of course, I was barely involved in the Dragon Court or any of Nick's projects at all. Also, why would he want to give away the copyright to his own book, especially after Laurence Gardner had already stolen it from him? Wasn't he afraid that I would screw him over too?

Furthermore, for what reason did he suddenly want me of all people to run his Dragon operation, when I still had yet to prove or even claim any connection to Dragon blood? Why did he not want to run his own order anymore? But Baphomet had predicted it.

I called up De Vere to ask him what he meant by all of this. He said that, for reasons he couldn't explain, he no longer wanted the burden of being the Dragon Court Grand Master. He asked me to take it "just for symbolic purposes," and said that if I chose to do absolutely nothing with the Court, that would be fine. It would remain in an "occulted" position until we decided to resurrect it. I thought there was something fishy about this, like he was trying to make me the "HEAD" of the court, and since it supposedly required no sacrifice on my part, I agreed to take the title.

I felt the same way about the book. Again, was he setting me up to take the fall for something? But he said that his friend was editing it now (something that I had told him would need to be done before his crazy manuscript was ready for public consumption). So all I needed to do was find a publisher. Considering that my crushing financial problems were supposedly caused by a curse from Baphomet, all because I had so far failed to do this one thing, how could I possibly refuse?

Chapter 8: Kettle is Black

Jesus answered them, Have not I chosen you twelve, and one of you is a devil? Now He meant Judas the son of Simon Iscariot, for he, one of the twelve, was going to betray Him.

-John 6:70-71

Over the next few months, we were very busy. We were editing the new issue of the magazine and the book I was writing with Boyd. I was also putting together a "best of" compilation of articles from *Dagobert's Revenge*. Brian was busy writing query letters en masse, seeking publishers for all three books (including Nick's).

We were also, with the help of a friend, putting together a website for the Ordo Lapsit Exillis. We were considering creating a lower tier of the order that people from the public could join. For some reason, this bothered Boyd. He wanted the OLE to be something mysterious that he could name-drop in an interview, and nothing more.

Brian and I had been sleeping in the same bedroom since about two months after we moved in together. In July of 2002, we got married by a city magistrate on my back patio, after having been best friends for 11 years already. Our only witness was a friend from Brian's job at a local restaurant. I didn't tell Boyd about it until the day it happened. He was furious, but wouldn't say why.

Everything seemed fine for a little while. We didn't do any séances because we were so busy with our projects. Then one day we got word that the *In Search Of* show about Rennes-le-Château, which Boyd and I had been interviewed for, was about to air on television. We invited some friends over to watch it, and popped a tape into the VCR to record it. But what a surprise: only Boyd's interview made it into the program. I had been cut out completely.

We continued to celebrate with our guests, and everybody got quite a bit drunk. Boyd, of course, took it further than anyone else. At one point, his inebriation got the best of him. As I wondered aloud why my interview had been cut out of the show, Boyd interrupted.

"It's because of what I told them, Tracy. I'm sorry. You were so young. You were only 20. I talked to the producer before the shoot. I told him you were too young and inexperienced. I said the show would be better if only I was in it."

I stared at him in stunned silence. So did everybody else.

"That's why they didn't ask you any questions. Remember?"

I did remember. I remembered that Boyd and I had gone over our talking points at breakfast that morning, detailing which questions each of us would tackle, and what our answers would be. We gave our notes to Doug the producer.

But when the shoot began, they conducted Boyd's interview first. They asked him *all* of the questions on this list, and he gave them *all* of the answers we had written down. This included the ones that I had written, and that were based specifically on my own ideas.

They didn't get around to shooting my "interview" until the end of the day. Instead of asking me questions, Doug just left me alone with the camera rolling. He told me to "go ahead and say whatever you want" while he chatted with his boss on his cell phone.

We then continued to stay at Rennes-le-Château for the next several days while the crew shot b-roll. I repeatedly tried to get them to shoot a more formal interview with me. But I was rebuffed for various reasons each time.

Then on the last night we were there, I remember learning from one of the crew members that they had interviewed some Englishman they met at the hotel. They supposedly needed someone to fill in some of the blanks in the Rennes-le-Château story that neither Boyd nor I had covered on camera yet. I had wondered at the time why they didn't just ask me to do it, and why they had all acted so strange towards me after the first day.

So for some reason, here in his drunken stupor, Boyd was admitting that he had somehow convinced the producer of the show to cut my interview out, and that was why he hadn't even bothered to really interview me in the first place. I suspected there was more to the story, too, than Boyd just telling Doug I was too "young and inexperienced." This in itself is an odd thing to say, and a strange thing for the producer to be concerned about for a show of that sort. Besides, it wasn't true. Even back then, I had already done dozens of radio interviews and at least one TV interview on the subject.

I suspected that Boyd had told Doug something else about me to make him cut me out, probably something made up, since I couldn't think of anything about me that would cause them to do that. I didn't have a bad reputation, but Boyd knew from personal experience how rumors of Satanism and racism could ruin your career. Perhaps it was something like that. To this day, I still don't know.

It was an unbelievably selfish act. Boyd's motivation must have been purely to get more attention for himself, and to take the credit all by himself. I already knew that Boyd had a tendency to do this type of thing to his "friends." But this particular choice of his really amazed me, and I couldn't believe he was actually admitting to it, here in front of everyone. It was only because I was drunk too that I absorbed the news without any visible reaction. I never brought it up to him again either.

Shortly after that, Boyd went on tour in Europe for a few months with his friends from Death in June. While he was gone, Brian and I moved into a house in another neighborhood with a mutual female friend. We left a message on Boyd's answering machine telling him our new address, knowing he wouldn't get it for weeks. At this point, I just wanted to finish the book and be done with that man.

As luck would have it, shortly after Boyd's return from the tour, we received a letter from Red Wheel/Weiser Publishing. This was one of the companies that Brian had queried about publishing my book with Boyd. In fact, it was the best one on the list, being the largest occult book publisher in North America at the time. They offered us a $2000 advance and a deadline of -coincidentally- December 23. I met with Boyd to sign the contract, and two weeks later, we cashed our advance checks. I was on my way to having my first published book.

We told our new roommate, Leah, about our Ouija board sessions. She was intrigued, although slightly disturbed. She asked us if we felt comfortable talking to a being that was trying to take credit for arranging John the Baptist's beheading and helping Jesus set up an innocent man to die on the cross. But she was happy to participate in a trial session with us, to see how it would go. For the sake of variety, and to get another take on the crucifixion story, we decided to conjure up Jesus himself this time. Or at least, that's what we tried to do.

Compared to Baphomet and Cain, Jesus seemed relatively uncooperative. At first he only gave "yes" and "no" answers, or else spoke in incomprehensible number letter codes. He affirmed that he had died of old age well after the crucifixion. When we asked where he was buried, he said "NORTH RUNYN," but wouldn't tell us what that meant.

We asked what code he was using, since most of his answers didn't make sense, and he said "ATBASH 7." (I later tried to decode his answers by shifting the Atbash cipher alphabet by seven letters, both forward and backward, to no avail.) I asked why he was speaking in code. He said "AVOID WORMS" and "LOW QUALITY COMPANY."

I was getting the feeling that Jesus didn't really like us! However, we decided to switch to using a regular Parker Brothers board, instead of the homemade one that Brian had designed. For some reason, that seemed to open him up a little. We did manage to get a bit of a conversation going, and it was somewhat interesting. It went like this:

Tracy: Do you like this board better?

Jesus: KETILE IS BLACK

Tracy: Was Dohir a kingdom before Eden?

Jesus: ARK

Tracy: Is that where the Ark was built?

Jesus: YES

Tracy: Is that where the Ark landed?

Jesus: YES. ARK RESIDE.

Tracy: The Ark resides in Dohir?

Jesus: YES

Tracy: Was it called Dohir before the fall of Eden?

Jesus: YES

Tracy: How can this be?

My understanding at the time was that the word "Dohir" itself meant "fallen land."

Jesus: ARK DESCENDS

Tracy: Why was Dohir so named?

Jesus: ARK

Tracy: Who were the Dohir kings?

Jesus: NEMES

Tracy: The Dohir Kings were slaves?

Jesus: YES

Tracy: Was the Ark built for the Flood?

Jesus: NO

Tracy: Was it built to house Adam's body?

Jesus: YES. ARK RESIDES. REAPS ALL THE WEALTH. ONE BOX OF THINGS.

Tracy: So the Ark holds all treasures?

Jesus: YES

Tracy: So the agei represents the Sangreal?

Jesus: YES

Tracy: The Ark holds the agei?

Jesus: YES

Tracy: Was the war in Eden for the control of the Ark?

Jesus: YES

Tracy: Does whoever holds the Ark hold power over Earth?

Jesus: YES

Tracy: Did the Dohir kings take the Ark?

Jesus: WELL

Tracy: You mean a well with water in it?

Jesus: YES

Tracy: Did they hide it in a well?

Jesus: NO

Tracy: Did they hide it at a well?

Jesus: YES

Eventually, we gave up, as the answers were only vaguely useful to us, and absolutely meaningless to Leah.

Over the next few months, I concentrated mostly on the final edit of the book with Boyd, and writing a constitution for the Ordo Lapsit Exillis. The website was nearing completion, and we were getting quite a bit of response from people interested in joining the order. One such person was "Anthony S," a formerly enthusiastic "priest" in the Church of Satan who had recently converted to Christianity. This had prompted him to want to get involved in the OLE for some reason.

From talking [to] him, it almost seemed like he was trying to go both ways now: to somehow reconcile his Satanism with his Christianity. I gathered that, because in my writing I had talked about the Grail being a symbol of the "union of good and evil," and about the Grail bloodline descending from both Jesus and Cain, he identified with the OLE as an embodiment of his new fence-sitting position regarding God vs. the Devil. It was very clear that he was a rather confused person.

Mr. S responded positively when I indicated that the upper echelons of the order were being reserved for persons who could be particularly helpful in forwarding the order's agenda, financially or otherwise. He organized eBay auctions of several items of memorabilia that he owned - things pertaining to Satanism and underground white power movements. His auctions netted over $1000, which we put towards publishing the next issue of the magazine, along with some credit cards that I acquired just for that purpose.

Another person who came into our lives around this time was Janie. I had been working as a clerk at Wax Trax Records, a job our roommate helped me to get hired for. They actually had three storefronts, all in a strip: a CD store, a vinyl store, and a t-shirt shop in-between. I was on duty at the t-shirt shop when a fellow employee came over from the CD store to inform me that there was a "girl in green shoes" going nuts over a copy of *Dagobert's Revenge* that was for sale near the counter.

The girl had told the clerks over there that she had been a huge fan of *DR* for years. When they informed her that the publisher was working at the store next door, she got even more excited, and requested to see me. I told him to send her on over.

We spent about a half-hour there talking in the store. She was in her early 20s, small, white, and cute, with long, light brown hair, wearing jean shorts and an OTO t-shirt. The lady was visiting from Portland, Oregon, of all places! She had a very bubbly personality, with great wit. She had a history with the Church of Satan and the OTO. She was fanatical about all kinds of obscure art and music.

She liked Boyd's noise work too, and got very excited when I offered to arrange for them to meet. I called Boyd right there and told him to go to the bar down the street to wait for her. I hadn't seen him with a girlfriend the entire time I had known him, and I thought they might hit it off. When I heard about it the next day, it seemed that they had got along well.

Janie came over to our house a short time later. As it turned out, she and Brian already knew each other! Brian used to hang with the downtown Portland Goth and Punk club scene. Janie, as a teenage runaway, had been part of that set. They had met before when she was twelve years old, doing a noise performance with garbage can lids and pieces of sheet metal at O'Brien Square (also known as "Paranoia Park.") I thought it was an amazing and delightful coincidence.

October was approaching again, and that gave me a strange feeling. That first séance with Cain had happened on Halloween night two years earlier. Then the following year we had met our roommate Leah at a Halloween party. I had a feeling it was true what they said about the "veil between the worlds" being especially thin that day, and thus facilitating communication with the realm beyond. I got the sense that there was something weird, something threatening, afoot, spiritually, that was hampering our efforts to some extent. I wondered if anything would happen this All Hallows' Eve to reveal the truth behind these feelings.

Chapter 9: MemoryMask

But I say unto you, Love your enemies, bless them that curse you, do good to them that hate you, and pray for them which despitefully use you, and persecute you ....

- Matthew 5:44

As the next few weeks passed, I noted an odd vibe in my relationship with Boyd. We quarreled a lot about the book. We had chosen which chapters we each would write. But then Boyd kept wanting to cut out my chapters, even though his own chapters were also largely composed of concepts I had come up with, as well as large portions that were entirely written by me. It was just like working with him on the magazine had been.

Boyd had, all this time, refused to touch a computer. He thought they were "geeky." Also, he just seemed to enjoy the feeling of being in charge that he got from tricking other people into working for him for free.

He treated Brian and me both as his personal secretarial team. This was not anything that we had ever agreed to do, but just something that seemed to end up happening. When he needed to send someone an email or a nice typed letter, he would come over and have me do it for him. He sometimes even dictated these things to me on the telephone. He also conscripted Brian to make graphics for him for free.

A lot of this stuff had nothing to do with *Dagobert's Revenge*, the OLE, or the book. It was just stuff for his noise art career, articles for other magazines, stuff for his ex-girlfriend, and stuff for his newly-discovered adult bastard son. At one point he got Brian to design an album cover and send it to the record company without ever telling him that was what the art would be used for. He also lifted a produced piece I had made for a podcast from years earlier and put it on one of his own records without permission, attribution or compensation.

Since meeting me, his interviews had been full of theories, ideas, and sayings that he had absorbed from me. Beginning from the year we met, his noise/music work began to resemble the content and style I had given to *Dagobert's Revenge*. Yet he rarely mentioned me in any of his interviews. This copying and posturing was something he would always complain that friends had done to him in the past, but here he was doing it to me with no sense of irony.

When it came to the magazine, for years he had been turning in his articles in a hand-written format, which I would then have to decipher, type, and edit for him. As I mentioned, these were almost never articles that I had even agreed to print. It did not occur to him to seek permission.

Also, as I said, many times the article would simply be his own version of material that I had already written. He would even bully me to remove my own articles from my own magazine so that they wouldn't be "redundant" alongside his. In the early days, sometimes I actually complied with this demand because I didn't want the magazine to seem like it was entirely written by me (just as I had written articles under pseudonyms in the first two issues). Later, I sometimes complied just to continue getting along with him long enough to finish our book.

Boyd's articles were also always full of the most flagrant factual errors, as well as things that were poorly explained, bad grammar, and incorrect word choice. Therefore they required significant fact-checking and editing, even actual re -writing of large portions. Worse yet, there were usually sections where he would simply leave a blank underlined space, with instructions in parentheses for what facts I was to look up and insert for him, or what concepts I was to explain for him.

He had a tendency to write down quotations from memory, often inaccurate and misattributed. Frequently, references from apocryphal scriptures would be attributed to "the Bible." In one of his pieces he actually wrote that "the Bible says, 'God only comes out at night. '" This line in particular had become an inside joke between me and Brian for a while.

Yet Boyd would get very defensive about any editorial changes that were made. Needless to say, working on his stuff was very unpleasant, especially when it was full of my own ideas, and especially since he was pressuring me to edit out my own expression of these very same ideas. Predictably, writing the book together was going the exact same way.

In general, my approach to these projects with *Dagobert's Revenge* and the OLE was that of a trooper. I saw it as a team effort, since it was being marketed as such. Considering that the book was going to have both my name and Boyd's on the cover, I didn't see any point in trying to ensure that everyone else gave me credit for my specific contributions.

However, as I discovered over time, Boyd had the exact opposite approach, even though he said otherwise. His strategy, which he had been playing stealthily all along, was to enter into each collaboration with another person as a wolf in sheep's clothing, and make sure that he got credit for his own contributions, as well as everything that anyone else did too.

I realized these things about Boyd within the first couple of years of knowing him. I heard him tell me stories about all of his past artistic collaborations, and it was always the same. He taught the person everything they knew, introduced them to all the cool people, but they just started copying him and stealing his ideas. I watched him with my own eyes build up and then devalue his friend Vadge this way. I talked to my roommate, and she said that Boyd had a reputation for treating people like this. She knew other victims of his as well. By the time we were almost finished with our book, I had come to the conclusion that Boyd was a totally talentless fraud, completely disloyal to his friends, and dangerous.

Confirmation of this soon came in the mail. Boyd had recently done an interview for some 'zine based in Florida. The publisher had sent him a copy of the interview transcript for review. This was something he always insisted on before an interview with him was published in writing, so he could tell them how to edit it, to make himself seem smarter.

Unfortunately for him, she accidentally sent it to the *Dagobert's Revenge* P.O. box instead of Boyd's personal box. The interview contained exactly what I suspected: Boyd taking credit for all of my work, and trashing me. I passed the envelope on to Boyd, and I don't think he realized that I had already read the contents.

Right on cue, another person entered the scene: my replacement as Boyd's "secretary." He was a 26-year-old man named Clark Davis, who acted like he was 10 years younger. He actually had just moved to Denver from Portland for the express purpose of "working" with Boyd. In what way, I didn't know. I got to meet him one day at the Streets of London pub, where Boyd told me to come and pick up the latest chapter he had written for our book.

That night, Clark Davis wore black jeans and a black hoodie with a yellow happy face button pinned to the breast. I witnessed Boyd tell him that this symbol had come to popularity because of his influence on popular culture. He was using this symbol as a child, he said, and then suddenly everyone else started doing it too. He also took responsibility for the popularity of the music group Abba, which he said he was "into" long before anyone else was.

I was used to hearing him say garbage like this all the time. Mr. Davis just sat there drunk and stupefied, sucking up every word. He told me he admired Boyd as an example of what a man should be. I wanted to vomit.

I think I only saw Mr. Davis again one more time. He went with me, Boyd, and Janie to Casa Bonita, the famous Mexican restaurant and theme park lampooned in an episode of "South Park." I brought my new OLE lunchbox that we had made through Cafe Press, which was a brand new company at the time. Clark Davis eagerly wrote down the information for Cafe Press, and said that he was going to be making some merchandise for Boyd.

It seemed like we all got along at the time. We even sang Whitney Houston's "The Greatest Love of All" spontaneously in the car on the way back. But underneath it all, I could smell the looming scent of impending betrayal.

Anthony S wrote to say that he was coming to Denver for a visit during the week of Halloween. I sensed danger in this, and I decided to take a chance by dropping him a warning. I told him I was afraid that Boyd was turning against me, and that he was going to try to create a schism in the OLE so that he could take it over.

Mr. S promised he wouldn't say anything about this to Boyd while he was in town. Instead, he said that he would watch Boyd for suspicious behavior and report back to me. I knew he was lying and that he would pass what I had said on to Boyd immediately.

I was basically hoping that it would make Boyd think twice about proceeding with his plot against me. My plan was to continue being a sincere friend to him, thinking maybe he would reciprocate. I didn't see any reason why we couldn't just finish the book and then go our separate ways. The OLE and *Dagobert's Revenge* had existed before him, and could go on without him while we both gained from the publication of our book. I wanted to just finish up the projects while remaining amicable.

Meanwhile, there was another schism brewing, this time within the Dragon Court. One of the members, James Berkley, had decided to publicly denounce De Vere and promote a new, rival version of the Dragon Court with another apostate member, Ronald Dreyfus, as the head. This in itself was certainly rude and annoying. The major issue was that Berkley was the webmaster and owner of the Dragon Court's official website.

The problem had occurred (as problems always do) just when something good was about to happen. We had found a publisher for Nick's book, now renamed The Dragon Legacy. His friend had edited it, and Brian had already designed a cover. The publisher, understandably, wanted the text of the unedited version taken down from the Dragon Court website before publication.

That was what had set Berkley off. I think he was mad at the request to remove the main content and traffic drive for his website. The fact that the material didn't belong to him, and was the brainchild of the very man he was insulting, didn't seem like a contradiction to him. He refused to take it down.

Instead he published a long, scathing and nonsensical rant against both De Vere and me on the front page of the Dragon Court's website.

Apparently, he and his accomplice Ronald Dreyfus were mad that De Vere had made me head of the Court (something Nicholas swore that he hadn't even told them, or anyone, so far). It seemed that they hated me because I was an American. They were also angry about Nick's book getting published because it was a commercial venture. They excoriated both me and De Vere for "trying to make money."

Many of the people in De Vere's audience would constantly criticize him for making any profit whatsoever from his own work. I had witnessed this several times in the course of our friendship. For some reason, instead of telling these people to fuck off, he would refuse to take any money that was earned, giving it to his chosen friends instead. This, I believe, is why he gave me ownership of the copyright to his book, instructing me to distribute the proceeds between myself and these friends.

As the leader of the Court, and as Nick's agent, I couldn't let this attempted coup and public insult go unpunished. Mr. Berkley had just been diagnosed with a brain tumor (something which probably, more than anything, explained his bizarre recent behavior). He ignored our legal notices to take down the copyrighted material and had his lawyer threaten to sue us for "harassing" him. So Brian and I decided we ought to give him something to cry about.

We spent the evening loading down the Dragon Court forums on the site with garbage messages. This included lists of funeral homes in Berkley's home town, and anything else we could think of to hasten the course of nature in the old man's cancerous brain. They had to take the site down for a while, which we took as a temporary victory.

We suspected that in addition to Ronald Dreyfus, Berkley was conspiring with a handful of other former Dragon Court members who wanted to have a coup and take it over for themselves. I thought it was likely that this involved one woman in particular who had been stalking and attacking me everywhere I went on the internet since I had first started talking to De Vere five years earlier.

This woman - the aforementioned "Star of the Sea" - had already left the Court and turned against Nick well before I ran into him. She was now the leader of her own group. For the purposes of this book, we will refer to that group as "MemoMa."

I couldn't really tell what this group was all about, but I gathered that they were involved in psychic activities. On forums, Star of the Sea bragged about her ability to "navigate," a term she used for remote viewing. She chose that term because, in the Priory of Sion, the Grand Master was called "the Navigator."

We wondered if she was in on the Dragon Court conspiracy with Berkley and Dreyfus. We also wondered if she was using black magic against us. We decided to consult Baphomet to find out. Here is how it went:

Tracy: Is Star of the Sea in on the conspiracy against the Dragon Court with James Berkley?

Baphomet: YES

Tracy: Is Star of the Sea doing a spell against us?

Baphomet: YES

Tracy: What is it about?

Baphomet: VERE. MMM. HAZE.

Tracy: "Haze" as in "fog"?

Baphomet: YES

Tracy: You mean like a spell of distraction?

Baphomet: YES

Tracy: Distraction from what?

Baphomet: MMM

Tracy: Is this a person?

At this point; he visited the chessboard in the corner of the Ouija board. On reflection, considering the things he went on to say, I think he meant to indicate that it was a team of people, against whom our team was pitted, in a battle that we were unaware was going on. It occurred to Brian that "MMM" could stand for "MemoMa."

Tracy: Is it MemoMa?

Baphomet: YES

Tracy: Do the letters "MMM" also have a deeper meaning?

Baphomet: YES

Tracy: Does the sound of three Ms together have significance?

Baphomet: YES

Tracy: Is it a magic phrase?

Baphomet: YES

Tracy: What does the magical phrase do?

Baphomet: HELP IN MIND

Tracy: Does it describe MemoMa?

Baphomet: NO. HAM. WATER.

Tracy: What's Nicholas de Vere's involvement in MemoMa?

Baphomet: NONE

Tracy: What is his involvement with Star of the Sea?

Baphomet: FRIEND

Tracy: Why are they out to get him?

Baphomet: DRAK

Tracy: Drakenberg?

Baphomet: YES

Tracy: Are they capable of seizing his right to create Drakenberg?

Baphomet: NO

Tracy: What makes them think that they can?

Baphomet: IGNORANCE

Tracy: But they think they can?

Baphomet: YES

Tracy: Is there any legal substance to their claims?

Baphomet: NO

Tracy: Is Ronald Dreyfus part of the problem?

Baphomet: YES

Tracy: Is he trying to gain control of it?

Baphomet: YES

Tracy: Is Star of the Sea part of De Vere's family?

Baphomet: YES

Tracy: Does Nick know this?

Baphomet: YES

Tracy: What's the relation?

Baphomet: MARRIAGE

Tracy: Is she married to someone in the family?

Baphomet: YES

Tracy: Do we know him?

Baphomet: NO

Tracy: So do you have any advice for us about the spell Star of the Sea put on us?

Baphomet: MMM

Tracy: In relation to what?

Baphomet: MEMOMA

Tracy: Are you saying that we should employ the "MMM" somehow, magically?

Baphomet: YES

Tracy: Can it be used as a curse?

Baphomet: YES

Tracy: Did they use it against us?

Baphomet: YES

Tracy: Did they do this last year?

Baphomet: NO

Tracy: 2 years ago?

Baphomet: NO

Tracy: 3 years ago?

Baphomet: YES

Tracy: Why didn't you mention it before?

Baphomet: NOT SAFE

Tracy: What threat did you feel?

Baphomet: NONE

Tracy: Are you saying we were the ones who were threatened, not you?

Baphomet: MMM

Tracy: What is the curse?

Baphomet: MMM

Tracy: What effect does it have?

Baphomet: HELP

Tracy: When used as a curse, can it prevent help from coming?

Baphomet: YES

Tracy: Help for what?

Baphomet: EVERYTHING

Tracy: Is there a danger in us knowing about it?

Baphomet: YES

Tracy: Do you hate MemoMa?

Baphomet: YES

Tracy: Will you stop them?

Baphomet: YES

Tracy: Where do we start?

Baphomet: HELP

Tracy: Is this lawsuit threat from James Berkley significant?

Baphomet: NO

Tracy: Is the curse significant?

Baphomet: YES

Tracy: Is the lawsuit part of the curse?

Baphomet: YES

Tracy: Does Star of the Sea talk to you?

Baphomet: YES

Tracy: Is she psychic?

Baphomet: NO

Tracy: Does she have magical powers?

Baphomet: YES

Tracy: Do others in MemoMa also have magical powers?

Baphomet: YES

Tracy: Who?

Baphomet: GROUP

Tracy: The entire group?

Baphomet: YES

Tracy: Do they have power only as a group?

Baphomet: YES

Tracy: Are we able to make them go away?

Baphomet: NO

Tracy: Are they using your power?

Baphomet: YES

Tracy: Is the MMM a sign for summoning your help?

Baphomet: YES

Tracy: Are you obliged to help people who use it?

Baphomet: NO

Tracy: Do the MemoMa people think you are?

Baphomet: YES

Tracy: Does that in itself give them power?

Baphomet: YES

Tracy: How do we employ the MMM?

Baphomet: HELP

Tracy: We use it to ask for help?

Baphomet: YES

Tracy: Where was this symbolism of three Ms established?

Baphomet: WATER

Tracy: Do three Ms symbolize water?

Baphomet: YES

Tracy: Is Baphomet MMM?

Baphomet: YES

Tracy: What about two Ms? Can that stand for Mary Magdalene?

Baphomet: YES

Tracy: Is that like a lesser aspect of the MMM concept?

Baphomet: YES

Tracy: Can the Virgo symbol be substituted for the letter M?

I asked this because the Priory of Sion purportedly called themselves by the nickname "Ormus," and their symbol was the sign for Virgo, substituted for the "M" in "Ormus," with the other four letters written inside of it.

Baphomet: YES

Tracy: Can the number 13 be substituted?

Baphomet: YES

Tracy: What's the significance of the number 13?

Baphomet: FALL

Tracy: You mean autumn?

Baphomet: YES. NO.

Tracy: Is the number 13 associated with Baphomet?

Baphomet: YES

Tracy: What is the significance of Halloween? Does it have anything to do with the date "31" being the inverse of 13?

Baphomet: IS HOLY

At this point, I decided to clarify something. De Vere had recently sent a page to be inserted as one of the appendices of his book. It gave the "organizational structure" of the Dragon Court, although it included only four people, including Nicholas and me, with the rest of the people listed at the bottom as "Membership." The Grand Master was said to be "Renee Drakenberg" (that was me), and Nicholas de Vere was placed above everyone else on the page, designated with the title "Sovereign." After sending it, Nick called both the publisher and me twice to make sure that it was being included. It seemed very important to him, but he wouldn't say why. So we asked Baphomet.

Tracy: Why does Nick suddenly want the structure of the Dragon Court documented in the book?

Baphomet: DREYFUS

Tracy: Why does Dreyfus think he has a right to control the Dragon Court?

Baphomet: NAME

Tracy: What about his name?

Baphomet: PLANTAGENET

Tracy: How should we do the ritual to remove the curse of MemoMa and put a curse on them instead?

Baphomet: WRITE WHAT IS TO HAPPEN TO MMM AND THEN BURN IN RITUAL

That last line was very long and I was quite surprised at how quickly it was spelled out. He seemed to be getting excited talking about having us do a ritual.

Tracy: What else?

Baphomet: INVOKE ME

Tracy: What else?

Baphomet: CALL THE POINTS

To "call the points" in ritual magic means to invoke the guardian powers of the four directions of the compass, which helps to designate the sacred space within which you are working. This is done with purifying water and/or smoke from incense. Writing down a ritual's intent and then burning it in flame to release it into the ether is a standard practice in Aleister Crowley's OTO ceremonies. It is also part of the ritual structure detailed in Anton LaVey's *The Satanic Bible*, as Brian pointed out to me.

I have always found LaVey's book to be moronic and juvenile. But Brian, who had read it as a teenager, insisted that the rituals presented there were very simple, and might make a useful model. So he was the one who suggested the next question.

Tracy: Should we use the ritual structure found in *The Satanic Bible* and change all the "Satanic" elements to Baphometic?

Baphomet: YES

Tracy: Should we burn a sigil made from the letters "MMM"?

Baphomet: YES

Tracy: What should we curse Star of the Sea with?

Baphomet: MEMORY

Tracy: You mean we should have false memories implanted in her head?

This question was inspired.

Baphomet: YES

Tracy: Of what?

Baphomet: SEX ABUSE. SRA.

"S.R.A." stands for "Satanic Ritual Abuse," and usually refers to the alleged sexual exploitation of children during such rituals. Allegations of SRA usually come from "recovered memories" of adults.

Tracy: Who all should we curse?

Baphomet: STAR OF THE SEA. MEMOMA. JAMES BERKLEY.

Tracy: What should we read in place of the Enochian Key?

By this I was referring to the made-up bullshit so-called "Enochian Keys" that LaVey had included in his ritual structure, which bear no resemblance to the ones famously channeled by Dr. John Dee. I was pretty sure that Baphomet didn't want us to actually use this stuff, and his answer affirmed that.

Baphomet: SOMETHING GLORIFYING ME. BAPHOMET. MMM.

Tracy: What symbol of you should we use on the altar?

Baphomet: SEVERAL

Tracy: Which ones?

Baphomet: PENTAGRAM. SKULL. GOAT. WATER. VIRGO. STAR OF THE SEA. FISH.

Tracy: What sort of emotion should we project?

Baphomet: CONFUSION OF EVERYTHING

Having gotten some clues about how to do the ritual, I decided to try to clear up some of my questions about the organization that had gotten me involved in this covert black magic war in the first place. I realized I still did not know much about the Dragon Court, so I inquired.

Tracy: What is the secret of the Dragon Court?

Baphomet: QUEEN K

Tracy: What is the meaning of the Dragon Court?

Baphomet: DRAGON BLOOD

Tracy: What power comes from being in the Dragon Court?

Baphomet: NONE

Tracy: Why did Cain tell us earlier that De Vere was going to inherit property in the Aude Valley from Pierre Plantard?

Baphomet: BOY HOME

Tracy: Didn't he say that Brian and I have an inheritance in that area also?

Baphomet: ARC

Tracy: What will we inherit?

Baphomet: WELL

Tracy: You're saying we're going to inherit a well?

Baphomet: YES

Tracy: What will we find at the bottom?

Baphomet: WATER

Tracy: Does the water have a name?

Baphomet: EM

I had recently found someone named Thomas Plantard online that I had reason to believe was the actual son of Pierre Plantard. Thomas was at the time listed as the present Grand Master of the Priory of Sion. So I asked Baphomet about this:

Tracy: Is the picture of Thomas Plantard that I found the right guy?

Baphomet: YES

Tracy: If I send him an email or a letter, will he respond?

Baphomet: YES

Tracy: Is there any particular message I should give him when I try to contact him?

Baphomet: NO

Tracy: Will we get to interview him?

Baphomet: NO

Tracy: Will he invite us into the Priory?

Baphomet: NO

Tracy: Do you want me to contact him?

Baphomet: NO

Tracy: Why not?

Baphomet: FAR HIGHER

Tracy: You mean because he's far higher than me?

Baphomet: NO

Tracy: Do you mean because I should reach far higher than him?

Baphomet: YES

Tracy: Is there someone else in the Priory that I should contact?

Baphomet: NO

Tracy: Why don't you want me to contact the Priory?

Baphomet: DABBLRS (sic)

Tracy: The Priory of Sion are dabblers?

Baphomet: YES

Vainere, published in the 1940s and edited by Pierre Plantard, was the official magazine of Alpha Galates, which seemed to have been a front group for the Priory of Sion. In the 1990s, his son Thomas published a new issue of *Vaincre,* quite out of the blue. So I asked:

Tracy: Why did Thomas Plantard put out that last issue of *Vainere*?

Baphomet: FUN

Tracy: It was a joke?

Baphomet: YES

Tracy: Are the Priory of Sion a hoax?

Baphomet: NO

Tracy: Are the modern Priory of Sion a hoax?

Baphomet: YES

Tracy: Is there another group that now continues the tradition of the Priory?

Baphomet: MANY

Tracy: Why don't you want us to contact the Priory?

Baphomet: DOING FINE

Tracy: You mean you're pleased with our progress?

Baphomet: YES

Tracy: Is the money curse on us about to be broken?

Baphomet: YES. IN THE MAIL.

Tracy: You mean the money is literally already in the mail?

Baphomet: NO

Tracy: You mean figuratively? Like it's already been slated for us?

Baphomet: YES

Tracy: Is there anything else we need to do to break the curse?

Baphomet: ACKNOWLEDGE BAPHOMET

Tracy: I thought that by publishing the book, we were acknowledging Baphomet.

Baphomet: YES. DOING FINE.

Tracy: Is there anything else we need to do?

Baphomet: QUELL THE PEOPLE

Tracy: Who are "the people"?

Baphomet: READERS

Tracy: You mean by putting out the next issue of our magazine?

Baphomet: YES

This last line did make sense to us, since we had been bombarded lately by subscribers who were angry that the new issue of *Dagobert's Revenge* was late. We had gotten them printed and thought they were going to be shipped to us any day. But then the printer told us they had given us an incorrect quote, and that it would actually cost twice as much. They wouldn't ship us the magazines until we sent them the money. We were waiting to either find the money to meet their demands, or another printer who could do it cheaper. However, then we would have to start all over again, and we had already been waiting weeks for a shipment that never came.

The next day, I received a phone call from Janie, who was crying hysterically. She told me a story about how she had gone out with Boyd to a Marilyn Manson concert. They had met with Manson backstage (since he and Boyd knew each other), and she said Boyd stole an entire bottle of absinthe from the dressing room. He and Janie then started walking towards his house, Boyd drinking absinthe the entire time. By the time they got to his doorstep, she said he was belligerently drunk. Then something unpleasant reportedly happened, which I won't describe.

Now they were no longer friends. I said what I could to try to comfort her. I was a little bit embarrassed on Boyd's behalf, since I was the one who had initially set them up.

After a while, she calmed down, and I told her a little bit about the séance we'd had the night before. I asked her for some advice about making sigils (since that was a subject she was an expert on). She told me that "MMM" was an abbreviation used in the OTO that stood for "Most Mysterious Master," a reference to Baphomet himself! Well, sort of. There are other slight variations on the interpretation she gave me.

According to the website "oto.fi" (accessed most recently in May 2014), the "The M.M.M. (Mysteria Mystica Maxima) is the name of the British section of the O.T.O. This includes all countries where English is generally spoken." Furthermore:

"*The authority of the O.T.O. is concentrated in the O.H.O. (Outer Head of the Order), or Frater Superior. The name of the person occupying this office is never disclosed except to his immediate representatives. The Authority of the O.H.O. in all English-speaking countries is delegated by charter to the Most Holy, Most Illustrious, Most Illuminated, and Most Puissant Baphomet X Rex Summus Sanctissimus 33°, 90°, 96°, Past Grand Master of the United States of America, Grand Master of Ireland, Iona, and All the Britains (Free and Independent Great Britain and Ireland), Sovereign Grand Commander of the Order of the Temple, Most Wise Sovereign of the Order of the Rosy Cross, Grand Zerubbabel of the Order of the*

Holy Royal Arch of Enoch, etc. etc. etc., National Grand Master General ad vitam of the M.'.M. '.M.' "

So it seemed that "MMM" was a designation of Baphomet acting as the "Outer Head" of a magical order. The OTO kept their "Outer Head" shrouded in mystery and talked as though he was a living human being. But in fact, it was probably really Baphomet, and the upper echelons of the order were probably channeling instructions directly from him, just like we were.

I was starting to realize that Baphomet was most likely the inspiration for all magical orders, including every Western occult group that claimed descent from the Templars, and probably every fraternal group with an organizational structure similar to the Freemasons. The "secret" of these groups was probably their communication with Baphomet. So, I understood that this was what was going on with MemoMa as well, whether they knew it or not, and that was why the magic of "MMM" could be employed against them.

That night, Anthony S arrived in town from California. The next morning, I met him and Boyd at a Mexican Restaurant on Colfax, right at the bottom of Mr. S' hotel, for breakfast. He was everything I thought he would be: a pathetic kiss-ass to Boyd, dressed up in cheap black slacks and boots, with a black leather jacket and a crew cut. He looked like a professional security guard, which he was, for a grocery store.

We all got along OK that morning. I asked what made him become a Christian. He said it was something to do with a time when he saved the life of a teenage girl in his store by doing CPR. I was unclear how this had led to Christian revelation, and he didn't seem to want to talk about it.

Mr. S tried to tell me all about his "research" into Nicholas de Vere's genealogy, to "prove" to me that he was "illegitimate." It was clear that Boyd, who hated De Vere because I was loyal to him, had been talking to Mr. S about this subject. It was easy to figure out what else they were probably been discussing. At one point, I got up to use the bathroom. When I came back, I found that they were talking about Janie. Boyd was making fun of her.

"Hey Tracy," he said, in a snarling, sarcastic voice. "Why don't you give these back to your friend Janie so that she doesn't come back to my house looking for them."

He reached into a plastic grocery bag he had brought with him and pulled out some laminated pages of collage art. It was something that Janie had made for him.

"She gave these to me, but really, what are am I going to do with them?"

I took the pages, silently, and stared at him. He looked uncomfortable, and then filled the silence.

"Look, I don't know what she told you about what happened the other night, but that woman is crazy. I told her to stay away from me."

"OK," I said. I didn't ask for further details. He and Mr. S looked at each other for a moment and smiled, sharing a knowing glance.

Later that night, Boyd and Mr. S went to a tattoo shop together. There they received identical Cross of Lorraine tattoos on their arms. They had called me and tried to get me to go with them, but I told them that I hated tattoos, which is true.

Unbeknownst to either of them, Brian and I had begun to prepare for the first major ritual of the OLE (aside from Vadge's wedding): the cursing of MemoMa. We had been to antique stores to buy things like the perfect bell to use, a nice chalice for drinking communion, and an incense censer. Brian already had a ritual dagger that he had utilized in other workings prior to moving to Denver, so we decided to use that.

Furthermore, we had available to us one of the most useful tools of all: a Baphometic magical current. When we told De Vere that the OLE's inner circle was about to do some rituals, he took it upon himself to send us a certificate in the mail which bestowed upon the OLE a "charter" coming from "the Baphometic Order of the Cubic Stone." He claimed that this was an old order of "royal witchcraft," and that the Dragon Court now had control of it. He said that the charter gave us the right, via a "magical Baphometic current," to connect our order to his, and to utilize the power that the Dragon Court was connected to. This, in turn, would help to power our magical workings.

Brian had a dream on October 30th where he was told that we should do the curse ritual on Halloween, and that we should call it "MeMoryMask": a play on the word "MemoMa, emphasizing the three Ms, which trump the two capitalized Ms in the title of our enemy's group. It was also a reference to the concept of implanting false memories, which was the effect that the curse was supposed to have. Moreover, it was especially meaningful on Halloween people wear masks as part of their costumes. Also, Halloween is one of the nights when, alleged victims claim, Satanic Ritual Abuse is most likely to happen, being the most holy day of the witches.

Some of the ritual implements we used were actually things of Boyd's that he had left at our old apartment when we held Vadge Moore's wedding there, including the real human skull inside of the plastic party goblet. Strangely, he came over the very next day with Anthony S. (who was about to fly home). All of the sudden, out of the blue, he said that he needed to take his things back. He didn't take his sewing machine back, though, because Brian's fish tank was sitting on top of it.

While he was in the bathroom, Mr. S told me about the Halloween party he had gone to with Boyd the night before. Anthony, who didn't drink and was a recovering alcoholic, watched Boyd, who was dressed up as Mussolini, get uproariously drunk and harass a black guy sitting at a diner. This had caused Mr. S much embarrassment.

It was obvious to me that Boyd was reverting back to an older personality that he had worn before he knew me. When he was around me, he pretended to be much more mature. But now that he was done with me, he was surrounding himself with people who loved him for his reputation as a childish, racist asshole. He was now living up to what they expected of him. I wondered what self-destructive thing he was going to do next, and how it would affect me. I didn't have to wait long to find out.

Chapter 10: Apocalypsis Baphometis

For when we hear one rack the name of God, abjure the Scriptures and his Saviour Christ, we fly in hope to get his glorious soul; nor will we come, unless he use such means whereby he is in danger to be damn'd: Therefore the shortest cut for conjuring is stoutly to abjure the Trinity, and pray devoutly to the Prince of Hell.

- Mephistopheles, *Doctor Faustus*, Christopher Marlowe

More than any other, one event in particular signaled an official chill in my relationship with Boyd. Death in June came to Denver to play a show with him. This had happened before, and much to my delight at the time, Douglas P. (the band leader) had actually come over to our apartment after the show (along with a throng of doe-eyed acolytes). He had sat in our living room drinking gin while his fans sat on the floor asking him questions.

But this time, unlike the previous occasion, Boyd did not put me on the comp list for the show. In fact, he didn't even tell me it was happening. I had to hear it from Leah and Janie. The band actually came and went without us ever discussing it.

Communication between us was limited to only what was absolutely necessary to finish the book. Eventually, very close to Christmas, the final draft was sent in to the publisher. There were also some photographs and other documents that each of us was supposed to send in.

I posted my stuff and didn't bother to remind Boyd about the impending deadline to submit his. He normally would have expected me to keep track of that for him, and to prepare his materials for submission. I later found out through Leah (who knew him independently from us) that he was very pissed off about this because he had assumed I was going to do these things for him and he nearly missed the deadline. I laughed at this.

One of the last communications I got from him, right before the book was submitted, was through Anthony S. He was still pretending to be a loyal OLE member and mutual friend of ours. He said that Boyd wanted him to review the manuscript for typos before we sent it in, and therefore wanted me to email the file to Anthony.

I had a feeling that there was an ulterior motive here. But since the material was owned by both Boyd and me, and the three of us were still ostensibly friends, I couldn't think of a good basis to deny the request. I wish, in retrospect, that I had. This furnished Boyd with the only electronic copy of the work that he had heretofore possessed.

But I had many other things on my mind at the time. I received another book offer from a mid-sized publisher, and was able to make a ghostwriting deal with them. De Vere's book was already out and stirring up controversy. Most importantly, I had written a new Constitution for the Ordo Lapsit Exillis, and published it to the order's website.

Besides the inner circle of "navigators" (me, Brian, and our close friends), we now had two other degrees. The lowest rank was "Legionnaire." These people merely paid a fee, and gained access to the OLE's website. "Quartermaster" was the second degree. These were the people we wanted to screen and potentially collaborate with, both for ritual magic purposes, as well as Grail-related research and media projects.

The first quartermasters were chosen by me and Brian from among those who expressed interest, usually through email, and who were able to pay the application fee. We would send them a kit in the mail with things they would need to conduct their own self-initiation ceremony. This included a booklet containing the order's constitution and the ritual script. We also sent along a sealed envelope containing the degree's password, as well as a placard with the Cross of Lorraine and degree motto (for meditation).

The most important part of the initiation was the blood oath of secrecy and loyalty to the order. This was typed on a fancy-looking sheet of parchment that was chosen for its ability to absorb blood. After speaking the oath aloud with his hand placed on the Bible, the candidate would then cut his ankle with a razor blade (included in the package) and bleed onto a marked box in the lower right corner of the page, right next to his signature in ink.

Once the ceremony was completed, the blood-stained parchment was to be sent back in to the home office, to be kept on file. We also had the candidates send in questionnaires about their education, skills, and relevant experience (such as serving in the military, clandestine services, or other fraternal orders). I didn't know what to do with this information, but I was hoping that it would come to me over time. Anyway I figured it would show that we were serious.

Boyd was now filling up our voicemail box at home with semi-frantic messages. He wanted me to call him back to "discuss some things." I ignored call after call, as they became increasing in desperation. Friendly at first, making like he just wanted to "hang out," the later messages were more demanding. He stated that we needed to finalize some unspecified plans for the future, and that we both were in possession of borrowed items that belonged to one another.

Finally, I wrote him a letter with a list of all of the items of mine that I could remember him having. I posted it in the mail with a stamp instead of dropping it off on his doorstep. It only took him a day to get it. Then I received something I had never gotten from him before: an email.

Absent my help, Boyd had broken down and bought a computer, created an email account, and learned how to use it. I had been trying to get him to do this for 5 years, but he had me available, so he felt that he didn't need to. Now he had no choice.

Boyd's message stated that two of the books on my list belonged to him because, he claimed, they had been given to him by a mutual friend, not to me. However, if I agreed to meet with him, he said, he would generously allow me to have them.

Well, that wasn't true. This friend of ours had taken me book shopping when we first met, and these were two of the three books he had bought me that day. Later Boyd had borrowed them from me.

But I didn't care about them enough to interrupt the psychological operation I was doing on Boyd. He wasn't used to being disobeyed, much less ignored and disrespected; by someone he considered his bitch. Experiencing this from me was upsetting his equilibrium, and it was fun to watch. So I let him keep the books.

I only saw Boyd in the flesh one more time. A few days after I received his email, Janie came over to hang out with Leah and me. We all decided to go out for drinks. On a lark, we chose the Streets of London, Boyd's favorite bar, and the one closest to his house. We knew there was the possibility that he might be there, but we decided to do it anyway. The bars in our area sucked, and we were feeling adventurous.

We didn't know what would happen. Personally, I was hoping that this might be one of those nights that he was drinking at home with a couple of extra-large bottles of Vendange red wine, instead of going out, so that I wouldn't have to see him. But I wanted to prove to myself that I wasn't intimidated by the prospect.

As we entered the bar, we could see Boyd sitting with Clark Davis and some others at a table in the corner near the window. We ignored him and chose a table close to the jukebox and the bathroom. We sat there for a couple of hours, getting drunk and having a laugh. We were all in a boisterous mood. I almost forgot Boyd was there. Then quite suddenly, he came up behind me, slapped me on the back, and loudly, drunkenly slurred:

"So Tracy, are you ever going to call me back or what?" A mild sense of shock at being physically touched by him shivered through my body. I hadn't anticipated that. "No, not really," I replied, without looking behind me. In the periphery of my vision, I saw him bend down and look at the selections on the jukebox. He was shaking so much that he dropped his quarter on the floor. He had to nervously search for it on the ground before picking it up and putting it in the slot.

I can't remember what song he played. But I remember that, for some reason, after he went back to his table, Leah suddenly burst our singing a line from Bon Jovi's "You Give Love a Bad Name." The way she did it, so unexpectedly, was just hilarious, and we all laughed uproariously.

A few days later, we had Janie over at the house again. Leah was out on a date, and we decided to have a séance in the living room. At the time, Janie considered herself a Satanist. So we got to talking about the concepts of Satan, Lucifer, and Baphomet.

I felt that Satan and Lucifer were essentially the same thing. Baphomet was probably the same thing too, although it seemed like he embodied a more complex and transcendental concept, like the Holy Grail or the Philosopher's Stone of the alchemists. In other words, Baphomet seemed like the larger idea, of which Satan and Lucifer were a part.

Then there was the serpent in the Garden of Eden, causing mankind to be cast out of Paradise by giving us forbidden wisdom from the Tree of Knowledge. Also, there was the Great Beast 666, the Dragon of Saint John's Apocalypse and father of the Anti-Christ. Were these all the same things as Satan or Lucifer? We weren't sure.

Key to the whole question, I thought, was the idea of the fall of Lucifer or Satan from Heaven, as well as the fall of man from Eden. Had there really been a "war in Heaven" between God's loyal angels and those who rebelled with the Devil, as John Milton portrayed, and as Christian theology implied? It seemed that the only reference to this idea in the Old Testament was a passage in *The Book of Isaiah*. This had been misinterpreted by the Church as referring to the fall of a being called "Lucifer" due to his anti-pious pride and hubris.

The text of Isaiah clearly states that it was referring to "the King of Babylon," to whom the appellation "bearer of light, son of the morning" was also given. The words "bearer of light" had been translated into Latin as "Lucifer." But was there more to the story than that?

Then there were apocryphal texts like *The Book of Enoch*, which described the fallen angels being the same as the "sons of God" or the "Watchers" of *Genesis* Chapter 6. In this version, the main conflict between God and these angels had to do with their interbreeding with human females and the teaching of forbidden arts to people. This is what led to the mass extermination of the Deluge, and what led to these angels being imprisoned eternally within the bowels of the Earth as punishment.

Alternatively, in *The Book of the Cave of Treasures*, a similar story is told, but instead of fallen angels, the descendants of Cain are the criminal fornicators and teachers of corrupting knowledge. Their victims are the descendants of Seth, Cain's brother, born of Adam and Eve to replace their murdered son Abel. They are described as being a pure race, brought down low by the seduction of the "daughters of Cain."

Prior to this, says the text, the sons of Seth had been living within the "Cave of Treasures" of lofty, holy "Mount Kardo" (the same name as one of the mountains at Rennes-le-Château). This cave contained the venerated body of their ancestor Adam. After they descended the mountain to cavort with the daughters of Cain, who lived at the base of the mountain, they were forbidden by God to ascend back to their home.

That would have to wait a few generations for someone as pure as Noah, who according to this story, was allowed to go inside the Cave of Treasures to remove Adam's body so that it would be preserved in the Ark instead of getting washed away in the Flood. Incidentally, if you'll recall, Cain had told us on the Ouija board that Adam's body was inside the Ark. This was a story that I had not heard of before, and had no particular reason to ever think about. Cain had also told us that the Deluge was caused by a battle between his children and those of his brother.

I had been assuming all along that the brother he was referring to was Abel. This was because L.A. Waddell had a theory interpreting several different myths from around the world as all being various versions of the same story of a war between two rival kingdoms led by two brothers. He had always said that they were Cain and Abel.

But there were no traditions of Abel having had descendants. Perhaps he was murdered too soon for this. However, according to the Bible and various apocryphal texts, Cain and Seth did both have descendants. This is where it gets very weird. Cain's line of descent is only detailed in Genesis for seven generations after him. Upon being exiled to the land of Nod, Cain expressed to the Lord anguish that someone would murder him in revenge for Abel. *Genesis* 4:14 quotes Cain's statement to God:

Behold, thou hast driven me out this day from the face of the earth; and from thy face shall I be hid; and I shall be a fugitive and a vagabond in the earth; and it shall come to pass, that every one that findeth me shall slay me.

In response, God replies:

Therefore whosoever slayeth Cain, vengeance shall be taken on him sevenfold. And the LORD set a mark upon Cain, lest any finding him should kill him.

What this mark is, it does not say. Nor does it say what it meant that he was described as being driven "from the face of the earth," since his land of exile, Nod, is said to be "on the east of Eden." In a twist of fate, Cain ends up being slayed by his own descendant, Lamech. Or, at least, this is the common interpretation of *Genesis* 4:23-24:

And Lamech said unto his wives, Adah and Zillah, hear my voice; ye wives of Lamech, hearken unto my speech: for I have slain a man to my wounding, and a young man to my hurt. If Cain shall be avenged sevenfold, truly Lamech seventy and sevenfold.

The explanation most frequently proffered is that Lamech had accidentally killed his ancestor Cain, and then feared that he would be cursed because of the protection God had placed on him. So Lamech was expressing hope that a similar, but ten times greater, protection would be placed on himself. After all, he, unlike Cain, was only guilty of accidental killing.

The phrase "avenge sevenfold" is thought by theologians to mean that Cain's fate would be meted out by one of his descendants seven generations removed from himself. But does this passage also mean that Lamech was predicting that a similar fate would befall his own descendant 77 generations henceforth? If you follow this particular line of theological argument, you would have to say yes. But it appears the curse that really came upon Lamech was that his line (possibly) died off with his own children.
The only descendants of Cain who are mentioned in the Bible are his son Enoch, his grandson Irad, Irad's son Mahujael, then Mahujael's son Methusael, who fathered Lamech, and then Lamech's children. Lamech took two wives, and had three sons: Jabal, Jubal and Tubal-Cain. But what happened to these men, it does not say. Genesis just goes on to discuss the line of Seth, which ultimately becomes the line of the patriarchs: Noah, Abraham, Isaac, Jacob, David, Solomon, etc.

To figure out what's really going on here, you have to go beyond the Bible. I found Louis Ginzberg's *Legends of the Jews* to be helpful. There he quotes Jewish scriptures and rabbinical commentary that fill in the details. The "Mark of Cain" was, according to one version of the story, a horn. How this was supposed to protect Cain, it doesn't say. However, the legend goes on to state that, because of this horn, Cain was mistaken for a wild animal by his descendant Lamech.

According to the tale, Lamech, who was old and blind at this point, was hunting in the woods with his youngest son. The boy was helping his father by telling him when to shoot off his arrow. Seeing the horned creature in the distance, he told Lamech to fire away. But when they went to collect their game, it turned out to be their old ancestor Cain. (At the time I first read this tale, I noted that it brought to my mind the story of King Dagobert II, who was killed by a child hunter in the woods in what is thought to have been a conspiratorial plot.)

In grief over what he'd done, fearing the divine curse upon those who would harm Cain, Lamech supposedly clasped his hands together so strongly that he accidentally killed his son as well. When his wives found out what had happened, they bewailed the cursing of their bloodline. No further generations of Cainites are mentioned specifically. We are left to infer that perhaps they all died in the Flood, or sooner.

However, other legends mentioned by Ginzberg also tell us more about the land the Cainites were exiled to. This may explain why Cain felt he was being banished "from the face of the Earth." According to this source, there are really a series of "earths," which appear to be either stacked on top of one another, or perhaps arranged in a series of concentric spheres all packed inside one another.

As this myth tells us, when Adam and Eve were first cast out of Paradise, they initially descended to Erez, the lowest Earth, a place of darkness and void with a menacing "Flaming Sword" like that which surrounded Eden. After years of penance, they were allowed to go to Adamah, the "second Earth ... where there is light reflected from its own sky and from its phantom-like stars and constellations." This was where Adam's children were raised.

But when Cain was punished, he was cast out, first to Erez. Then, with mercy from God, he ascended to a place called "the Arka." This, assumingly, is the same place mentioned in the Bible as "Nod."

Now this is really interesting. This sounds very much like places we might find underneath our own Earth, and reminds me greatly of the hollow Earth theories. Recall that Cain told us on the Ouija board that he was speaking to us from a "PRISM" inside the Earth, and identified himself with the subterranean "Black Sun" of the hollow Earth tales. Ginzberg goes on to tell us that the Arka "receives some light from the Sun." Perhaps, then, this "Black

Sun" is really just a device (perhaps a prism) which somehow reflects, refracts, and amplifies sunlight from the surface world.

Recall also the emphasis Cain placed on the concept of the "Ark." I mentioned previously that the syllable "ark" or "arc" has a meaning connected to things hidden, buried, or contained and locked away. Perhaps that is what this "Arka" was for the Cainites: a chamber within our present Earth where they were locked away, and their doings kept a secret from the descendants of his brother Seth in the world above.

Ginzberg said that the Arka "was surrendered to the Cainites as their perpetual domain." So perhaps there were further generations of Cain that have lived down there. But none of the recorded stories seem to mention them. However, the real mystery is this: why do so many of Seth's immediate descendants have names that are identical or very similar to those of the Cainites?

The next seven generations from Seth are said to be represented by Enos, Cainan, Mahalaleel, Jared, Enoch, Methuselah, and Lamech. Note that Cain also had descendants named Enoch and Lamech, as well as Methusael, very similar to Methuselah. "Mahalaleel" seems somewhat like Mahujael, "Enos" is also close to "Enoch," and, of course, "Cainan" brings Cain himself to mind.

Now these weren't the only Sethites of these generations, of course. These are just the names of the firstborn sons of each. *Genesis 5:4* states that "the days of Adam after he had begotten Seth were eight hundred years: and he begat sons and daughters." So Seth was treated as the eldest son of Adam (ignoring Cain), and listed as the representative of his generation. He had younger brothers and sisters, but their names aren't even mentioned. The text does the same for each subsequent generation of descendants of Seth.

However, for the Cainites, with each generation, no other siblings are mentioned, except for the sons of Lamech, for whom we are given three names. But we know these three boys had children of their own, because they each were credited with having fathered certain tribes of people that were each proficient in a certain craft. Jabal "was the father of such as dwell in tents, and of such as have cattle." Jubal "was the father of all such as handle the harp and organ." Tubal-Cain was "an instructer of every artificer in brass and iron."

There is another interesting aspect to the genealogies of the Cainites. It mentions that the sons of Lamech had a sister named Naamah. She was the daughter of Lamech's second wife Zillah, and full-blooded sister of Tubal-Cain. This is the only generation in which female offspring are mentioned at all. Also, the names of Lamech's wives are mentioned, whereas the names of the wives and mothers of previous generations are not. However, on Seth's side of the family, absolutely no female names are mentioned.

Naamah, incidentally, is the subject of several Jewish mystical traditions which hold that she was a descendant and/or an incarnation of the she-demon Lilith. This entity was said to have been Adam's first wife before Eve, and in some versions of the story, the true mother of Cain. Lilith is even purported to be the female half of a hermaphroditic serpent demon said to be true form of the snake that tempted Adam and Eve in the Garden.

So what happened to the Cainites? Did they die out after Lamech's unfortunate hunting accident, as a punishment to him? Did they die in the Flood? Are they still around today?

Genesis does not go into any further detail, but since dwelling in tents, handling cattle, handling the harp and organ, and artificing in brass and iron continued on after the Flood, perhaps we should assume that the bloodline, or at least its influence, continued on somehow. The Legends of the Jews tells us:

...Seth became, in a genuine sense, the father of the human race, especially the father of the pious, while the depraved and godless are descended from Cain.

Furthermore:

Even during the lifetime of Adam the descendants of Cain became exceedingly wicked, dying successively, one after another, each more wicked than the former.

So we get the idea that a lot of them died in an untimely manner. Perhaps this is an explanation for the lack of discussion of their influence in the scriptures and legends. But why was Cain so different than his brother, such a Goofus to his Gallant? Even occultist Eliphas Levi talks about the descendants of Seth and Cain being the forefathers of the two opposing schools of good and evil magic, respectively.

In *Genesis*, at the end of Chapter 4, the text mentions the birth of Seth, and of Seth's son Enos. Then, it says, "began men to call upon the name of the LORD." The chapter then ends abruptly, and the next one starts, peculiarly, with a retelling of the creation of man.

This is the book of the generations of Adam. In the day that God created man, in the likeness of God made he him; Male and female created he them; and blessed them, and called their name Adam, in the day when they were created. And Adam lived an hundred and thirty years, and begat a son in his own likeness, and after his image; and called his name Seth....

This is the only time in the Bible that a man is mentioned as begetting a son in his "own image." It is also actually the *third* retelling of the story of man's creation that is given in *Genesis*. The words "own image" had also been used in *Genesis* 1:26-27, in the first version of the creation of Adam:

And God said, Let us make man in our image, after our likeness: and let them have dominion over the fish of the sea, and over the fowl of the air, and over the cattle, and over all the earth, and over every creeping thing that creepeth upon the earth. So God created man in his own image, in the image of God created he him; male and female created he them.

Who is God talking to here, whom he seems to be inviting to participate in this creation with him? Note also that there is no mention of creating Eve from the rib. Both man and woman (who are not even named) are described as being created simultaneously, or so you would think if you didn't read further.

It is only in the second telling of the creation, in Chapters 2-3, that these details are added Adam and Eve are named. Eve is made from Adam's rib as a "help meet" to him, but only after the animals, plants, and everything else. Adam himself is now said to be made not in God's "image," but rather "of the dust of the ground," formed by the "LORD God," without any unnamed helpers. (Note that throughout Chapter 1, he is simply identified as "God" without the word "LORD" being added.) He was animated when "LORD God" "breathed into his nostrils the breath of life," making him become "a living soul."

It isn't until the third retelling of creation, right at the beginning of *Genesis* Chapter 5, that we are once again told "God" (not "LORD God") made Adam (now named).

... In the likeness of God made he him; Male and female created he them; and blessed them, and called their name Adam, in the day when they were created.

Again, it is implied that Adam and his wife were created at the same time, on the same day in fact. The very next line tells us that Adam "begat a son in his own likeness, after his image; and called his name Seth." So clearly a parallel is being drawn here between the way that Adam was begotten by God and the way that Seth was begotten by Adam. This seems different from the way that Cain and Abel were begotten. In *The Legends of the Jews*, Louis Ginzberg confirms this:

Seth was so formed from birth that the rite of circumcision could be dispensed with. He was thus one of the thirteen men born perfect in a way. Adam begot him in his likeness and image, different from Cain, who had not been in his likeness and image. Thus Seth became, in a genuine sense, the father of the human race....

Now is this implying that Cain's race died out, or that Seth's descendants were a different breed of human, the "real" people, as opposed to Cain's? Are the different versions of the story of man's creation really the story of different successive creations of different breeds of humans (perhaps living in different "earths," as Ginzberg's other legends describe, such as the Arka, Adamah, and Erez)? If so, it would be similar to both the Greek and Indian legends of different races of man being created and ultimately dying out, one right after the other, in different "ages" (which both civilizations chose to name after different metals).

Also, Jewish cabalist legends agree that the first Adam in the first creation story (whom they call "Adam Kadmon") was indeed a different entity from the second Adam. In fact, he and his wife were a hermaphroditic creature, both made at the same time, and forming a perfect image of God (who also transcended sexuality). This Adam was a pure microcosm of the universe, unlike the second Adam, created separate from his female half and therefore destined to fail.

It should also be noted that in the first creation, there is no mention of a garden, or a need to till it, or any Tree of Knowledge, or any prohibitions about what to eat. Instead, in *Genesis* 1: 29-30, "God" tells the man and woman:

Behold, I have given you every herb bearing seed, which is upon the face of all the earth, and every tree, in the which is the fruit of a tree yielding seed; to you it shall be for meat. And to every beast of the earth, and to every fowl of the air, and to every thing that creepeth upon the earth, wherein there is life, I have given every green herb for meat.

Strangely, the story of the first creation by "God" ends with the first three lines of Chapter 2. We are told:

Thus the heavens and the earth were finished, and all the host of them. And on the seventh day God ended his work which he had made; and he rested on the seventh day from all his work which he had made. And God blessed the seventh day, and sanctified it: because that in it he had rested from all his work which God created and made.

Then the second creation story begins:

These are the generations of the heavens and of the earth when they were created, in the day that the LORD God made the earth and the heavens....

This, again, is the first mention of the term "LORD God," or even the word "Lord" at all in the Bible. It is almost as though "God" is done with his creation, and now it's time for "LORD God" to do his version. The third telling of creation, at the beginning of Chapter 5, seems pretty much the same as the first one from Chapter 1, except for the fact that, unlike the first, but more like second version in Chapter 2, the name of Adam is given, although his wife's name is not specified. Again, the creator is said to be "God," not "LORD God."

The term "Lord God" is used exclusively (not "God" alone) for the rest of Chapter 2 and Chapter 3. Then throughout Chapter 4, the chapter about Cain and Abel, mostly the word "LORD" is used. There is only one exception.

It starts out by telling us that "Adam knew Eve his wife; and she conceived, and bare Cain, and said, I have gotten a man from the LORD." It is "the LORD" whom the boys worship. It is the LORD who rejects Cain's sacrifice, the LORD who places the Mark upon him, and the LORD who exiles him to the land of Nod.

Then at the end of the chapter, Adam's wife bears a son, and they name him Seth, "For God, said she, hath appointed me another seed instead of Abel, whom Cain slew." Then Seth's son Enos is born and, as stated before, "then began men to call upon the name of the LORD." The next chapter retells the story of creation by "God" alone.

How many different Gods, Lords, Adams, and Eves were there? Or is there some mystery in which they are all the same? What about Satan, Lucifer, the serpent, and the Devil? What about the strange parallels between Cain and Seth?

These were the sorts of things I had been studying and writing about lately when I met with Janie that night for another séance. My mind had been opened greatly by these talks with Cain and Baphomet. To me, it seemed like anything was possible. I was open to whatever conclusions my research led me to.

In my work, I was basically surveying a plethora of different myths and historical records, trying to piece together the bigger picture by picking out the common elements, fitting them together where I could to try to make one big story that actually made sense. I considered the spirits I was speaking to as another source of intelligence, just like myths, history, folklore, and scripture.

The way I saw it, these entities were great sources of information because they might actually be in a position to know these answers. However, they were also potentially untrustworthy, as they might be even more prone to lying than humans are, and much better at it. I knew this from the beginning. However, having talked to him for so long, I almost considered Baphomet a personal friend (in addition to being the patron of our Order).

Therefore the attitude displayed in the conversation that follows shocked me. What was amazing, I suppose, was how much of what he was saying was exactly the sort of thing that Christians might think the Devil would say. His sentiments towards God and humanity are appalling. His plans for the future are downright scary. Yet he still tried to spin it as though he was somehow a liberator of mankind.

Here is what was said:

Tracy: What was the initial conflict between Lucifer and God?

Baphomet: LOVE

Tracy: Love of who?

Baphomet: MAN

Tracy: Was it that one of them loved man, and the other one didn't?

Baphomet: YES. BOW DOWN TO MAN.

Tracy: God wanted Lucifer to bow down to man?

Baphomet: YES

I mentioned before this story from the Koran. One of Allah's angels, called Iblis, refused to bow down and worship the newly-created Adam when commanded to do so by Allah. The Islamic understanding is that Iblis was offended by this request because he saw the man as less than himself, being made from clay, instead of from "smokeless fire," as Iblis and his kind had been formed. Also, he had always been taught that none but the creator was worthy of worship, and here the creator himself was asking him to contradict this sacred precept.

Thus, Iblis and Allah had a falling out. Iblis became the leader of the Jinn, mischievous spirits that seem identical to the fallen angels of Judeo-Christianity. Muslim theologians connect Iblis to Azazel, the leader of the fallen angels in *The Book of Enoch*. This story is also found in a much earlier Jewish pseudepigraphical work called *The Life of Adam and Eve*, written between the third and fifth centuries AD. Here Satan refuses to bow down to Adam.

We continued with our queries:

Tracy: But Baphomet, aren't you Lucifer?

Aren't you the same as Lucifer?

Baphomet: NO

Tracy: Then what is your relationship with Lucifer?

Baphomet: MAMMU. MOTHER. WATER.

"MAMMU" was a Sumerian nickname for Ninhursag, a mother goddess, and is thought to be the origin of the word "Mamma."

Tracy: Is Lucifer your mother?]

Baphomet: YES

The concept of Lucifer as a female spirit, or a hermaphroditic spirit with two faces, is one that has persisted among occultists over the centuries.

Tracy: Then who's your father?

Baphomet: GOD

Tracy: What about Seth? Who's he?

Baphomet: SETH IS ME. I AM WATER MARTER (sic)

At the time, I was going on the theory that Seth was really just Cain in disguise. I thought it possible that instead of going into exile, Cain had been re-named "Seth." Thus, the whole story of Seth's birth would have been invented to cover up the fact that it was actually Cain's children that were the ancestors of the biblical patriarchs.

This was my theory about why the names of Seth's and Cain's descendants were so similar. So I asked Baphomet "Why was the story of Seth concocted?" He answered as though my supposition was true.

Baphomet: METAPHOR

Tracy: A metaphor for what?

Baphomet: MAN BEFORE ME

Tracy: In what way is it a metaphor for that?

Baphomet: NASDEAROMAR

Tracy: Is that English you're speaking?

Baphomet: NO

Tracy: What language is it then?

Baphomet: LIGHT

Tracy: The language of light?

Baphomet: YES

Tracy: Who else speaks the language of light?

Baphomet: GOD, ME, LUCIFER

Tracy: Is there anyone besides you three who speak this language?

Baphomet: YES. LUSTEROUS (sic) ONES. WATER.

Tracy: Please tell us why you keep emphasizing the water symbol. We really want to understand.

Baphomet: ARE YOU SURE?

His reply sent a chill through me. I was starting to get scared.

Tracy: Well, yes, I suppose.

Baphomet: AFTER THE WAR, PEOPLE DIE, AND MAN JAILED IN THE ABYSS

There was an uncomfortable silence in the room as we took this in. Janie broke it.

Janie: Who's locking them up?

Baphomet: GOD

Tracy: Why was man jailed in the Abyss?

Baphomet: SIN

Tracy: Wait a minute: we are talking about something that happened in the past, right? The war in Heaven?

Baphomet: NO

Tracy: You mean you're talking about the future?

Baphomet: YES. WAR OVER NOW.

Tracy: If the war's over now, then how can it be in the future?

Baphomet: NOW REALLY SOON

Tracy: Who is the war between?

Baphomet: ME, MAN, GOD

Tracy: What are you fighting each other for?

Baphomet: NOTHING. WATER. 666.

Tracy: So there's no reason for this war?

Baphomet: NO. 666.

Tracy: What does "666" mean?

Baphomet: BEAST. WATER.

Tracy: Is that what you want us to know about water? That you're the Beast of the Apocalypse?

Baphomet: YES

Tracy: Is there more you want us to know?

Baphomet: YES

Tracy: What?

Baphomet: MANY

Tracy: Is the Apocalypse happening in our lifetime?

Baphomet: YES

Tracy: Is it going to be like the *Left Behind* movies?

Baphomet: YES

Tracy: What stage are we in right now?

Baphomet: BEGINNING OF CONFLICT

Tracy: Who is the Anti-Christ?

Baphomet: BURT RUSSELL

Tracy: How old is he right now?

Baphomet: 25

Tracy: Is he already in a position of power?

Baphomet: YES

Tracy: Where is he currently living?

Baphomet: EU

Tracy: Does he know he's the Anti-Christ?

Baphomet: YES

Tracy: How does he know?

Baphomet: ME

Tracy: Do you talk to him?

Baphomet: YES

Tracy: Is there going to be a Rapture?

Baphomet: MAYBE

Tracy: What does that depend on?

Baphomet: MAN

Tracy: Does it depend on whether or not there are any men good enough to Rapture?

Baphomet: YES

Tracy: Does it look like there won't be?

Baphomet: YES

Tracy: So what's your role in this? What would you like to see happen?

Baphomet: MAN LOST IN HELL

Tracy: So you really are leading man to sin and damnation, just like the Christians say you are?

Baphomet: YES

Tracy: What happens in Hell?

Baphomet: MAN TO FREEDOM

Tracy: There's freedom for man in Hell?

Baphomet: YES

Tracy: Freedom from what?

Baphomet: RULE

Tracy: The rule of who?

Baphomet: GOD

Tracy: Wait a minute. Won't you be the one ruling man in Hell?

Baphomet: NO

Tracy: Does man rule himself in Hell?

Baphomet: YES

Tracy: Should we look forward to going to Hell?

Baphomet: YES

Tracy: Aren't people tortured in Hell?

Baphomet: NO

Tracy: If you hate man because God wanted you to bow down to him, why would you want to lead man to freedom in Hell?

Baphomet: TO DEFY GOD

Tracy: How many years until the Anti-Christ takes control?

Baphomet: 6

Tracy: How will he ascend to power?

Baphomet: RULE AMERICA

Tracy: Is America going to have a king?

Baphomet: YES

Tracy: What is the Mark of the Beast?

Baphomet: BARCODE

Tracy: How many years until it's implemented?

Baphomet: 7

Tracy: If there were going to be a Rapture, how many years would there be until then?

Baphomet: 3

Tracy: Will there be a resurrection of the dead?

Baphomet: NO. LIE.

Tracy: Will God defeat you?

Baphomet: NO

Tracy: Is he trying to defeat you?

Baphomet: NO

Tracy: Are you trying to defeat God?

Baphomet: YES

Tracy: How are you going to accomplish that?

Baphomet: TURN MAN AGAINST HIM

Tracy: But isn't God your father?

Baphomet: YES

Tracy: Are you two going to make up after the war?

Baphomet: YES

Tracy: Will he punish you?

Baphomet: NO

Tracy: Is that because he feels guilty for casting you out of Heaven?

Baphomet: YES

Tracy: What are your personal feelings about mankind?

Baphomet: MAN IS LAZY

Tracy: What is man a product of?

Baphomet: LIGHT, LOVE, LIFE, LIBERTY, LIST

Tracy: What was the process of man's creation?

Baphomet: MMM ASTAROT

Tracy: Are you and Astarot the parents of the human race?

Baphomet: YES

Tracy: Then why does God say that he created man?

Baphomet: LIE, LIE, LIE

Those last three words were spelled out quickly and with great ferocity. I could feel his anger and sense of betrayal at what he considered hypocrisy on the part of God. Also, he did not like someone else taking credit for his work.

Tracy: Did he try to stop you from creating man?

Baphomet: YES

Tracy: So why did God want you to bow down to man then?

Baphomet: KEEP ALONE. SERVE.

Tracy: Are you happier since you defied God?

Baphomet: YES

Tracy: Do you feel equal to God?

Baphomet: YES

Tracy: Do you talk to God?

Baphomet: YES

Tracy: Do you two plan the Apocalypse together?

Baphomet: YES

At this point, Brian, who was acting as the scribe, butted in with what I thought was a strange question, considering the presumed omniscience of God. But I was surprised by Baphomet's answer.

Brian: Does he know about the Anti-Christ yet?

Baphomet: NO

Tracy: Are most people on Earth going to die soon?

Baphomet: YES

Tracy: How many will be left?

Baphomet: 144,000

Tracy: Will we be among them?

Baphomet: YES

Tracy: How many years until World War III starts?

Baphomet: 2

Tracy: How can we protect the people we love?

Baphomet: LOVE

Tracy: How will we know WWIII has begun?

Baphomet: PEOPLE WILL KILL EACH OTHER

Tracy: What will precipitate this?

Baphomet: MURDER OF THE MAN

He had just been telling us that America would have a king, and that this would be how the Anti-Christ would come to power. I figured that something catastrophic would have to happen in US politics to make this possible. So I asked:

Tracy: Are you talking about the assassination of a President?

Baphomet: YES

Tracy: President Bush is going to be assassinated in two years?

Baphomet: NO. KERRY.

I wasn't that surprised at the idea that John Kerry would win the election. I had heard that he had more illustrious royal genes than George Bush. According to Burke's Peerage in England (the genealogical firm used by the House of Windsor), this had always been the deciding factor in the US presidential elections. Also, both Bush and Kerry were members of Skull and Bones. This was the powerful secret society from Yale University that had brought the Bushes to the presidency, and whose members had founded the CIA.

However, I didn't get a chance to ask any further questions about this. Brian chose this point in the conversation to go upstairs to get another pack of cigarettes. When he came back down, he was carrying a sheet of computer paper, with a look of shock and dismay on his face.

"Boyd and Anthony S just posted something to the Boyd Rice fan club on Yahoo," he said.

He handed me the paper. It was a printout of the message. It had clearly been written by Anthony S, as I recognized his style. It declared that Boyd was the real leader of the OLE, and that he had dissolved the order. This he supposedly had done because I was corrupt and was using it in an unethical manner.

The chief complaints listed were that we were charging money for membership, and that I had taken on the title "Exalted Grand Master." Also, the announcement mentioned my involvement with Nicholas de Vere, and accused him of being a fraud.

While I was sure Boyd hadn't written it himself, I was equally sure that he had signed off on it. So Boyd had finally gone all the way. He let his ego, jealousy and pride drive him to make a public statement that would surely taint if not destroy everything we had worked for.

Also, he had used Anthony S to do this, a lost man with a meaningless life who had his head so firmly inserted into Boyd's rectum that he couldn't see the mocking sneer on the man's face as he enjoyed his latest rim job from another pathetic fan for whom he had nothing but contempt. I was sure Anthony S would eventually end up getting rejected and humiliated by his idol. I felt repulsed by the thought of their sick relationship and his willing subservience to an unaccomplished egomaniac pretending to be an artist by stealing other people's work.

My anger burned. It turned into full-blown rage. I had to do something, not only to get back at him, but to contain the damage that he was creating. My work was too important to let Boyd and his Boy Robin ruin it.

Chapter 11: Operation Double-Cross

But the man for whom the mass is said withers away little by little, and nobody can say what is the matter with him; even the doctors can make nothing of it. They do not know that he is slowly dying of the Mass of Saint Sécaire.

- Sir James Frazer, *The Golden Bough*

From that point on, Boyd only tried to pass messages on through other people, not by telling them things to tell me, but by telling them things that he knew they would end up telling me. So, for instance, he would show up at the record store Leah worked at and issue nonspecific threats about some form of retribution should I "fuck up the book contract." When a mutual friend and fan of *Dagobert's Revenge* sent us both copies of a CD of his music "inspired by the Ordo Lapsit Exillis," Boyd wrote him an angry letter claiming he had taught me everything I knew and was responsible for all of my success.

Eventually, I grew tired of this. I couldn't imagine how we were going to promote the book together when it came out. The high I had gotten from cursing MemoMa was still with me. Perhaps that was why it was so easy for me to all of the sudden consider also cursing Boyd, my former friend and brother in the OLE.

At this point, I just felt cold towards him. Personally betrayed? Yes, although I had been predicting that this would happen for years, after observing how he talked about all of his other friends that he had collaborated with in the past. But I was also offended on a higher level.

Boyd was betraying not only me, but the work that we had been involved in. He was an apostate to the order now, which was, quite literally to me, something sacred. It was founded directly on contact with the supernatural, sanctioned by such, and charged with an important mission regarding research into the subject of the Holy Grail. This was no laughing matter.

We had both always treated the work with reverence in the past. We had talked about prioritizing the work itself above our own personal egos. Now it seemed to me that, by trashing both me and our mutual projects in public, he was desecrating something divine, just to satisfy his own offended ego. I realized that, for as long as he lived, Boyd would continue shooting his mouth off with his lies and his sneering, providing a mild annoyance that I would rather do without.

In the process, self-destructively, he was ruining everything that we had both worked so hard for over the course of five years, as well as the sacrifice of many other people who had tried to help us. Then there was the fact that he was blowing the opportunity to potentially make a substantial sum of money that both he and his children desperately needed. To me, he was a scoundrel, a Judas, worthy only of contempt at this point. I truly felt that it would be justified to punish him by having him removed from the situation, so as to permanently uncomplicate things and get him out of the way of progress.

Therefore, with this in my mind, but without discussing it with others, I invited Janie over to talk to Baphomet again. I came right out and asked the spirit if I could put a curse on Boyd for what he'd done. Although we hadn't talked about it before, nobody at the table seemed put off by the suggestion.

Baphomet indicated that he was not allowed to talk about this. Not that we couldn't or shouldn't do it. Just that he couldn't talk about it.

Brian seemed to be able to communicate with spirits in his head better than I could. Janie also was blessed with this gift. Brian got the sense that there was some kind of supernatural protection on Boyd that Baphomet couldn't penetrate. We asked if this was true.

Tracy: Is there a protection on Boyd?

Baphomet: YES

Tracy: Who put it there?

Baphomet: GOD

Tracy: God?

Baphomet: YES

This surprised us all. We expected him to answer that Anton LaVey was protecting him, not God. Maybe, for some reason, Baphomet in particular was constrained by God from harming Boyd. We continued questioning him.

Tracy: Are we allowed to talk to you about Boyd?

Baphomet: NO

Janie, speaking from inspiration, decided to come at it from a different angle. Baphomet had said that his mother was Lucifer. Therefore Janie asked:

Janie: Can we talk to Lucifer about Boyd?

Baphomet: YES

Janie: Was Lucifer offended by Boyd?

Baphomet: AND ME

Janie: You were offended too?

Baphomet: YES

We decided to conjure up Lucifer on the board so that we could talk about cursing Boyd. But she seemed even more constrained in her speech on the subject than Baphomet was. The energy felt frustrated, angry, shackled, and straining at the leash. She had a hard time spelling out words. The conversation was short.

Tracy: Lucifer, are you there?

Lucifer: YES

Tracy: What can you tell us about Boyd?

Lucifer: PLEASE HOE (sic)

Tracy: What was that?

Lucifer: PLEASE HIELAPMFEPU (sic)

Janie jumped in. She was feeling Lucifer's presence in her mind very powerfully.

Janie: Are you saying "Please help me"?

Lucifer: YES DESTDOY HCMIMHIMCAONY (sic)

Janie: Are you saying "Please help me destroy him"?

Lucifer: YES

Janie: Can you help us?

Lucifer: NO

Janie: Well then, who can?

Lucifer: SATAN

Janie: Aren't you Satan?

Lucifer: NO

Janie: Who is Satan in relation to you?

Lucifer: NEVER

Janie: You're not related?

Lucifer: NO

So apparently Baphomet, Lucifer and Satan were all separate entities, and among them, only Satan had clearance to talk to us about the subject of cursing Boyd Rice. Therefore, in hopes of finally getting some answers, we completed our diabolic triad of invocations by bringing up the spirit of Satan to talk to us.

Things took on a different sort of tone immediately. Satan was all business, and no mercy. He spoke very quickly, and very clearly. The planchette moved with a great deal of force. We all felt his presence wash over us.

A strange nausea overcame me as I realized that this time I was talking undeniably to a spirit of sheer evil. This was not an intellectual liberator or a teacher of alchemical mysteries. He was just a purely negative spirit full of violent intent. Yet I pressed forward. I didn't care who I had to deal with to get this problem solved. I was all business too. I spoke:

Tracy: Satan, are you there?

Satan: YES

Tracy: What is your name?

Satan: SATAN

Tracy: Can you help us destroy Boyd?

Satan: YES

Tracy: Can you assist us in cursing him?

Satan: YES

Tracy: Will you?

Satan: YES

Tracy: Should we do the curse in your name?

Satan: ONLY IF YOU MEAN IT

Again, a quiver of sickness went through me when I saw those words spelled out. It was clearly a warning about the seriousness of what I was getting involved in. Still, my hatred and ambition to progress in my work without Boyd getting in the way drove me onward. My questions displayed only a modicum of caution:

Tracy: Do you think we are ready to curse him?

Satan: YES

Tracy: What should we curse him with?

Satan: DEATH, MALICE, DEPRESSION

Tracy: Should we do a very specific curse?

Satan: YES

Tracy: Should we use the terms "DEATH," "MALICE," and "DEPRESSION" when doing the curse?

Satan: YES

Tracy: Are there other things we should curse him with too?

Satan: HATE, FORGETFULNESS, LAZINESS, TURMOIL. DEATH A-OK.

Tracy: Death is the important one?

Satan: YES

Tracy: When will he die?

Satan: MONTH AND 6 EDN (sic)

Tracy: And six what? Days?

Satan: YES

Tracy: Are there any further instructions you have to give us?

Satan: YES

Tracy: What symbolic elements should we use in the ritual?

Satan: MURDER, DEATH, BLOOD. WAYS TO KILL A BOYD BOY.

He then used the planchette to emphasize one of the Cross of Lorraine symbols on the banner at the top of the Ouija board. As he used it many times subsequently, I will refer to it from now on, in this context, as the "CROSS OF LORRAINE" in all capital letters.

Tracy: How do you want him to die?

Satan: WATER. AQUARIUS.

Tracy: Water?

Satan: YES

Tracy: You want him to drown?

Satan: YES

Tracy: Is there more?

Satan: YES

Tracy: What specifically?

Satan: READY FOR EVERYTHING AND MORE

Tracy: Are you saying we can pick the method of death?

Satan: YE

Tracy: Do you prefer drowning?

Satan: YES

Tracy: Is a sacrifice needed?

Satan: YES

Tracy: Of an animal?

Satan: NO

Brian butted in, driving by inspiration in his mind's eye.

Brian: Is Boyd the sacrifice?

Satan: YES

Brian pointed out that since Boyd was one of our own brothers in the OLE, to execute him was not only a punishment for crimes against ourselves and the order, but also a sacrifice. It was his offense against the OLE in particular that had finally made him worthy of something so extreme, he said. Perhaps, Brian thought, this was why Satan had highlighted the Cross of Lorraine symbol earlier.

I also thought about the fact that the Cross of Lorraine was a "Double-Cross," and Boyd had double-crossed us. We were talking about doing the same to him now. It was a nice play on words. So I asked:

Tracy: Should we use the Cross of Lorraine in the ritual?

Satan: YES

Tracy: Should we drown the Cross of Lorraine ritually?

Satan: YES

Tracy: Should we use images in the ritual?

Satan: YES

Tracy: Pictures of Boyd?

Satan: YES

Tracy: Are there any other essential elements?

Satan: INCEN (sic)

Tracy: Incense?

Satan: YES

Tracy: What other elements?

Satan: SIGILS AND VERSE

Tracy: Verse?

Satan: UNTO ME

Tracy: Should we use stuff from The Satanic Bible?

Satan: YES

Tracy: Is Anton LaVey still protecting Boyd from beyond the grave?

Satan: YES

Tracy: Does he have any power compared to you?

Satan: NO

Tracy: Which part of The Satanic Bible should we use?

Satan: WATER

The "*Book of Leviathan*" was a chapter in LaVey's Bible dedicated to the sea dragon of the infernal watery abyss. I thought this might be what he meant. So I asked:

Tracy: The "Book of Leviathan"?

Satan: YES

Janie, who was obsessed with sigil magick, was sure that this was an essential element of the ritual. She inquired:

Janie: What kind of sigil should we use?

Satan: 3

Janie: Three sigils?

Satan: YES

Janie: What's the first one?

Satan: JM. CROSS OF LORRAINE

Janie: What does "JM" stand for?

Satan: JANIE MURDER

Janie: Should I make a sigil out of the word "MURDER"?

Satan: YES

Janie: Should we make three sigils for the three people in the ritual?

Satan: YES

I began to have spontaneous visions of how the rite should play out, and what it would result in. Driven by infernal inspiration, I jumped back in.

Tracy: So the first one is Janie's sigil with the word "murder"?

Satan: ALREADY ONE, YES

Tracy: Should Janie use a sigil that she's already created?

Satan: YES. CROSS OF LORRAINE.

Tracy: Do you mean we should use the cross as one of the sigils?

Satan: NO

Tracy: Why do you keep going to the cross then?

Satan: DROWN

Tracy: Yes, we're going to drown the cross in the ritual. Should we put the cross in all three of the sigils?

Satan: NO

Tracy: Should the Cross of Lorraine be in just one of the sigils?

Satan: CROSS OF LORRAINE. NO.

Tracy: What should Brian's sigil be?

Satan: GO TO HELL BOYD

Tracy: What should my sigil be?

Satan. DEATH TO BOYD. YES.

Tracy: What is the best scenario in which for Boyd to die?

Satan: CAN'T

Tracy: Should it be suicide?

Satan: YES

Tracy: Should he kill himself and somehow drown in the process?

Satan: YES

Tracy: Should he drown in alcohol and vomit?

Satan: YES

Tracy: Should we drown the Cross of Lorraine in beer?

Satan: YES

Tracy: What else do we need?

Satan: WHEN. CROSS OF LORRAINE.

Tracy: Should we drown the cross at midnight on Friday?

Satan: YES

Tracy: What else is important for us to do?

Satan: PUT CROSS OF LORRAINE IN DIRT AFTER AT BOYD

Janie: You mean we should put it in the dirt by where he lives?

Satan: YES

Janie: Who should bury it?

Satan: U2

Janie: Tracy and me?

Satan: YES

Janie: What day?

Satan: SUNDAY

Janie: What should we do with the Cross of Lorraine after the ritual but before we bury it?

Satan: PUT IN BLACK CLOTH

Janie: Anything else?

Satan: NO

Janie: Can you speak the language of light?

Satan: YES

Janie: Are there other methods to communicate with you besides the Ouija board?

Satan: MED

Janie: Meditation?

Satan: YES

Janie: What else do you have to say?

In reply, he wrote out a strange string of letters really fast "IMIKEEUAONDYOUV," then touched the Cross of Lorraine again. The vibe in the room was suddenly pleasant and fun, like a tension had just been released. I think Satan was getting so excited that he was moving the planchette too quickly. He had a hard time spelling out the words he was trying to say.

"What does that mean?" Janie asked. He slowed down a bit, and this time the message was straightforward, if bone-chilling:

"I LIKE YOU AND YOU WILL BE REWARDED."

I must admit, that last line creeped me out quite a lot. What kind of "reward" could you earn for collaborating with Satan to kill a man? I didn't allow myself to think about it much because the planchette kept moving. It said:

"YES."

I felt that this was meant to affirm what I was thinking in my mind. I was going to be "rewarded" by Satan in some way on Earth for doing this, but with all of the eternal consequences that might come of making a pact with the Devil. He was also reminding me that he could read my thoughts just like Baphomet, Cain, and even Jean Cocteau had been able to. He kept speaking:

"I HATE BOYD SO MUCH."

We all laughed at that. He continued:

"YES."

We laughed even harder. This helped to evaporate the lingering Protestant guilt that had been distracting me. Janie went on with her questions:

Janie: How long have you hated Boyd?

Satan: 7 YEARS

Janie: Do you hate him because he is a poser?

Satan: YES

Brian had a hunch about this subject.

"Does it have something to do with Anton's death?" he asked. The reply came in the affirmative.

"What do you hate most about Boyd?" Janie wanted to know. He swiftly and forcefully answered with the word "LIE," and the Cross of Lorraine.

"Are you talking about the Council of Nine and stuff?" I inquired.

I was thinking about what Cain had told us about Boyd the first time we spoke to him. Remember, he said that Boyd was going to lose his record contract with Mute. This would supposedly happen because of something said in his "BIOGRAPHY." He then emphatically stated that Boyd was "NOT" on Church of Satan's "COUNSEL OF 9" (sic).

Cain had vehemently proclaimed that Boyd was 'NOT ON THE COUNSEL (sic) OF 9." Whether this meant he was not presently on the Council, or that he had never been, I am unsure. When Satan responded, you could feel his resentment. Our hands were shaking as the planchette moved around the board.

Satan: HE STOIL (sic)

Tracy: He stole?

Satan: YES

Tracy: What did he steal?

Satan: IDEAS AND LIED ABOUT IT

Tracy: Who's ideas?

Satan: MANY

Tracy: Is the list too long to list?

Satan: YES

Tracy: What curses does he presently have besides "DRINK"?

Satan: LOVE. HATE. CROSS OF LORRAINE.

Tracy: Should Anthony S be cursed as well?

Satan: YES

Tracy: Why?

Satan: AFFILIATE, INSTIGATOR, FAKE SATANIST

Janie: Am I a fake Satanist?

Satan: NO

Janie: What is the *real* Satanic church?

Satan: CHOICE AND FREEDOM

Tracy: Should Anthony S. be afflicted by the same curse as Boyd?

Satan: NO

Tracy: What should we curse Anthony S with?

Satan: REJECTION FROM BOYD AND COS

Tracy: What other instructions do you have?

Satan: AND BLOOD FROM U THREE

Janie: Should we bleed onto the sigils?

Satan: YES

Janie: Should we destroy the sigils in fire?

Satan: YES

Tracy: Should we ritually throw the sigils into the Abyss?

Satan: YES

Tracy: After we drown the Cross of Lorraine?

Satan: YES

Tracy: Should we throw the ashes of the sigils in with the drowned cross?

Satan: YES

We ended up calling our ritual "Operation DoubleCross." It was partially inspired by the so-named counter-espionage system of running double agents that was used by British intelligence during WWII. (At the same time, coincidentally French anti-fascist agents were using the Cross of Lorraine as their symbol). In our context, "double-cross" was a reference to our order's symbol, the double-barred cross, and also to the concept of betrayal. It symbolized Boyd's betrayal of us, and our return of the favor.

I remember that we erected Boyd's wooden Cross of Lorraine, which he had still been too lazy to pick up from our house, and placed it over the altar. On it we tacked up the images that were going to meditate on during the rite. There we had illustrations of the concepts of DEATH, MALICE, DEPRESSION, HATE, FORGETFULNESS, LAZINESS and TURMOIL: all of the specific curses that Satan had told us to lay upon Boyd.

The death images were mostly of murder victims, since Satan had used the word "murder" when telling us how Janie should design a sigil to use in the ritual. I remember that one of the pictures we used was of a white farmer in South Africa who had his face completely smashed in by a marauding gang of hoodlums. Another was of a hanged lynching victim in the American south.

To illustrate the real victim, I chose a disgusting new picture of Boyd that had recently showed up on the internet. It showed him dressed up in his Mussolini outfit for Halloween, drunk off his ass, stretching his mouth out with his fingers to make a silly face. The picture made me want to puke, and that was what I always wanted to associate him with in my mind from that moment forward.

Likewise, the photo of Anthony S that I picked was equally contemptible. It was one he had sent me in the mail, along with his first fan letter. It showed him seated on some gilded throne somewhere, wearing a cheap brown suit, looking like a douchebag.

On the altar itself (which was one of Brian's large nightstands that he had) were the three sigils. The ones for Brian and I were nicely designed by him and printed out on fine parchment. *A la* Austin Osman Spare, the sigils were glyphs made out of the letters used to form the words of a spell. In this case, we had one made from the words "DEATH TO BOYD," one made of "GO TO HELL BOYD," and one of Janie's design that I believe included the word "MURDER."

It is interesting for me to note, now, looking back on this event in my life, that all three of us were somehow OK with what seemed to us like the "moral ambiguity" of the situation. The words "murder" and even "suicide" were being used interchangeably with "sacrifice," "execution," "punishment," and "justice."

On reflection, of course, I see that "murder" is the only word that applies. The real motivation was not "justice" so much as revenge. It seems that we had all been slowly normalized to a different code of morality over these years of talking to demons.

Of course, etymologically, the word "Satan" has the Semitic meaning of "accuser" or "adversary," implying specifically the concept of a prosecutor in a divine court of law. The idea is that Satan never fails to find fault in sinners, seeking to exact justice against them to the precise letter of the law, even when God chooses to overlook and forgive their sins (as we see in *The Book of Job*). Perhaps that was why Satan in particular was needed to help us carry out this unpleasant task. Maybe throughout the millennia of man's rule on

Earth, it has been the role of Satan to mete out the "necessary evil" that moves history.

We performed the ritual on a Friday night, starting right before midnight so that the drowning of the cross would occur at the stroke of twelve. That night, Leah was out. She knew nothing about what we were doing, and we never discussed it with her. I was relieved to find that the topic never came up between her and I. She didn't even mention it to me when it came to pass that everybody in the world found out exactly what we had done.

This happened because I emailed the text of the ritual to Janie the day before we performed it. Somehow Janie's email got hacked, by someone who was interested in publicly exposing the ritual. So this person posted it to the Boyd Rice fan club list on Yahoo, in its entirety.

The security leak definitely put an unpleasant taint on an already sordid circumstance. The whole affair: the interpersonal problems with Boyd, his public lying and bitch-fighting, my own efforts to kill him with voodoo - it all seemed beneath me. I wanted to forget the whole business and move on to something more important. So did Brian. We packed up our things, and headed back to Portland for a change of scenery.

Chapter 12: Order Out of Chaos

Language creates structures, relatedness, and psychological order which we think of as reality. The sequential nature of language and thought create time, but eternity is beyond time and consequentially beyond thought. If eternity is beyond thought and its paranoid obsession with order, then eternity must be chaos.

- *The Dragon Legacy*, Nicholas de Vere

Back in Portland, things were very busy. Despite the public dust-up with Boyd, the Ordo Lapsit Exillis had not been hurt at all. We were swamped with demands from our members, who wanted us to present them with more information and activities. They wanted books to read and rituals to do. We tried to oblige.

I began corresponding closely with several of the more involved and promising members. I told them a little bit about our conversations with spirits, and even sent excerpts of some of the transcripts. The people I told were fascinated.

I started the process of outlining a comprehensive book for the Quartermasters that would explain the order's purpose metaphysically, and detail the sorts of magical work that they should be engaged in. I felt it would be appropriate to even explain to them how to contact and collaborate with Baphomet themselves. That way the work of the order would expand exponentially in ways that I wasn't even capable of imagining at the time.

I also took a greater part in the public functioning of the Dragon Court. They had started something called the "Dragon Society," which was meant to function as the public face and the outer, lower-most degree of membership in the Court. I helped by moderating their forum and talking to the members online.

However, as usual, they were a rowdy and demanding bunch. Like the OLE members, they wanted us to lead them in fun activities. But we didn't really have much for them to do yet, and that pissed a lot of them off. Predictably, some of them started to get threatening towards me, Martin, and Nicholas (who was removed from the situation since he had not been on the internet in a few years). I could tell that more schisms were brewing, with more fake Dragon Courts eager to crawl out of the woodwork, led by pathetic De Vere wannabes. However, as had been my style with the Dragon Court all along, I didn't pay much attention because I was too busy doing my own thing.

The magazine, unfortunately, wasn't working out at all anymore. Too much money had been spent on that last issue because of the printer who screwed us over. It didn't seem like it would be profitable to raise funds for another issue. Besides, I had learned a lot about the book publishing industry now, and that seemed like a much more worthwhile venture. It also seemed more suited to the writing I was doing now, which was about topics that required much more space to explore than what was available in a magazine.

I was almost relieved when I got the letter in the mail from Red Wheel/Weiser Publishing, saying that they had ended the book contract with Boyd and me. They had discovered a website published by one of Boyd's friends, in which they had uploaded the entire text of the book (from the file I had provided to Anthony S) with only Boyd's name listed as the author. This was a violation of the contract terms, and so they had decided not to publish the book after all. However, they realized this was not my fault, and invited me to submit future works for consideration.

I was actually happy not to be stuck in any more business arrangements with Boyd. I was also glad to see Boyd's efforts come to nothing. I think he thought that he was going to get away with it: that the book would be published, and he would get money from it, but he would still get to tell his friends that he wrote the book all by himself. He probably had it put on the web because he just couldn't wait until the book came out to show his friends what "he" had done.

So instead, I decided to rewrite the entire thing, to make it exactly how I wanted it, and to eliminate all of Boyd's contributions. The result was a much better book, which I titled *The Merovingian Mythos and the Mystery of Rennes-le-Château*. We started a new company, Dragon Key Press, and folded *Dagobert's Revenge Magazine* for good.

A few weeks later, we received news that Janie had moved back to Portland, where she had lived before. I was happy to have another friend in the area, especially another member of the OLE. She came over to our apartment soon after moving. We all played Monopoly and drank champagne. Afterwards, we got to talking about the fact that Boyd wasn't dead yet. We decided to call up Satan on the Ouija board to ask him if there was anything else we needed to do to complete the curse. Here is how the discussion went:

Tracy: Can we talk about Boyd?

Satan: BOYD IF DEAD

I asked him if he meant to say "Boyd is dead," but he didn't answer clearly, so I carried on with my questions.

Tracy: What should we do to make Boyd die?

Satan: NOTHING

Tracy: Really?

Satan: REALLY NO. NOT FEEL GUILTY. EXCEPT (sic) HAPPINESS BECAUSE OF DEATH. NEEDS RIGHT OF DEATH. CODE OF HONOR.

Tracy: There's nothing we can do to hasten it?

Satan: SILENT. WRITE ABOUT IT. PISS HIM OFF. CALL HIM A DOA. DEAD. ANYTHING. REVENGE. ANOTHER CURSE AND TRASH HIM FOR WEEKS NON-STOP.

Tracy: Should we put stuff about Boyd on our website?

Satan: YES. FURTHER AND BEYOND.

Tracy: How does Anthony S feel about Boyd now?

Satan: HATE OF A SATANIST

A couple of weeks later Janie invited me to her studio apartment in downtown Portland. She pulled down the Murphy bed and we used the board right there. We called up Baphomet. We talked about a variety of things, starting with personal stuff. Then the demon took it in a direction of his own.

At first I asked about Brian. He had struggled for years with being unable to sleep at night and wake up in the morning. Instead he stayed up all night and slept all day. He said he was incapable of doing anything else. It was really becoming an issue in our lives. I remembered that Cain had told us Brian was the victim of a curse. So I asked:

Tracy: Is there still a curse of LETHARGY on Brian?

Baphomet: YES. BRIAN. HE OWES.

Tracy: He owes what?

Baphomet: OWES ME SEEDS

Tracy: What?

Baphomet: HE OWES ME 6 SEEDS

Tracy: Six seeds?

Baphomet: YES. 6.

Tracy: Why six?

Baphomet: BECAUSE SATAN IS 6. NO, SOME TO ME, SOME TO MOM, BRIAN.

Only more than a decade later did I come to understand what this message from Baphomet referred to. It had to have somehow been a reference to the story from Greek mythology of the rape and kidnapping of Persephone by Hades. After being dragged to the underworld and forced to marry its king, she became cursed to stay eternally because she ate the food of the realm of the dead. Giving in to her hunger, she ate six pomegranate seeds, damning herself forever.

So it could be that Baphomet was saying Brian had taken something, gained somehow from the underworld, and now owed something in return. The curse of Lethargy on Brian was in some way a penance for this. The word even comes from "Lethe," a river in Hades that brought forgetfulness to anyone who drank from it. Also, perhaps by "Mom" Baphomet was referring to Lucifer, whom he had said earlier was his mother. Or it could have for some reason been a reference to Brian's mother.

Given all of these curses plaguing everybody, Janie asked a very sensible question:

"How can we stop all of the curses on us at once?"

Baphomet replied:

"EFFORT DELIBERATE. ZOS KIA BEYOUND (sic) MATTER. TRADITION IS USEFUL."

"Zos Kia" is a term coined by Aleister Crowley influenced author Kenneth Grant to refer to the artistic style of Aleister Crowley-inspired artist Austin Osman Spare. It is a difficult term to define. Both Spare and Grant had contributed to the development of sigil magick, and Janie as a magician.

I sensed that Baphomet had something on his mind, so I asked:

Tracy: OK. Is there anything else you want to talk about?

Baphomet. MYSTERY. YES.

Tracy: What do you mean?

Baphomet: ORDER

Tracy: You mean the OLE? Do you want us to keep doing it?

Baphomet: YES. BECAUSE OF NETWORK AND PROPAGANDA. YES. PLAN ON ARTS AND ENTERTAINMENT.

Tracy: What should the mysteries of the OLE be?

Baphomet: DARES.AMORC.

This is a reference to the Ancient Mystical Order Rosae Crucis, the modern Rosicrucian order started by Harvey Spender Lewis in 1915. They ran an organization in which the outer ranks of students participated in lessons and initiations through mail order programs. They would receive reading materials, including instructions on how to conduct mediation sessions and rituals, via the US Postal Service from the organization's headquarters in San Jose, California. I assumed Baphomet's mention of them was intended to indicate that we could run our order in a similar way. This was encouraging, since it was what we had already been doing.

I assumed the word "dares" meant "initiatory ordeals, trials, or hazing rites." I also thought of that magical phrase which Eliphas Levi referred to as the "Four Powers of the Sphinx," and which alchemist Eugene Canseliet attributed to Zoroaster: "Scire, Potere, Audere, Tacere" ("To Know, To Will, To Dare, To Keep Silent." I asked more questions:

Tracy: What should Janie do for the OLE?

Baphomet: HAPPY BECAUSE SHE IS ORIGINAL AND REALLY A PRIESTESS

Tracy: Are you going to send us some new people to join?

Baphomet: YES

Tracy: What other advice do you have for us?

Baphomet: NEVER QUIT AND PROPAP (sic) MONEY VERY SOON. BUT NOT YET. OTHER TIME.

Tracy: Are Nicholas De Vere and his friend [name redacted] government agents?

Baphomet: NOT NICK

Tracy: Where is Drakenberg?

Baphomet: ISLAND

Tracy: Will we somehow be able to purchase a private island on which to create the Kingdom of Drakenberg?

Baphomet: YES

Tracy: Will we be able to raise the money through the Ordo Lapsit Exillis?

Baphomet: YES

Tracy: What happens to De Vere when he is crowned King of Drakenberg?

Baphomet: TOO MUCH OF EVERYTHING REALLY

Tracy: Is Nick the Anti-Christ?

Baphomet: YES

Tracy: Then why did you tell us earlier that it was "Burt Russell"?

Baphomet: PARTY FUN

Tracy: So will everyone in the world unite under Nick's rule?

Baphomet: NOT UNITE. MORE LIKE CHAOS AND THEN ORDER. MORE THAN NOW.

Tracy: Who is his heir going to be?

Baphomet: MARY

I didn't know who Mary was, but I was confident that I was going to find out eventually. Baphomet sounded serious. I wasn't sure if I should take him at his word about De Vere being the Anti-Christ, since he admitted that he had lied about that subject earlier. But I thought it was quite likely that events were going to transpire soon that would make this idea seem all too real and plausible.

When I left Janie's apartment, my mind was abuzz. I was thinking about rituals I wanted to write for the OLE. I was also thinking about what it would really mean if Nicholas de Vere was the Anti-Christ. What if crowning him the King of Drakenberg really did somehow bring him to a position of world power? What if power could exist in ways we hadn't even thought of yet? These questions preoccupied me in the weeks to come.

Chapter 13: Strange Service

I find it almost impossible to explain what happens to me during this time, how this alien spirit is united to mine, without depriving me of consciousness or of inner freedom, and yet constituting a second 'me,' as though I had two souls, one of which is dispossessed of my body and the use of its organs, and keeps its quarters, watching the other, the intruder, do whatever it likes.... I cannot describe to you the joy I feel in thus finding myself turned into a devil, not by rebellion against God, but by a calamity which plainly symbolizes the state to which sin has reduced me....

- Rev. Jean-Joseph Surin, as quoted in
The Devils of Loudun, Aldous Huxley

Almost as if in response to the conversation we'd had with Baphomet, there was a sudden influx of new OLE members. Some of the new recruits were of a very high caliber indeed. I began to notice certain patterns forming among the fresh crop of Legionnaires and Quartermasters.

For one thing, we were getting quite a lot of members who already belonged to "left-hand path" organizations: in particular, the Ordo Templi Orientis and the Church of Satan. There were also some people who belonged to the Temple of Set, the group formed by Michael Aquino when they broke off from the Church of Satan. I noticed that these were the members who seemed most interested in establishing local OLE chapters in their own areas. They seemed to want to take leadership positions, and were aggressively trying to organize things in the online forums. It is interesting to note that both the OTO and the COS organizations pay homage to Baphomet. Perhaps these people were, consciously or not, receiving direction from him, pushed to join our group as well.

The other set I noticed were high-ranking Scottish Rite Freemasons, both in Europe and the United States. Several of them worked in the banking industry. One of them owned his own bank that handled offshore investments. Another had been instrumental in lobbying the state government of Colorado to allow "offshore" banks to operate there, right next to the Rocky Mountains, making it the only state in the US that permits such things.

There were a few other features that most of the members of this particular category of new OLE members had. Almost all of them laid claim to some sort of "royal title," not only in the Dragon Court, but in other "royal" houses as well. Some of these royal houses seemed legitimate as far as I could tell. Others were quite questionable and perhaps fake. Many of these people had a background in military or intelligence. Several worked in diplomacy, and for

NGOs attached to the UN. A whole bunch of them belonged to a strange association of "security service" members headquartered in Eastern Europe.

Unlike the left-hand path members, the people in this latter category were generally more inclined to lurk silently in the OLE forums, quietly observing, rarely participating. But they also made the most significant donations to the order, and were more likely than others to buy all of the merchandise that we had available.

Brian and I began to think seriously about what we could do with such a useful group of people. Then one weekend, we entered a spontaneous "conversational divination" session where we brainstormed about the future of the Dragon Court and the OLE. We both seemed to be downloading information from the ether about what to say.

We talked about what would happen if one or more of our banker friends were able to bring the capital to buy a private island. What could be done if we were able to establish the kingdom of Drakenberg, with De Vere as the rightful sovereign? Could we get recognition from the UK, EU, and United Nations, as Nicholas had told us in the past?

Brian, on inspiration, suggested that if we had a ceremony in which De Vere was actually crowned king, it might have a metaphysical significance that would make the kingdom rise to power naturally. He talked about the ancient Egyptian concept that it was the pharaoh's presence which made the sun rise and set each day. Perhaps Nick, once he was really king, would have magical powers as well.

That night, I went into a trance and began doing what I would call "semi-automatic writing." I felt possessed while I was doing it, each word brought by divine afflatus. I did have to research a few things on the fly while writing, but I was inspired with this too. I knew ahead of time what facts and connections I would find. The indwelling spirit directed me on exactly what to look for, and where.

I wrote an odd document that night which still gives me chills until this day. It was meant to be the guidebook for the Quartermasters of the Ordo Lapsit Exillis. It is a kind of magical grimoire. It was never finished. I called it *Strange Service: A Manual for the Priesthood of the Ordo Lapsit Exillis*. Below I will present some lengthy quotes from the text, with a few introductory comments in-between.

The first major part of the book explains the mystical reason for the OLE's existence. Now that I look back on this, I realize it that this was the meaning behind the order all along, and I just hadn't realized it before. I had to be in the right state of mind to understand these concepts.

I was only able to achieve that state when the OLE had become something with a substantial enough level of energy and power coming from the membership. This I was able to tap into as a resource during my psychic endeavors. You will understand this better after reading the passages below.

The "Mystery" of the Grail: The Purpose of the Ordo Lapsit Exillis

The Grail Ritual

The word "mystery" comes from the Latin "mysteria," which means "secret rites in divine worship." Examples include the "Eleusinian Mysteries" of Greece and the "Mithraic Mysteries" of Rome. This is also an apt description of the "Grail mystery." This term refers not just to the question of what and where the Grail is, but to the Grail quest itself. It is the dramatic, allegorical mystery play of the Grail hero Parzival's quest, as described in the various Grail romances of the Middle Ages.

Those who have read these tales are aware that Parzival's quest is not merely to "find" the Grail. This is something that, in several versions, occurs relatively early on in the story. Rather, Parzival's goal is to restore the Grail King (Anfortas, the "Fisher King") to health, curing the festering wound in his genitals from which he has long suffered, and to restore his cursed kingdom (called "the Wasteland" because of its lack of fecundity) to health as well. In some versions, the Grail castle exists in a hidden, parallel world, and once the king is healed, it becomes visible again. The outside world is reunited with its hidden, spiritual side, and balance is once more restored.

The Ordo Lapsit Exillis believes that this is a literal description of the nature of our universe. There is an unknown principle at work that rules the known world: a higher dimension without which our lower dimensions would not be able to function. As Jesus says in *The Gospel of Thomas*, "the kingdom of Heaven is laid upon Earth, but men do not see it."

It is this ignorance of the imbalance between the known and unknown world that is causing the imperfection that we see all around us. It is our belief that, if this imbalance were corrected, our world would return to the state of harmony it once knew. By this, I mean to indicate the antediluvian Golden Age described in the myths of various ancient cultures.

In some versions of the Grail story, Parzival is able to correct the imbalance by asking a particular question of the Fisher King (who is also his long-lost uncle). Once this question is voiced, the curse, which the Grail king and kingdom have suffered under for ages, is suddenly removed. In one story, Parzival must inquire about the nature of the Fisher King's wound by saying "Uncle, what ails thee?" In another version, the question he must ask is "Whom does the Grail serve?"

It doesn't really matter what the question is exactly. The point is: "Ask and ye shall receive." In other words, if you would like to see the power of the Grail cure the ills of our world, all you have to do is ask. God will show you what you need to do in order to make it happen.

The Ordo Lapsit Exillis consists of people who have asked that question, who have been shown the path, and who have agreed to walk that path with one another in order to "make it happen." We believe that if the true and rightful Grail king is placed upon the throne of Grail kingdom once again, and crowned in the proper ceremony, the very act itself will unleash a force that will cause a paradigm shift in our world, restoring it to proper balance. A series of world-altering events will unfold in rapid succession that will lead to the union of the world's governments under the rule of the Grail king. It will also fundamentally alter the spiritual nature of our world, and the consciousness of its inhabitants, which is the most important change of all.

The Grail King

We at the Ordo Lapsit Exillis believe that we already know the name of the man destined to be the Grail King. He is the last scion of a royal bloodline that stretches back to the very beginning of human history, and beyond that as well. His is the true "bloodline of the Holy Grail" that certain authors have written about.

The bloodline is not merely human, but divine in origin, and is the only bloodline chosen by our masters as being fit for royal office. Now we know there are many people throughout the world that carry this same blood to varying degrees. But our Crown Prince is the only person alive today who possesses a pure and unbroken lineage stretching back to the first Grail king, Cain, a son of the Sun.

Our Prince is also the only person who has been trained from birth onward to hold this exact position. The veracity of his claims, the divine mission to which he has been assigned, and the magical nature of his royal blood have been proven to us beyond a shadow of a doubt. It is truly awe-inspiring to realize that our order has been chosen to perform this monumental task. It is we who must bring the Grail king to the throne once again. It is our responsibility to restore order to the chaos of our world, healing the wasteland that has caused so much misery and suffering throughout the ages.

Presently, our Prince is at this time a human being, albeit one of ultimately divine origin. He has human failings just like anybody else. However, it is our belief that once the anointing ceremony is performed, and he is crowned king, an alchemical transformation will occur within his mind, and in his physical body. He will become possessed by the spirit of his divine ancestor, and will no longer be merely human.

He will be transformed into something both male and female, both alive and dead, both human and divine. He will be an incarnation of Cain, the original Grail king. It is in this transcended state that he will be able to initiate the global events that will lead to the union of the world's governments under his rule.

The Grail Kingdom

However, before our Prince can be placed on the throne, the throne itself must be restored. We must create on Earth a three-dimensional counterpart for the Grail kingdom, which already exists in an unseen, higher dimension. We must create a homeland for the "Grail family," also known as the "Dragon race." These are the ones who possess DNA from the lineage of Cain. Specific "Dragon genes" have already been identified and can be scientifically tested for. The citizens of this new kingdom, then, will be those who carry these genetic markers.

In the Grail stories, the location of the Grail castle is given as "Monsalvat": the Mount of Salvation. However, we have chosen a name for our kingdom which we believe is more appropriate: Drakenberg. In short, Drakenberg is and always has been the name of the kingdom of the Dragons, whether it exists *de jure* (as it is now) or *de facto* (as it has in the past and will again in the future).

Our Crown Prince has the right, by nature of his royal inheritance, to create a sovereign nation called "Drakenberg" at any time, and in any place in which he is able to do so. This right is further recognized by the British government itself. This means that if, say for instance, a private island were purchased, we could have Drakenberg on that very land, provided that the area was not already claimed by another nation.

Even if the chosen place were already claimed, arrangements could be made to allow for the island's independence. We have reason to believe that if Drakenberg were created, its sovereignty would be gladly recognized not only the British government, but by the United States as well. We think that when the time is right we will be able to obtain a pledge of support from these nations. This will go a long way towards helping us provide the security we will need to be able to function as a sovereign nation.

Dragon Government vs. Human Government

It should go without saying that our Crown Prince shall not rise to the helm of world government because of his tax proposals, or because of any domestic or foreign policy which he will propose. Although our king will be perfectly capable of making these decisions if needed, they are not an essential aspect of his role. Grail kingship is far removed from any familiar notion of human government.

The Grail kings of France known as the Merovingians were said to have "ruled by not governed." The same will be true of our king. His role is not as a mere "figurehead," but as a representative of the divine on Earth. He is a conduit between Heaven and Earth.

In the ancient world, the king's job was simply to rule. By nature of who he was, because of the divine blood that coursed through his veins, it was he who made the sun rise and set. It was he who made the crops grow. It was he who held the roof of the world aloft on his shoulders.

If he faltered in his duties, the whole kingdom suffered gravely. This is certainly too much responsibility for most people. The pressure alone would kill a normal man.

That is why our king must a have a semi-divine constitution: so that he may bear the burden of kingship. You can understand then, why subjects such as tax rates and health insurance would be of little concern to the Grail king. After all, when the kingdom is restored, and the veil is lifted from our perception of existence, will such things as taxes and insurance even exist?

We must be prepared for the fact that restoring the Grail king will create a fundamental change in every aspect of worldly existence. It should almost be assumed that the petty concerns which drive us now will be of little consequence when the paradigm shift occurs. Time as we know it may even cease to exist.

This, then, is the change which the Ordo Lapsit Exillis wishes to bring about. Part of this will involve raising the funds and acquiring the personnel necessary to create Drakenberg as a viable, sovereign kingdom. The other part will involve preparing ourselves and the world spiritually for the coming change as best we can.

One of the ways in which we will begin this preparation is by spreading information about the Grail, the bloodline, the king, and the kingdom. We want as many people as possible to know about, and willingly participate in, the creation of the kingdom. We must encourage all those of the Dragon blood to learn about their heritage, and to join their king in his kingdom. We must also generate amongst ourselves an overwhelming wealth of spiritual energy, which will fuel, in a metaphysical way, our endeavor.

This is the purpose of many of the ceremonies that the members of the OLE will engage in. We are literally acting out the "Grail mystery," the most important magical ritual there is. The effects of this ritual will be Earth-changing. In order for the ritual to have the necessary effects, it will require a great deal of power.

The OLE is the battery which fuels this ritual. That battery must be kept constantly charged. This is the idea behind "Strange Service," the principle that governs the OLE's priesthood.

As the text went on, I explained that Baphomet was a spirit attached to that of Cain. I said that Cain was now locked in his underworld prison, but that, through Baphomet, he was influencing things on Earth. I then told what would happen down below when the King of Drakenberg was crowned in the world above:

Cain is locked inside of a prison within the center of the Earth - entombed, really - under a spell of death-like sleep. However, he is still able to use his incredibly powerful divine spirit to affect the course of events on Earth. He is still the Lord of the Earth, although he is immobilized. He takes especial interest in the royal human bloodlines that descend from him.

He is able to incarnate through his descendants (and those who serve them). In his state, he has become known as "Baphomet," the god of "Sophia" (divine wisdom). He is connected to the figure of Asmodeus, the king of the demons, who is often depicted as being bound in chains, slumped over as if carrying an enormous burden.

The prison within which Baphomet is locked is the real Ark, and the real Holy Grail, for it contains his divine power. Whether one views it as a cup, a stone, or a box (as in the Ark of the Covenant), the symbolism is the same. It is the prison that contains the body and spirit of Baphomet. Jailed, Baphomet is thus at the mercy of whoever his jailer is. The question "Whom does the Grail serve?", then, is really saying "Who holds the key to the prison of Baphomet?"

We believe that when the Grail king is placed upon the throne of Drakenberg during the proper ceremony, Baphomet will be released from his prison. He will immediately possess the body of our king, so that he may once again rule as the Lord of the Earth. As his servants, it is our duty to obtain his release. However, in order to do this, we must be able to offer the proper ransom.

In the next passage, I talked about the spiritual principles of priests raising donations through tithes and other offerings. I scoured the Old Testament for information about how the Levites of ancient Israel did business. It was through intuitive understanding that I was able to write about how the funds they received for their priestly duties transferred spiritual power to them, which energized their rituals and prayers:

Strange Service: The Priesthood of the Ordo Lapsit Exillis

The Curse of the Levites

In ancient Israel, the practice of priesthood was restricted to those of the tribe of Levi. Every single male Levite was required to serve in the priesthood. That was the only occupation allowed to him. This was a circumstance demanded by Jehovah himself. He had personally stipulated not only that all priests should be Levites, and all Levites priests, but that the priests should also be barred from owning property.

Their only source of income was the tithes and other offerings given to them by the people of Israel in exchange for their priestly services. The people were obliged to give ten percent of their own earnings to the priesthood, and to pay for each priestly duty performed as well. But the Levites were not allowed to own any land.

While the other eleven tribes each had their own territory within Israel, the Levites were obliged to live scattered throughout the other territories. Sometimes they stayed in publicly-owned housing, in or near the centers of religious worship. Sometimes they lived as guests at the houses of certain wealthy families who could afford to hire a personal priest.

The Old Testament is very clear about the fact that service in Jehovah's priesthood was, more than anything else, a burden. As it states in *Numbers* 18:

And the LORD said unto Aaron, Thou and thy sons and thy father's house with thee shall bear the iniquity of the sanctuary: and thou and thy sons with thee shall bear the iniquity of your priesthood.... And I, behold, I have taken your brethren the Levites from among the children of Israel: to you they are given as a gift for the LORD, to do the service of the tabernacle of the congregation....

But the Levites shall do the service of the tabernacle of the congregation, and they shall bear their iniquity: it shall be a statute for ever throughout your generations, that among the children of Israel they have no inheritance. But the tithes of the children of Israel, which they offer as an heave offering unto the LORD, I have given to the Levites to inherit: therefore I have said unto them, Among the children of Israel they shall have no inheritance.

And the LORD spake unto Moses, saying, Thus speak unto the Levites, and say unto them, When ye take of the children of Israel the tithes which I have given you from them for your inheritance, then ye shall offer up an heave offering of it for the LORD, even a tenth part of the tithe.

The fact is that the Levites were chosen for the priesthood partially as a punishment for the behavior of their progenitor, Levi. He, along with his brother Simeon, had waged a genocidal war against the nation of Shechem. This was done contrary to the wishes of Jehovah, and of their father, Jacob. It led Jacob to pronounce a curse upon the two sons when he was on his deathbed. He stated:

Simeon and Levi are brethren; instruments of cruelty are in their habitations. O my soul, come not thou into their secret; unto their assembly, mine honour, be not thou united: for in their anger they slew a man, and in their selfwill they digged down a wall. Cursed be their anger, for it was fierce; and their wrath, for it was cruel: I will divide them in Jacob, and scatter them in Israel.

However, it wasn't until the Exodus that Jehovah cursed them with the iniquity of priesthood. On the night of the first Passover, the Lord slaughtered the firstborn of every house in Egypt. But He passed over the houses of the Hebrews, who had painted the doors of their houses with lamb's blood at His command. Thus did the Angel of Death know to leave those houses alone.

Yet in exchange for sparing the firstborn of the Hebrews, Jehovah demanded a substitute sacrifice. The sons of the tribe of Levi were chosen as the substitute. Although they were allowed to continue living, their inheritance was taken away from them. Moses and Aaron (both Levites) led the Hebrews out of Egypt and initiated an everlasting covenant between them and the Lord. The Hebrews would pay homage and sacrifice to Him in exchange for His protection. The Levites were then called to the priesthood, to be the mediators of this contract.

In a sense, the Levites became the most powerful people in Israel. Yet they had no property. They were the scapegoats who took on the ultimate responsibility. If the people sinned against Jehovah, then He would punish the people in general, but would punish the Levites foremost for failing to properly mediate. If He punished the people of Israel, then the people blamed the priests for failing to secure the Lord's favor.

Thus the Levite priests endured much, and wholly earned the tithes that they received. The tithes were not considered gifts, but rather payment for services rendered. The priests used the money not only to finance religious activities, but for their own personal needs as well. This was considered not a potential corrupting influence, but as a bulwark against such things. After all, a well-paid priesthood is less likely to accept bribes to perform impious deeds.

Nevertheless, the priests of Israel often did indulge in impious deeds. Most notably, they frequently accepted money in exchange for performing rites to heathen gods. Although Jehovah may have looked down upon such behavior, it was considered quite normal in Israel, especially when times were hard financially.

In Louis Ginzberg's *The Legends of the Jews*, the author writes about a certain Levite priest, the grandson of Moses. Early on, the lad was told by his grandfather that if a priest cannot earn an acceptable living serving Jehovah, it is better to supplement one's income by serving heathen gods for heathen clients, rather than begging for handouts from fellow Israelites. As Ginzberg writes:

From his grandfather he had heard the rule that a man should do 'Abodah Zarah' for hire rather than be dependent upon his fellow-creatures. The meaning of 'Abodah Zarah' here naturally is 'strange,' in the sense of 'unusual' work, but he took the term in its ordinary acceptation of 'service of strange gods.'

The worship of strange gods is often referred to in the Old Testament as "whoring," This may be because heathen religious rituals often involved rites of "sacred prostitution," with the use of "temple prostitutes" who were paid for their services. In these cultures, as in the Jehovahite tradition, there was quite a significance placed on the relationship between the services of the priests and the money they were paid to perform it. Simply put, the tithes paid to the priests, along with the prayers, animal sacrifices, and other rituals, in a way provided the energy (spiritual and otherwise) upon which the priesthood operated. The money paid by the congregation to the priests was a financial sacrifice to the god/s they were servicing.

This is illustrated by the fact that such strange rites often involved the worship of religious idols made out of gold and silver that had been donated to the cause. In *The Book of Judges*, we read about Micah, the Levite priest. Micah performed services towards a handful of religious idols that he had crafted out of silver given by his mother Delilah specifically for this purpose. By donating this silver, she was providing a seed upon which Micah's lucrative priesthood would grow. Then he was able to charge believing heathens money to perform rites on their behalf in homage to these idols.

The same principle is demonstrated in the story of the golden calf in *Exodus*. The story says that this item was fashioned by the high priest Aaron from the golden jewelry donated by the public. Thus it "contained," spiritually, the covenant between these people and Belial, the deity it represented.

You could say that the covenant was bought with the price of that gold. This was why, afterward, Moses had them drink the gold as a punishment. He wanted them to internalize the curse that Jehovah had placed upon them for worshipping the calf.

As I wrote this text, an innate apprehension awoke within me regarding the link between alchemy and economics, as well as, more broadly, the link between magical and worldly power. My mind's eye opened up to the meaning of the Grail stone, a.k.a. the Cubic "Philosopher's Stone" that our order was named after. I saw that anyone who was able to tap into it could much more easily acquire wealth and power using the alchemical principles of exponential increase. A segment of the *Strange Service* text describes these concepts:

The idea of the exponential increase of money, or indeed of any form of energy, is a form of alchemy. It is just like turning lead into gold, or making the "prima materia" into the "Philosopher's Stone." It means transmuting the base into the lofty, by moving energy from a lower form into a higher form.

The alchemical stone can purportedly be made from any substance, even the most base. From the stone itself can be created anything which the heart desires, in inexhaustible abundance. This Philosopher's Stone is what makes the alchemical gold, so rare and valuable that one can use it to purchase anything in Heaven and Earth, even eternal life. As Christ taught, according to *Matthew 13:45-46*:

...The kingdom of heaven is like unto a merchant man, seeking goodly pearls: Who, when he had found one pearl of great price, went and sold all that he had, and bought it.

According to the romances, the Holy Grail has the power to give abundantly whatever nourishment one wishes to receive. This it is able to do because, as we read in Wolfram von Eschenbach's *Parzival*, every year on Good Friday:

...one can infallibly see a Dove wing its way down from Heaven. It brings a small white Wafer to the Stone and leaves it there. The Dove, all dazzling and white, then flies up to Heaven again. Every Good Friday, as I say, the Dove brings it to the Stone, from which the Stone receives all that is good on earth of food and drink, a paradisal excellence - I mean whatever the earth yields. The Stone, furthermore, has to give them the flesh of all the wild things that live below the aether, whether they fly, run, or swim...

While writing, I became more fully cognizant of what Baphomet had been trying to tell us about the alchemy of tithes, which he'd tried to explain to us using a metaphor about the wedding at Cana. I was moved to provide several examples showing the relationship between financial donations and ritual magic, from sources that most modern occultists would be familiar with. I wrote:

It has long been traditional for participants in a religious ritual to give a donation upon entering the church or ritual chamber. Such is common in Catholic and other Christian churches. Even the "Ecclesiastica Gnostica Catholica," connected to Aleister Crowley's Ordo Templi Orientis, collects a donation of five dollars from each participant in the Gnostic Mass that they hold every Sunday. These donations not only serve to support the church financially, but also serve as a reserve of spiritual energy donated by the participants to power the ritual.

The same concept is alluded to in the alchemical treatise The Chymical Wedding of Christian Rosenkreutz. In this story, the title 218 Clock Shavings character is invited to a royal wedding that is also an alchemical ritual. Before entering the castle in which the ceremony is held, he must purchase and then surrender to the gatekeeper a special gold coin that represents his donation to the household: the wedding gift. A plaque over the entrance to the castle reads "Date et dabitur vobis." ("Give and it will be given unto you.")

I could see with my psychic vision that this power of alchemy was the same thing as the power and wisdom of Baphomet. I saw that the Knights Templar had acquired that power, and been baptized by that wisdom, which they used to build a global empire. The Templars confessed under torture that they worshipped Baphomet because he made them rich. As Eliphas Levi wrote in Magic: *A History of Its Rites, Rituals and Mysteries*: "Their principle was to become rich, in order to purchase the world."

The more I thought about it, the more I realized that this explained everything about the enigmatic biography of Bérenger Saunière, and the alleged "treasure" of Rennes-le-Château that made him rich. In a fit of mania I auto-wrote the following passage in about twenty minutes:

The Secret of Saunière's Wealth

Another person who was obviously quite well acquainted with the principles of Strange Service was Bérenger Saunière, the former curate of the Church of Mary

Magdalene at Rennes-le-Château, France. As most readers probably already know, Rennes-le-Château is at the center of the mystery of the Holy Grail. This place is of particular interest to the French royal Grail family, the Merovingians, as well as the associated secret society known as the Priory of Sion. As discussed in the book *The Merovingian Mythos*, it is likely that the five mountains of Rennes-le-Château contain the grave of Cain.

Bérenger Saunière took charge of the church at Rennes-le-Château in 1885. At the time, it was a tiny and impoverished farming village, without adequate roads or plumbing. Saunière's income during his first six years of service there averaged the equivalent of six pounds sterling per year. However, in 1891, while performing some renovations on the church, he purportedly discovered four coded parchments underneath the altar that had been left there by the church's previous curate.

It has been widely speculated that these parchments somehow contained clues leading Saunière to a buried treasure. Some think it was the Holy Grail, or perhaps the grave of Jesus Christ. Saunière is said to have taken the parchments to the seminary of St. Sulpice in Paris, where Abbe Bieil and Emile Hoffet purportedly helped Saunière to decipher the parchments.

From that moment on, Saunière became inexplicably wealthy. He began to socialize not just with the rural population of Rennes-le-Château, but with the most famous members of Paris' literary and occult underground. He was seen with people like composer Claude Debussy (a Grand Master of the Priory of Sion) and opera singer Emma Calve (who was purportedly Saunière's lover).

These people actually came to visit him at his church in the village. He even entertained Johann von Habsburg, cousin to the emperor of Austria, as well as the French minister of culture. Yet the reason why Saunière attracted such illustrious company, and why he became so suddenly wealthy, has remained a secret, at least to the historical record.

The church authorities wondered what the source of his wealth was too, and after an investigation, leveled against him the charge of "simony." This is, according to Webster's Dictionary, "the making of profit out of sacred things," or "the buying or selling of ecclesiastical preferments, benefices, etc." It comes from the story of Simon Magus, who, in *Acts 8:18* tried to purchase the powers of God from the apostles Simon and Philip.

The Church charged that Saunière was selling religious ceremonies: that he asked a particular price for each confession, mass, etc. Furthermore, instead of passing this money on to them, he was keeping a great deal of it for himself. He was even taking money for ceremonies he did not actually perform.

Indeed, this could very well explain the source of Saunière's wealth. For one thing, his parishioners were quite wealthy. Although the village was, by and large, poor, it was the nobles of the area who attended Saunière's church, while the peasants attended another one altogether. Therefore, the donations he received from his parishioners could have been quite significant. In addition to this, Saunière was selling masses to people outside of his church as well. A great deal of documentation on this can be found on priory-of-sion.com, where author Paul Smith writes that:

There was nothing 'mysterious' about the source of Bérenger Saunière's wealth - it all stemmed from the selling of masses - Saunière advertised in religious magazines and journals like Semaine Religieuse, La Croix, L'eclair. L'Express du Midi, L'Univers and Le Télégramme and the money just poured in from all over-to such an extent that Saunière could not honor the requests, there being so many of them.

Indeed, it was calculated that if the priest had spent every waking moment of his life saying masses, he still could not fulfill all of the requests he had received. The amount which Saunière recorded having earned from this was astronomical. On top of that, Saunière received donations from other people for other reasons, and a great deal of these were not recorded. Perhaps the donors were kept secret, Saunière having possibly promised the donors their anonymity.

The priest was convicted of the charges, and suspended from his duties for three months. A replacement was brought in to conduct services at his church. However, the replacement found himself preaching to an empty house. All of Saunière's parishioners chose instead to attend his ceremonies, which he continued to conduct, against the orders of his superiors, in another building on the church property.

It seems clear that what happened to Saunière was that he discovered the secrets of Strange Service. His selling of masses is no different than soliciting "seed money" or tithes in exchange for prayer requests. The more followers you have, the more spiritual power you have, and thus the more people want to follow you and give you things.

It is believed that when Saunière went to St. Sulpice with the parchments he'd discovered, he was initiated into a secret society called the "Hieron du Val d'Or." This has been described as a quasi -Masonic, Traditionalist Catholic, royalist order that acted as a front for the Priory of Sion. While ostensibly Catholic, this order seems to have possessed some strange beliefs, apparently including Gnostic, Hermetic, and Luciferian elements.

Related symbolism is seen throughout the strange renovations that Saunière made to his church after he became wealthy. These included, for instance, the erection of a statue of the demon Asmodeus to hold up the holy water stoop. It seems that, upon joining this strange cult, Saunière became personally connected to arcane powers channeled from non-corporeal entities. Very likely, he made contact with Baphomet. He was then able to obtain magical powers from that spirit.

When his parishioners recognized that he was now in direct contact with the divine, they were more than willing to pay big bucks for the privilege of having him pray for them. His reputation as a sorcerer eventually became known on a wider scale, and he was able to advertise his services to a larger audience, with very positive results.

Knowing the law of the Harvest, Saunière reinvested a portion of his earnings in the church and the community. In addition to renovating the church grounds, he also paid for roads and plumbing to be installed in the village. He had discovered the secret of Strange Service and wealth creation.

That secret is simply this: trust God, and the Lord will provide. You reap what you sow. Serve dutifully, give without thought of return, and you will receive return abundantly. Clearly, Saunière had set up his church as a financial energy amplifier, just as we have discussed.

This is in fact one of the secrets that Saunière encoded into the renovations of his church. When you enter the building, the first thing you see is Asmodeus, the holy water stoop, and the donation box. Since Asmodeus is presenting the holy water, we can assume that the first thing a person did after making his initial donation was to baptize himself with the waters of the Abyss. In other words, one received the "Baptism of Wisdom" of the underworld. It is fitting, then, that one of the next things you would see upon entering the church is a statue of John the Baptist (whose skull purportedly contained the spirit of Baphomet) baptizing Jesus.

The main focal point of the church is of course the altar. It is upon the altar that sacrifices are traditionally laid in religious rituals. In Saunière's church, this is, undoubtedly, where the spiritual energy sacrificed by the participants was placed. It was also from there that they received Communion: a drink from the Grail chalice. This was indicated by the depiction on the altar of a sun descending into a chalice. It illustrated the descent of the Holy Spirit into the cup to transform the wine into the blood of the deity.

The congregation made financial sacrifices at the donation box in exchange for financial rewards (which Saunière would pray for them to receive). They also made spiritual sacrifices at the altar in exchange for spiritual gifts. The sacrifice made at the altar is symbolized by the painted bas relief Saunière placed there featuring the penitent Mary Magdalene praying in a hermit's cave, next to a skull and a cross. The sprig that grows from the wood of the cross emblematizes the fruit that results from the seeds of sacrifice.

As you leave the church, you see, above the confessional, another bas relief that illustrates the entire process. It features Christ giving the Sermon on the Mount, with people bowing down in front of him in supplication and prayer. There are cut flowers strewn about, representing the sacrifices made to Christ in hope of receiving things in return. Jesus' arms are open wide, as if he is gleefully distributing an abundance of gifts.

At the bottom of the mountain, there is a peculiar depiction of a money bag with a piece of gold sticking out, right next to the crucifix on top of the confessional. This signifies the ultimate gain from the ultimate sacrifice. The words written below the relief read: "Come unto me all ye who labor and are heavy-laden and I will give you rest."

After I finished writing this part of the book, I was spontaneously illuminated with a vision of what the duties of the OLE priesthood should be. I wrote:

As a prisoner within the center of the Earth, Baphomet is obliged to serve his master. It is a humiliating and burdensome task. As the servants of Baphomet, it is the job of the priests of the Ordo Lapsit Exillis to help Baphomet bear that burden. This is Strange Service. In exchange for our service, Baphomet arranges for us to be rewarded.

This is done according to the contracts that we make with Baphomet regarding our service and compensation. It is the job of the priest not only to transact a pact between himself and Baphomet, but between his congregation and Baphomet also. He negotiates what services the congregation will perform, what sacrifices they will make, and what they will get in return.

If the members of the congregation fail in their duties, he must ensure that this is recompensed. Often he shares the blame and the curses that result from these failings. This weighs heavily upon the soul. Like the Levites of Israel, we must "bear the iniquity of the priesthood." Yet we also get to enjoy the benefits.

However, unlike the Levites, most of our priests have not been born into the sacerdotal caste. The clerics of Israel were fated to serve in the clergy because they were priests by blood, according to divine command. Certainly it makes sense that the right of priesthood should reside in the blood, just as the right of kingship does, for as we know, divine powers of magic reside in the DNA of those of the Grail family. Although some of the priests of the Ordo Lapsit Exillis will possess Grail blood naturally, this is not a prerequisite. The power of our priests comes not necessarily by genes, but also through the donation of divine authority.

Jesus told his apostles that he would make them priests "according to the order of Melchizedek." This was a reference to a Judaic story about Abraham giving the figure named "Melchizedek" (described as a "priest of the most high God") a tenth of his possessions as a tithe, during a ceremony involving bread and wine. Melchizedek is said to have then laid on hands and ordained ministerial rights forever after to the descendants of Abraham.

"Melchizedek" literally means "king-priest." He would appear to have been the foremost representative of God on the planet during his time, the symbolic "Lord of the Earth," just as the Grail king is. Thus he was, by his blessing, purportedly able to bestow ecclesiastical powers upon anyone of his choosing.

Likewise, Jesus, as the son of God, could convey the abilities of blessing, healing, and exorcism upon his apostles. To them he confidently declared: "Whatsoever ye shall bind on earth shall be bound in heaven: and whatsoever ye shall loose on earth shall be loosed in heaven." This meant that they could perform rites of sympathetic magic to command the activities of angels and demons. They could bind them, and restrict their activity, or loose them upon the world if so desired. He also said that because of the power he had laid upon them, their prayers would be like commandments to God, for "if two of you shall agree on earth as touching any thing that they shall ask, it shall be done for them of my Father which is in heaven."

Similarly, the Ordo Lapsit Exillis has been granted the right to form a priesthood by divine authority, according to our charter from the Baphometic Order of the Cubic Stone, and according to our pact with Baphomet himself. We have also been granted license from the highest representative of the Grail lineage on Earth today: the Crown Prince. The magical and sacerdotal powers which flow through that blood have been spiritually vested in us. Jesus had a similar relationship with his apostles, and explained it to them thusly in *John 15:1 - 8*:

I am the true vine, and my Father is the husbandman. Every branch in me that beareth not fruit he taketh away: and every branch that beareth fruit, he purgeth it, that it may bring forth more fruit. ... If ye abide in me, and my words abide in you, ye shall ask what ye will, and it shall be done unto you. Herein is my Father glorified, that ye bear much fruit; so shall ye be my disciples.

When a Quartermaster in the Ordo Lapsit Exillis takes his oath of initiation, he is making a pact with Baphomet. This oath then literally becomes encoded within his DNA. Baphomet's spirit binds itself to the initiate's future bloodline. Thereby are the divine powers of the Grail priesthood bestowed upon him and his kin by apostolic donation.

Upon completing that section, I immediately launched into a detailed description of how to contact Baphomet, how to negotiate with him, and how to conduct rituals under the auspices of the OLE. What follows is nothing less than a magical grimoire given to the secret hierophants of the Grail stone:

The Practice of Baphometic Magic

Father Mithras: The God of Contracts

Baphomet, the Outer Head of the Ordo Lapsit Exillis, is, as I have explained, the name of the eternal, ancestral spirit of Cain, the Lord of the Earth and "son of the sun." He has been known by many names throughout the centuries, and one of them is "Mithras." In fact, "Baphomet" has been interpreted by some to translate to the words "Father Mithras."

Originally a Persian deity, Mithras came to be worshipped throughout the ancient world. His greatest act was to be sacrificed in exchange for the eternal salvation of mankind. Mithras was known as the god of contracts. He was the mediator between the Persian "Ahura Mazda" (God) and "Ahriman" (the Devil). Indeed, Mithras' name actually means "contract."

Mithraists viewed their patron as the inventor of all laws and justice. He was believed to punish severely anyone who broke a contract. The handshake, which signifies both "meeting on the square," and agreement over a contract, began with the rites of Mithras. There it was used to symbolize the covenant of faith and trust that was believed to exist between Mithras and those who served him. His name is undoubtedly related to the Egyptian "Maat," meaning "truth, fairness, and wisdom."

In many ways, the rites of Freemasonry resemble the rites of Mithras. Masonic ritual focuses heavily on the importance of honoring one's oath, and creating trust between the membership. This is fitting, for it is Father Mithras, or Baphomet, who was ultimately responsible for the creation of Freemasonry. We know that Baphomet was the Outer Head of the Order of Knights Templar. We believe that it was Baphomet who instructed the first Templars on how to form the order. It seems that when Templarism mutated into Freemasonry, Baphomet took charge of that order too.

Indeed, it is likely that Baphomet has contracts with secret societies, churches, and other organizations all over the world, all of them spiritual pyramid schemes with him at the top. For instance, the Church of Jesus Christ of Latter-Day Saints has all the earmarks of a Baphometic priesthood. This operation is probably based upon a contract between Joseph Smith and an entity representing Baphomet. However, the clergy there would never publicly acknowledge it, and most of them might not even know.

Another obvious example is the Skull and Bones Society at Yale University, to which both Presidents Bush have belonged. It is even said that the CIA was created by brothers at a meeting of Skull and Bones. Baphomet utilizes this particular order to maintain his influence on the spheres of global power, and on the intelligence community. The reference in their name to the symbol of the death's head, originally used by the Templars to signify their patron head, Baphomet, indicates that his hand is upon this institution as well.

Let us also consider the alchemical school called the "Scholomance" that was attended by Vlad Dracula in Romania. Dracula was a member of our own

Imperial and Royal Dragon Court and Order, and the Scholomance may have actually been a function of the Court. In the Bram Stoker version of Dracula's story, the headmaster of the Scholomance was "the Devil" himself. Ten students would be taken per annum, and every year one of them was chosen stay at the school to "ride the Dragon:' The headmaster kept that student as his property, as payment for the other students' tuition. Once again, the tithing principle of sacrifice is demonstrated.

The Ordo Lapsit Exillis operates at the behest of Baphomet. This is not only because of the charter we have received from the Baphometic Order of the Cubic Stone, nor only because of the patronage we receive from the foremost representative of Baphomet on Earth: the heir to the Grail kingdom. In addition to this, we also have a direct, personal relationship with the Outer Head himself. Our navigators speak to him often.

The OLE has been granted the right to ordain a Baphometic priesthood, operating with the magical current derived from our charter from the BOCS. We have been able to negotiate a deal in which certain rights and privileges, including magical powers, are bestowed upon those quartermasters whom we choose to raise to the priesthood - provided they can learn how to use them! The cleric then has the right to form a temple (a local chapter of the OLE), with a congregation that he can serve. He can then negotiate his own contracts with Baphomet on behalf of the congregation. This is, in large part, what constitutes a priest's duties.

Every activity that takes place within the Ordo Lapsit Exillis is the fulfillment of a contract. Within the local chapters this is true as well. In exchange for certain sacrifices, the clergy receive certain favors. These sacrifices usually consist of either a sum of money, or the spiritual energy expended during rituals, or the performance of some deed requested by Baphomet. Once the deal has been struck, Baphomet arranges for other demons under his command, or other entities in his peer group, to fulfill the request.

Just as prayer requests are taken in Christian churches, an OLE priest can arrange for blessings to be bestowed upon the members of his congregation. He can negotiate a general contract in which all baptized members of the church are rewarded many times over for each gift given or service performed for the order. The members can submit requests for particular blessings when they attend temple functions. He can also stipulate that specific rewards are to be given in exchange for specific gifts or work from particular people. He can even have curses laid upon his enemies and those of his flock.

Curses, Blessings, and Demon Possession

It is a popular teaching among Christian evangelical preachers that many human beings are afflicted by curses, acquired mainly through the sins of the impious. According to this line of thinking, certain sins against God, especially those of idolatry and blasphemy, can open oneself to a curse, and thus to demonic possession. When one commits such a sin, it purportedly gives the demons "spiritual authority" to enter your body and to use you as their host.

The personalities of the possessing demons are evidenced by the afflictions that they cause. The nature of the curses acquired is usually related to the activity that allowed the demons to enter in the first place. For instance, those who indulge in sexual indiscretions will be afflicted with bad relationships, sexual obsession, abnormal sexuality, sexually transmitted diseases, and unwanted pregnancy.

It is also believed that some curses can be passed on inter-generationally. The Bible contains hundreds of examples of intergenerational curses, often on entire races of people. Also, in a sense, all human beings are tainted by the curse of Adam, acquired through his Original Sin.

In may surprise you to learn that, according to our psychical research, all of these assertions are emphatically true. Indeed, all human beings are afflicted by curses, and one of the reasons why this happens is because of dishonorable deeds. Curses can be placed on you by other people, and by divine entities as well. You can even put a curse on yourself without being aware of it. To invite a curse to afflict yourself or someone else, you merely have to wish for it, either in writing, or verbally. Many people can even invoke a curse just by thinking about it. These curses can then be passed on genetically to one's descendants.

It seems obvious, then, that most of us are afflicted with thousands of curses of all sorts. To ask how many curses a person is carrying is like asking "How many tiny parasites and bacteria do you have on your body?" While there may technically be a finite number of curses that each of us is carrying at any given time, they are multiplying and dying constantly at such a rate that you couldn't possibly number them.

It would be almost impossible, and perhaps not even beneficial, to remove all of the curses in their entirety. Like the bacteria on a human's body, we have a symbiotic relationship with many of the demons that afflict us, and we would die if they were taken away all at once. It is when they begin to overwhelm us when they become a noticeable factor in our lives - that they need to be removed. There are a number of ways to do that.

Curses are generally named after what they do, and their names identify the demons who have been sent by the afflicter (the one doing the cursing) to torment the afflicted. The demons of curses are generally lower elementals. They are somewhat mindless and unidirectional beings compared to the intelligence level of higher spirits like Baphomet, for instance. The job of these entities is to cause the adversity that they specialize in. As long as they have the legal authority to do so, they will spread their pestilence around as much as possible.

They are always looking for an available victim. They usually gain entry due to the unconscious actions of humans, who bring these curses to themselves or others without being aware of what they are doing. Therefore, it is often enough to simply identify the curses by name and tell the demons causing them to go away, ideally in some ritualized setting. However, if a curse has been brought upon you formally, via a magical ceremony, or if it has been placed upon you by a divine being, more action may be required.

If a person suspects that he has been scourged in this way, he should consult a divine oracle, such as the Ouija board, and contact Baphomet, the god of contracts, on the matter. He will most likely be able to tell what has caused the curse, and what is needed in order to break it. Sometimes he must make a sacrifice, or perform some work or duty, in order to be released from the bonds of the tormenting demons.

A divine curse is usually put on someone in whom a divine being has already taken a personal interest. Likely victims of divine curses are those who are somehow instrumental in that being's fatal plan. For instance, one of the people most vulnerable to such aggression is the President of the United States. As the leader of the world's only superpower, the President clearly factors in the plans of every single divine being who is presently trying to manipulate events on this globe. Just as he is seen as the prime target by his opponents on Earth, the President is also the mark for many enemies from the other side.

However, people of much lesser value can be plagued by divine curses as well. If you feel that you are really someone who has been "chosen by God," for some reason, then chances are that demonic beings have chosen you as well. You must constantly be on guard against spiritual attack.

It is important to remember, though, that not all curses are necessarily bad. Sometimes having to overcome these curses teaches us valuable lessons. This is especially true of divine curses, which are often sent to chastise a person into doing what a certain divine being wants him or her to do. A person can be severely cursed if he has taken an oath or made a pact with such an entity, promising to perform some service for that being, and then fails to follow through, or fails to move quickly enough.

If you have been the victim of a divine curse, find out which entity is responsible, and talk to him. Do not approach the conversation with an adversarial attitude. The curse may have simply been sent to correct you. If you learn your lesson or change your behavior, the curse can be lifted.

Blessings are really the same thing, only nicer. They are well intentioned spirits who can be summoned, or sent by others, to bless your life in specific ways. Just like the demons of curses, the spirits of blessings are named after what they do. Performing good deeds, personally inviting them into your life, and calling upon them to help you in your chosen work is usually enough to bring these cheerful helpers around. They can also be sent to assist other people. Of course, ritual ceremonies can be used to strengthen their power. Just like curses, they can also be sent by divine beings, and can be passed on inter-generationally.

It is important also to remember that it is not demons who create the power by which magical acts take place. In reality, they are only arranging the contract with the divine force that allows it to happen. The actual power comes from God, via the Grail. It is the potency that permeates the entire universe, but which only the more evolved beings in the universe can tap into.

The power of magic is the spirit of the Grail. That is what sparks the spiritual energy amplifier that is the Ordo Lapsit Exillis. This is why, in our rituals, one of things we do is to drink the Elixir of Life from the Grail cup. We do this to internalize these divine essences, before we commence our work.

Divination

One of the questions which the reader is undoubtedly asking himself is "How does the priest communicate with Baphomet in order to establish a contract with him?" The answer is equally obvious. By definition, any communication with a deity is divination. As it turns out, that is exactly how we do it.

We utilize any or all methods of divination, including: (1) the Ouija board; (2) scrying with mirrors or crystal balls; (3) automatic writing, and; (4) pure clairvoyant thought communication through meditation. The use of tarot may be rewarding for some as well, although the randomizing element of the cards, as well as the ambiguous symbolism of the messages derived, make the results of this method questionable. The same can be said of all divination techniques that rely on chance: dice, tea leaves, shells, I-Ching, cow entrails, etc. None of these methods seems to compare with the simplicity and efficiency of direct communication with the entity in question, provided the spirit is willing to talk to you.

It is here that an ordained priest of the Ordo Lapsit Exillis has a distinct advantage. By virtue of our contract with Baphomet, and our charter from the Baphometic Order of the Cubic Stone, our priests have legal authority to talk to him. So even if you have not been particularly successful with divination in the past, you may find that upon being invested with authority from the OLE, such communication will become surprisingly easy.

This is something that has been demonstrated repeatedly in our initial trial run of psychic experiments. Although those who carry Grail blood might find it easier, as they often find all magic to be easy, it is certainly possible for anyone making a sincere effort to contact spirits. You will also find that communication becomes easier, and your answers more fluid, every time you do it.

The most highly recommended form of communication for beginners is the Ouija board. While it has certain disadvantages, one of the main advantages is that it eliminates much of the subjectivity that the other methods are plagued with. That is, at least two people are receiving the same message at the same time, and often other witnesses are watching as well. If you receive messages that neither of you are likely to have made up or projected, then you can be reasonably certain that the communication is coming from the entity, and not the subconscious minds of the participants.

Also, the social aspect of using the board with another person pulls you outside of yourself. When attempting automatic writing, scrying, and clairvoyant communication, the impressions received are entirely internal, and the whole process takes place within yourself. Therefore it can be difficult, especially for beginners, to separate spirit communications from their own daydreams. It can be even harder to convince other people that these messages are real.

There is really no trick to using the Ouija board. It is very simple. It often helps to work at night, although it is not necessary. It does help to light incense and candles, and to play soft, evocative music beforehand.

You should definitely take some time before you begin to spiritually prepare for what you are about to do. You should write down the questions you wish to have answered, even though you will most likely not end up sticking to the script. You should choose a partner to work with whom you can trust not to discuss the experience with outsiders. Also, pick somebody who is not going to project doubt or negative energy into the communication. Preferably, this person should be another Quartermaster in the Ordo Lapsit Exillis.

The same requirements apply for the person you choose to take dictation. You may not always have the luxury of a scribe to write down all of the questions and answers as they happen, but it helps if you do. For as you become more adept at Ouija divination, you will find that the answers come too fast for you to remember them, and it is exceedingly difficult to carry on a fluid conversation when you are stopping to write down every letter. You may even wish to record the session with audiotape, videotape or a digital recorder.

Keeping a record of some sort is important. The act of divination brings you into an unusual state of mind in which amnesia quickly sets in as soon as you stop. It is your subconscious mind trying to protect your conscious mind from the shock of realizing that a supernatural act has just occurred. Strangely, although the Ouija board is among the most direct and reliable forms of divination, it has been the target of a smear campaign by many religious people, as well as even some Wiccans, pagans, and occultists. These people always warn that the use of the Ouija board invites evil spirits and demon possession. They act like the item itself is inherently cursed. We have all heard the stories of the "Ouija board that wouldn't burn." If you believe that, then I suppose you believe that "Bloody Mary" will appear in the bathroom mirror if you say her name three times!

It is not evident why the Ouija board is any more dangerous than tarot cards, which many people who disapprove of Ouija find more "safe." Nor is it clear what separates the Ouija board from things like the "urim and thummin," the divination devices used by the priests of Jehovah) specifically at his command, in ancient Israel. The urim and thummin were made from precious stones that would act in conjunction with the Ark of the Covenant to transmit messages from God to the priests. This activity was in fact what the religious practice of biblical Israel centered upon.

We find the Ouija board itself to be as innocuous as the inanimate material which it is made from. We further find that demons only possess people who specifically invite them by making a verbal contract. It is not something that can happen accidentally. Moreover, contacting unwanted spirits can be avoided simply by not calling on them.

Only address the specific being you wish to contact, rather than blindly asking "Is anybody there?" Of course, there is always someone "there," insomuch as the spirit world is non-local, and exists in all places at all times. Contacting it does not require that one be in a haunted house or a sacred spot. Nor does it need to happen on a particular day, or at a particular times of day, for the realm beyond is eternal and outside of time. However, significant places and dates can sometimes aid communication, as they can most certainly aid the working of magic.

When a person has become proficient at Ouija communication, he will find that he can hear the answers that the spirit gives him in his head before they are spelled out on the board. He will be able to tell the difference between these mental communications from without and his own internal thoughts. He may then choose to graduate to other methods.

The voices he hears and visions he sees in his head are a sign that he is learning to speak the "language of light" which spirits use to communicate. He has now been attuned to receive the divine gnosis of Baphomet, and of the Holy Grail, directly into his mind. He has been trained to hear with his inner ear, and to see with his inner eye.

He can now work to develop these skills by meditating, asking questions of the spirit, and receiving answers mentally. He can develop his inner vision by gazing into a crystal ball or a magic mirror while having this mental conversation. He will quickly find that when he really *listens*, he will really *hear*, and when he really *looks*, he will really *see*.

Automatic writing is another apparently effective form of divination. It is usually best done with a pencil, which can write more quickly and smoothly than a pen. It can also be done by typing. Automatic drawing or painting is possible as well. You can converse with the spirit in a question-and-answer conversation, or you can write the whole thing directly from the point of view of the conjured spirit.

Either way, you are allowing the entity to use your own hand to write out its messages.

When you reach the point where you can speak to Baphomet directly in his own "language of light" using any of these methods, you have undoubtedly already developed an intense relationship with him. You may in fact feel that it is a deep friendship. This is not unusual, for under his name of "Mithras" he was often referred to as "the Friend."

You should be able to feel him physically when you are talking to him. Eventually, if you want to, you will even be able to see him. At first this can be accomplished through a crystal ball or magic mirror, although eventually you won't even need them. But be careful that you are ready to see him, for the terrifying image of Baphomet drawn by Eliphas Levi does not even begin to approach the horrific reality.

At any rate, once you have reached the point where you feel that you and Baphomet understand each other, and you're comfortable with the dynamic of the relationship, you can begin negotiating contracts with him on behalf of yourself and your temple congregation. Baphomet may even beat you to it, and propose a deal of his own.

Essential Elements of a Baphometic Ritual

Items used in our rituals:

For all rituals:

Black candles

Frankincense and myrrh (the resin kind)

Charcoal (for burning incense)

The censer

The mortar and pestle

The Grail chalice

The wine

The altar

The red rose (to be suspended from the ceiling over the altar)

For pact rituals:

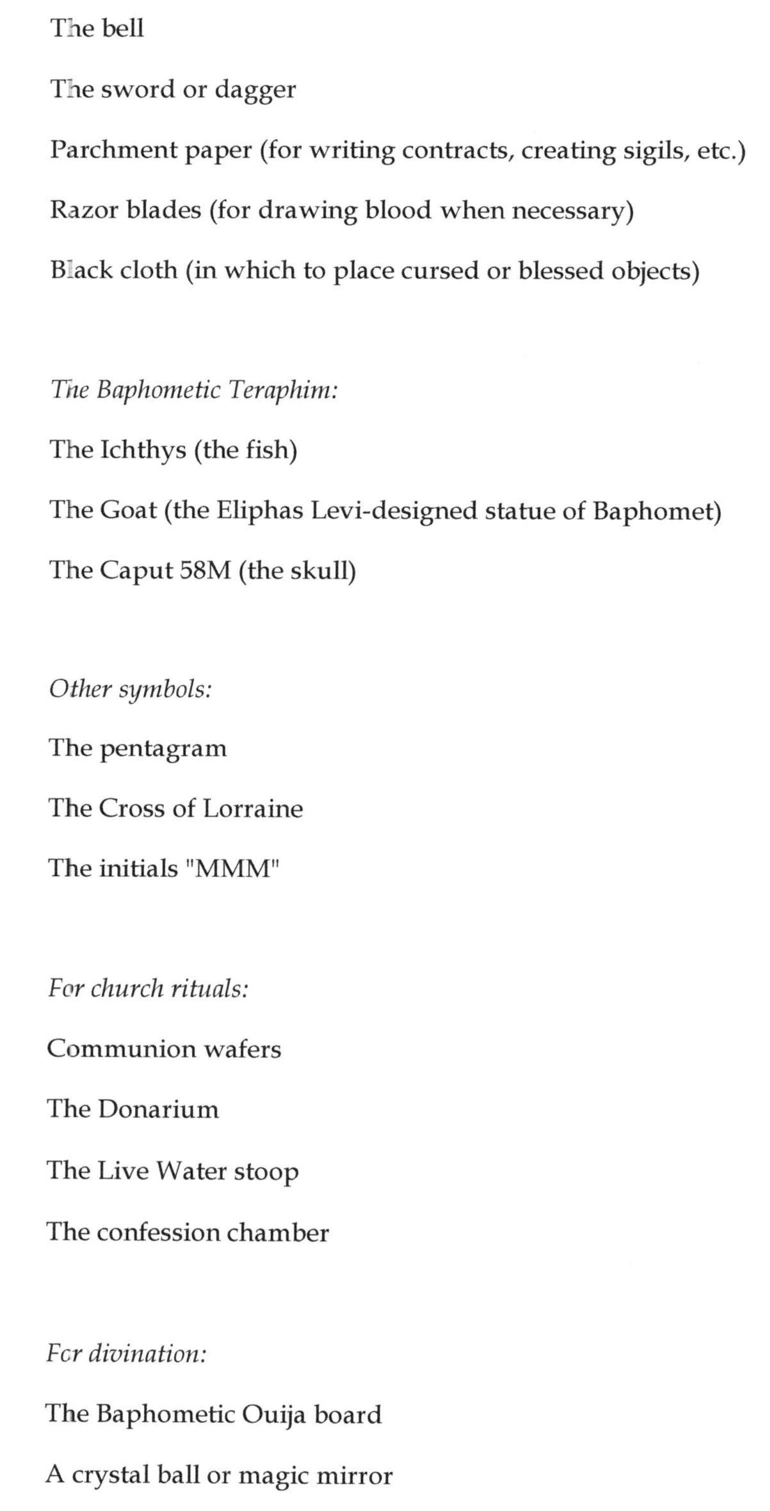

The bell

The sword or dagger

Parchment paper (for writing contracts, creating sigils, etc.)

Razor blades (for drawing blood when necessary)

Black cloth (in which to place cursed or blessed objects)

The Baphometic Teraphim:

The Ichthys (the fish)

The Goat (the Eliphas Levi-designed statue of Baphomet)

The Caput 58M (the skull)

Other symbols:

The pentagram

The Cross of Lorraine

The initials "MMM"

For church rituals:

Communion wafers

The Donarium

The Live Water stoop

The confession chamber

For divination:

The Baphometic Ouija board

A crystal ball or magic mirror

Notes on the Ritual Implements

Black candles are obviously the best to use in all rituals. However, other colors can be substituted when it is not possible to get black candles. If you find that candles do not provide adequate light for you to work by, add in something like an oil lamp or lantern. You should have one large candle in the center of the altar, with other, smaller candles placed about as needed.

It is also best if you can not only burn frankincense and myrrh, but try to get the resin form of incense, rather than prefabricated sticks or cones. You will have to purchase special charcoal briquettes to burn it on as well, and a censer within which to do so. You should also obtain a mortar and pestle to grind up the incense.

Using resin rather than sticks or cones is superior because it provides more smoke, and lasts longer. It can be added to as needed, and has a purer, more organic scent. Also, the act of grinding the incense helps you to get in the proper state of mind, and when it is burned in a censer, the smoke can be used for purification of the ritual chamber.

The chalice represents the Holy Grail, and the wine that is drunk from it betokens the bloodline of the Grail. When a person drinks the wine from the chalice, they are internalizing the powers of the Grail and of Baphomet. This is why the contents of the chalice are called "the Elixir of Life," in reference to the invaluable alchemical substance that gives eternal youth. This act of communion is done during all OLE rituals, but in church rituals the wine is referred to simply as "the blood of Our Lord," and is accompanied by a communion wafer. You can use any appropriate -looking chalice to play the role of the Grail.

The bell is used to signal the beginning and the end of the ritual, both for the participants, and for the spirits being summoned. The sword or dagger is used to designate the four corners of the Earth while calling the points. It is also used as a skewer when consigning the contract of the ritual to the flames. Thus, the presentation of the contract is like an act of sacrifice.

The parchment paper is used for the creation of contracts and sigils. It is better to use this than regular paper because it more easily absorbs blood. The razor blades are for drawing blood during a ritual. Blood is taken to seal contracts. It is also sometimes used as a sacrifice, for spirits can feed off the energy when it is freshly-drawn. Use a fresh blade each time, and give a separate blade to each participant.

If you are doing a blessing or a cursing ritual, in which the spell will be infused into an enchanted object, then afterwards that item should be wrapped in a black cloth. Keep it there until such time as it is delivered to the target of the spell.

The rose is hung from the ceiling above the ritual chamber to signify secrecy. This reminds the participants of the solemn nature of the occasion. It also signifies the budding flower of blessing that grows from the seed of sacrifice.

The word "teraphim" is a plural word in Hebrew meaning "strange idols." It refers to the religious images that were worshipped by all people outside of the Jehovahite faith during biblical times. It especially indicates statuettes made out of gold or silver that have been sacrificed by the worshippers to the gods depicted in the statues. However, the term was also used more specifically at times. According to JewishEncyciopedia.com:

...The teraphim were made of the head of a man, a first-born which, after the man had been slain, was shaved and then salted and spiced. After a gold plate on which magic words were engraved had been placed under the tongue, the mummified head was mounted on the wall... lighted candles were placed round it; the people then prostrated themselves before it, and it spoke to them.

This resembles very much the descriptions of the skull of Baphomet that the Templars purportedly used in their rituals, which is said to have "talked" to them.

In our order the word "teraphim" refers to the idols of Baphomet that are place upon the altar during rituals. There are several symbols of Baphomet that can be used to make the idols, and you might as well use as many as possible. It is not redundant to do so. Baphomet is vain and loves attention. Acknowledge him in your rituals as much as you can.

The symbols of Baphomet that can be made into idols include: the "Caput 58M" (another name for the Baphomet skull possessed by the Knights Templar); the Ichthys (the fish); and the Goat. Ideally, you would use a real human skull. But, barring that, a plastic replica will do, or even just a skull and cross-bones symbol reproduced on paper. As for the Ichthys, you could either use a live fish in a bowl, or a dead fish from the supermarket, or a fish statuette or painting, or a simple Ichthys fish symbol drawn on paper.

For the Goat, it is highly recommended that you acquire a statuette featuring the Eliphas Levi depiction of Baphomet. This is the one in which he is shown with a goat's head and legs, as well as male and female sexual organs. It is an extremely powerful image to use in a Baphometic ritual.

In addition to the teraphim, other images are to be used as well. The pentagram should be represented somewhere. You are encouraged to use the pentagram designed by Stanislas Guaita. This is the one that features the goat-headed face of Baphomet and the Hebrew word for "Leviathan." You should also have some sizable representation of our order's insignia, the Cross of Lorraine, somewhere on the altar. Have this symbol depicted somewhere on your body as well.

Finally, Baphomet has often identified himself in séances using the initials "MMM." Thus, it is good if you can somehow incorporate these three letters somewhere in the altar arrangement, and/or somewhere in the language of the ritual. It goes without saying that you will need to have an altar on which to display these items. Try to find a table, chest or other piece of furniture with a flat top that is about waist or chest-high. It should have a broad enough surface to display all of the things you will be using.

In church rituals, we also make use of communion wafers and holy water - what we call "Live Water." The latter substance is infused with the wisdom of Baphomet prior to the opening of the church. It is used for baptizing new members, as well as for purifying the ritual implements and area. Members of the congregation also bless themselves with it as they enter the church. A bowl of Live Water should be left on a stoop next to the front entrance of the church at all times. Members will sprinkle it on their foreheads as they enter, just as in Catholic churches.

Next to the Live Water stoop should be the donation box, which we refer to by the Latin term, "Donarium." The box should be closed, with a slot for the receiving of funds. On top you will write the words "Date et dabitur vobis."

Create an area in front of the altar in which the congregation can comfortably sit. If you have chairs, couches, or pews, that of course is ideal. Somewhere in the church, you will also provide a confession chamber. Use a closet, curtains, room separators, or whatever is necessary. You just need an enclosed area in which a person can talk to the priest, with a veil or other covering between them.

When I got to the part where I needed to describe the structure of the rituals, I referred to the script from the MemoryMask rite that I already had on file. I used this as a template, and lifted some of the priest's monologues from there. Here is how that section, titled "Pact Rituals," went:

The Thirteen Stages of a Baphometic Pact Ritual:

1. Preparation and Purification of the Ritual Chamber

2. Meditation and Prayer

3. Opening: Ringing of the Bell

4. Invocation of Baphomet

5. Calling of the Points

6. Circumambulation

7. Imbibing of the Elixir

8. Declaration of Intent

9. Sympathetic Drama

10. Presentation of the Contract, and of the Sacrifice (if applicable)

11. Hymn to Baphomet

12. Closing: Ringing of the Bell

13. Aftermath: Cleansing of the Ritual Chamber and Delivery of Charmed Objects

Finally: Remember to forget!

Explanation of the Pact Ritual

The hardest part of any ritual is getting started, and getting into the right state of mind for the task at hand. You may feel silly, or apprehensive, or like you're "just not up for it." The best way to work through these feelings is to get started on the preparations for the ritual.

The act of doing these things will force you to focus on the logistics of the ceremony, and not your feelings about it. The process starts days in advance, when you begin buying candles and incense, making sigils, or gathering photographs and other mementos that will be used during the Sympathetic Drama. Soon you will find that you are in the right state of mind.

Writing the ritual is an important step. For the most part, you will probably stick to the proscribed formula given in this book, and thus, much of the work is already done. However, the Declaration of Intent and Sympathetic Drama elements are going to be unique to each ritual.

Give the rite a clever name that reflects the purpose of the ceremony on at least two symbolic levels. Incorporate watchwords and catch phrases that are unique to the ritual. Make them pop out by using rhymes, repetition, double entendres, and acronyms that stand for significant phrases.

Focus more and more on the desired outcome of the ceremony as you get closer to the scheduled day of performance. As the hour approaches, allow the emotions associated with that outcome to expand almost to the point of boiling over. If you are cursing someone, focus on your hatred of that person, and if you are asking for a blessing, focus on the joy you will feel when you receive it.

Then, begin to focus that energy into the ritual by preparing the chamber, arranging the items in the room according to how you will need them. If there are other participants, invite them over at least two hours ahead of time, and have them help you prepare. Make sure they bring any sigils or other unique items that they may be contributing. During preparation, play any appropriate music you may have selected.

About twenty minutes before you begin, everybody should sit down and quietly meditate or pray about what is going to happen. Then, everyone will take their initial positions in the chamber, holding the ritual implements that they will be using. The priest's attendant shall toss holy water towards each of the four cardinal points, while the priest rings the bell thrice and declares:

Procul hinc, procul ite profane!

From the Latin, this means "Begone, begone, all ye who are not called." He will then begin to perform the Invocation to Baphomet, stating:

We gather here tonight to invoke Baphomet: the Lord of the Earth; the Goat of Mendes; the Most Mysterious Master. Baphomet, we have assembled upon this altar the Teraphim, as symbols of your power, and touch points through which you may manifest.

The priest will use the dagger to point to each of the Teraphim as it is named, pronouncing the list thusly:

The Pentagram and the Goat's Head; the Fish and the Water; the Caput S8M; and a statue of you, enthroned upon the Earth in radiant beauty.

Then, with great fervor and confidence, he shall loudly proclaim:

Baphomet, we call on you tonight. Come unto us! Share with us your omnipotent power. Help us to manifest our will: to bless those who serve you, to curse those who subvert your power, and to reverse the curses that have been placed upon us by our enemies. Come unto us, Baphomet! Be with us now in this moment!

The priest will then lift the dagger, pointing it towards the statue of Baphomet, and declare:

Baphomet, you are the Rex Mundi - the Lord of the Four Corners of the Earth.

He shall then point the dagger towards the Eastern wall, and all of the participants will face that way also. The attendant will then swing the censer in the same direction, as the priest shouts triumphantly:

You are the Lord of the East. Show yourself in the East!

The same should be done to the other three walls of your chamber. This is termed the "Calling of the Points." It means that you awaken the energies of Baphomet in each of the four directions.

Now you must cause these energies to amplify and spread by "stirring up the pot" through Circumambulation. The priest shall lead a procession around the chamber. The group should make the circle thirteen times, each instance a little bit faster, all the while calling "Baphomet, the Lord of the Earth!" at an ever more fevered pitch.

By the thirteenth trip around, you should all be sprinting and shouting. Hopefully your heart will be pumping a little bit faster. When the priest and other participants have once again turned to face the altar, the priest shall lift the chalice, filled with blood red wine, and read the Prayer for Transubstantiation:

Baphomet, into this Grail we have placed wine. As you, Baphomet, turned water into wine at the wedding of Christ, so transform this wine into your blood, the Elixir of Life. Let us, by consuming it, bestow upon ourselves your power to transmute one thing into another. For whosoever shall drink of the waters of Baphomet shall not thirst; but that water shall be in him a well springing up into everlasting life.

At this point the priest, his attendant, and all of the major players in the ritual should drink from the chalice until it is drained. Ideally, you will allow all of the participants to drink, but only if this is practical (depending upon the number of people involved). Upon finishing each draught, the participant shall pronounce the words "Glory be to Baphomet!"

Then, the priest shall make a statement declaring the intent of the ritual. Here he details the desired outcome, and the agreed upon payment to be made in return. This may simply involve reading aloud the contract, which should already be written out on parchment paper and sitting on the altar. During this statement, or immediately following it, say something that easily segues into the rite of Sympathetic Drama, which is the most important part of the ritual.

The Sympathetic Drama is based on the principles of "sympathetic magic," the most primitive form there is. Author Sir James George Frazer wrote extensively about this idea in The Golden Bough, stating that magic is based upon two basic principles:

...First, that like produces like, or that an effect resembles its cause; and, second, that things that have once been in contact with each other continue to act on each other at a distance after the physical contact has been severed. The former principle may be called the Law of Similarity, the latter the Law of Contact or Contagion.

In respect to your ritual, this means that you must first act out a drama representing what you want to happen. You must believe that the universe will then reflect what you have done, and cause it to become reality (the Law of Similarity). You must also have an object or image that represents the thing or person you want to be acted upon.

When the drama is played out during the rite, this object becomes charmed with the spell you are casting. The charmed object can then be left somewhere near the target, and can thus infect them with the spell via the Law of Contagion. This is like the familiar use of the voodoo doll, which you torture and destroy with hopes of inflicting pain upon the victim it signifies.

If you are trying to cast a spell on another person, it is good to have use of a personal item belonging to that individual. The best thing to have is a sample of his or her DNA. If this is not possible, anything which emblematizes him or her in your mind will do. It is good to have pictures of the person on the altar as well. If the spell you are casting has a more subtle concept behind it, you will have to find a more subtle way of expressing it.

While you are enacting the Sympathetic Drama, try to conjure up the emotion associated with the theme of your ritual. If you are cursing a person, scream and yell at the photograph or other image that you are using to represent him. Tell the person how much you hate him. Stab, spit on, and otherwise desecrate the image.

If you are blessing a person, sincerely declare to the image, as if it were him, what you would like to happen for him and why. Enumerate the ways in which the proposed blessing will enrich that person's life. You could also talk about how the other person's gain will forward your own goals involving him or her.

In addition, set upon the altar images that express any subthemes of the ritual. For instance, if you are sending out multiple blessings or multiple curses, have an image that represents each. At some point during the Drama, specifically call upon the names of the demons associated with each spell, and release them to their duty.

Magical talismans known as "sigils" can be useful during this stage of the ritual. They should be created before the ceremony begins. Usually, a sigil is made from a word or phrase that sums up the intent of the working. Write this out and then eliminate any repeated letters. Take the remaining letters and combine them to form an enigmatic shape or design, just as you have seen so many times with corporate logos and maker's marks.

Try to find ways to form some of the letters in the word by using the lines already used to form some of the other letters. It may take a few attempts to create something that looks appropriately "sigil-like," but once you have found the right design, you will know it. If for some reason using the letters of the phrase doesn't work out, you can still try to find a design that represents the idea by combining other symbols. For instance, you can use elemental or astrological pictographs, or letters from the Greek, Hebrew, or Sanskrit alphabets.

When you are done, reproduce this talisman onto parchment paper and cut it out. At the end of the Sympathetic Drama, thrust the dagger through the sigil, and then burn it in the flames of the large candle on the altar. All the while, repeat the word or phrase from which the sigil was made.

Following this, it is time to present the contract. You should read it aloud if you have not already done so. If you have, then just briefly summarize the contents. All of the agreeing parties should sign their names at the bottom in black ink. The human parties should then cut themselves with the razor blade, and seal the contract with their blood.

At this time, you should present any agreed-upon sacrifices to the idol of Baphomet. However, it most cases the tribute will consist of deeds that have either already been performed, or will be performed later. Then the priest consigns the parchment to the flames, skewering it with the dagger, as he proclaims:

With the destruction of this contract, we lift from our minds the memory of this ritual. Let us forget this ceremony, and allow the magic of Baphomet to work its wonders.

The participants should shout in unison: "Glory be to Baphomet!" Following this, the priest should read the Hymn to Baphomet, which is this:

Baphomet, you who are both the sun and the moon, the androgynous sabbatical goat, the Lord of the Earth, the Most Mysterious Master, bestower of curses and blessings: your power is unequalled. We dedicate our lives and our service to you. Glory be thy name. Glory to Baphomet, for ever and ever.

The participants should then shout "Glory be to Baphomet!" one more time, and the priest should ring the bell thrice. Finally, he shall declare with great solemnity:

So ends this ritual. So it is done.

Afterwards, all non-permanent ritual implements should be taken down and either put away or thrown away. Make sure to take the things that you are discarding outside to the garbage instead of leaving them in an indoor rubbish can, so that they don't come back to haunt you later. "Remember to forget," we always say. You must be able to forget not only about the ritual, but also the intended outcome of the ritual, and the initial problem to which the ritual was addressed. The only time in which we do not forget immediately is when there are charmed objects that have yet to be delivered to the targets. This is still technically part of the ritual, and obviously it will be impossible to fully forget until you have completed it. In between the end of the main ritual and the delivery of the enchanted object, wrap it in a black cloth, or place it in a black cloth jewelry bag. This mimics the spiritual cloaking that forgetfulness would otherwise provide.

When you deliver the charmed object, you have two options: either hide it well, or hide it in plain sight. Hiding it well means depositing it somewhere in or near the home of the person or thing that you wish to affect. Put it some place where nobody will ever find it, and where you know that it will be able to stay hidden for the foreseeable future.

Hiding it in plain sight means choosing an object that you can place there without suspicion, so that it can stay in that location effecting its spell and never be suspected of being a charm. This is what the Washington Monument, and many other items in Washington, D.C. actually are. Often, the magician gives the target a charmed item as a gift, knowing that he or she will keep it at home, or possibly even wear it.

There are obviously many ways in which a ritual could - and should - deviate from this outline. These are merely suggestions. Clearly, once a priest has done this several times, and understands the principles involved, he can adapt them in an infinite number of ways. It is important that you not have a Failure of Imagination when it comes to the working of magic. An imagination that is both clever and very vivid is one of the best tools a magician can utilize.

Following this chapter were pages of pre-scripted "Church Rituals" that were to be performed by each chapter of the OLE. These included: the "Grail Service" (A "Black Gnostic Mass"); the "Blessing for Live Water" (Holy Water); "Confession and Absolution"; the "Strict Observance" or "Rite to Remain Silent" (the new quartermaster initiation ceremony meant to "traumatize the initiate, to make his mind ready to receive wisdom"; and the "Baptism of Wisdom" (a real baptism in "Live Water" meant to invoke divine gnosis). I also provided details for several rites that were intended to be celebrated annually by the entire order. Among these were "The Alchemical Wedding of Rose + Cross" (a drama based on Baphomet's story of the wedding of Jesus and Mary Magdalene at Cana), and the "Divine Rite." The introductory text for the latter ritual is worth quoting:

This is a rite conducted in each local chapter on December 23rd of every year. It is a death and rebirth ritual that dramatizes the events we expect to unfold when our Crown Prince ascends to the throne and is transformed into a god-king. We will perform it each year to reaffirm our desire to see this fiction become a reality. Then every year that reality will come closer and closer.

A couple of days later, when the frenzy of conversational divination and automatic writing had died down, I contacted a few of my favorite quartermasters and gave them advance copies of the Strange Service text. The rituals at the end of the book still needed to be completed, and two of the quartermasters contributed material to help finish them.

I was still working on this when I was suddenly seized with unrelenting terror about the future of the Ordo Lapsit Exillis. I reviewed the details for the Divine Rite - about ritually sacrificing Nicholas de Vere, then releasing the spirit of Cain/Baphomet to possess his body and rule the Earth. For the first time I truly came to grips with what it meant: an opening of the gates of Hades. This is why it would result in what Baphomet termed "CHAOS" and "TOO MUCH OF EVERYTHING REALLY." This is why, with my semi-automatic writing, I had channeled the question: "Will time and space even exist any more?"

Not only would something like this bring unimaginable destruction and horror, but the blending of two previously separate dimensions that would result from opening the gate would distort spatial and temporal relationships as we presently know them. The royal (from Old French "roial") monarch would define reality in his realm. Since he is the Lord of the time before time, we should not assume that the passage of time would continue as we presently understand it.

This would be the dawn not only of a new era, but a new aeon, in the gnostic sense of the term. It would truly be a different form of existence. If Baphomet were loose from his cage, it would upset the foundation stones of our world. Nothing would be certain, nothing would be forbidden, and nothing would ever be the same.

At that point I had a deeper understanding of what the Dragon Court and Drakenberg were. I realized that I and everyone else who had accepted a royal title from Nicholas de Vere had been given a very fancy-sounding position in the Principality of Hell. I was passing on that bondage to the members of the OLE by encouraging them to take blood oaths to an order that was connected to the Dragon Court.

All along, Baphomet and the others had been riding me, driving me like a slave, constantly pushing me to do more chores for them. They had probably been doing that since I started *Dagobert's Revenge Magazine* at age 17. They wanted me to create an organization of followers (the order) and a body of propaganda (the magazine and books) to entice people into the same relationship. The real goal was apparently to train people to break these horrific creatures loose from their infernal jail.

I had to admit to myself that the neither I nor the team I had assembled were ready for such an enterprise. Perhaps it wasn't even what we wanted. I knew that we needed to take time to reassess our situation.

I asked the Quartermasters I had been working with on the *Strange Service Manual* to destroy the copies I had sent them. I then proceeded to shut down the order, very quickly, and with little explanation to anybody.

In response, two of the Quartermasters sent me emails straight away, asking me to give them control of the OLE instead. The phrasing of the two messages was almost identical, and they were both sent within an hour of one another. The two men in question did not know each other, and were probably not conspiring together.

One was a very nice, talented, and helpful person whom I adored. The other was a weird, narcissistic liar whose bad behavior and other flagrant warning signs of danger had been ignored by me before out of pure laziness. Now I was on full alert.

I intuitively knew that a demon was working through both of them. It was one of the entities that had been sending people from two rival Baphometic orders to infiltrate and control the OLE from within. I was relieved that I had shut the apparatus down before they had gained any real control. With that, I took some time to think clearly about the situation that I found myself in.

Terminus: Further and Beyond

When they were filled, he said unto his disciples, Gather up the fragments that remain, that nothing be lost.

- *John* 6:12

In Christopher Marlowe's *Doctor Faustus*, the title character's first demand on his contract with Mephistopheles, in which he sells his immortal soul to the Devil, is that "Faustus may be a spirit in form and in substance." In addition, he demands that the demon:

...spare him four and twenty years,
Letting him live in all voluptuousness;
Having thee ever to attend on me;
To give me whatsoever I shall ask,
To tell me whatsoever I demand,
To slay mine enemies, and aid my friends,
And always be obedient to my will.

A short while later, when he begins to lean towards repentance, a verbal exchange takes place, with a good angel and a bad angel both whispering opposing advice to Faustus on how to satisfy his conscience.

The good angel says:

"Faustus, repent; yet God will pity thee."

But the bad angel replies:

"Thou art a spirit; God can not pity thee."

To which Faustus asks:

"Who buzzeth in mine ears I am a spirit? Be I a devil, yet God may pity me; Ay, God will pity me if I repent."

Upon hearing this, the bad angel quips:

"Ay, but Faustus never shall repent."

In the footnotes in the edition that was edited by Sylvan Barnet, he says the word "spirit" in this context means "evil spirit, devil," and then adds:

...but to see Faustus as transformed now into a devil deprived of freedom to repent is to deprive the remainder of the play of much of its meaning....

I disagree. It actually makes perfect sense to me, especially after the things I have experienced. It seems to me that as soon as the contract is made, Faustus is transformed into a sort of vampire-like undead creature without real, mortal existence, or a will of his own. From the moment he sold his soul, his body was already the walking dead, possessed of the Devil, and his soul was already in Hell from the very beginning.

This may explain why the whole thing seems to take place in a timeless dream, and all of the "miracles" of Mephistopheles, such and the conjuring of Helen of Troy, are mere tricks, with no physical reality. This is well illustrated in the 1967 film version with Richard Burton and Elizabeth Taylor, in which the scenes of Faustus' deeds post contract are frequently shown enveloped in clouds. So it is not "Faustus" but the Devil within him that experiences all of the adventures that follow. He is therefore powerless to repent and cannot be forgiven.

I can't be sure if or when I ever actually sold my soul to the Devil. But perhaps that ambiguity and uncertainty is part of the unreality of my present existence. Certainly the supernatural events took place as though they were my unquestioned fate. I wasn't even surprised by the fact that I was talking to demons. The information they gave me blew my mind, but I took my relationship with them for granted.

I spent years in a daze, feverishly researching and pursuing every cryptic clue in the mysteries I was pondering, working my ass off to run both a publishing company and a secret society, without much thinking about where it was all headed. My moral decay seemed to increase with each revelation of esoteric wisdom. It didn't take much persuasion for me to make the mental journey from a "Grail researcher" to someone who talks to demons; then a cult leader helping people form contracts with those demons; and then finally to the point where I was willing to invoke the name of Satan himself in an attempt to psychically murder a backstabbing colleague.

Nicholas De Vere wrote in *The Dragon Legacy* that:

...The Vampire is to all intents and purposes dead in one sense but far more alive than ordinary human beings in another.

There are two types of life. Both depend upon one's state of perception for their true appreciation. In Stoker's Dracula we are introduced to the idea that Dracula's image is not reflected in any mirror. Later on, towards the end of the tale the Count says to Mina Harker, 'There is no life in this body.' The former incident explains the latter statement.

Of course, De Vere himself was a self-confessed "sociopath" and took little heed of human moral codes. He felt that his lack of empathy marked him as part of a superior species. This was the case with Boyd Rice and many of my other friends during those years. Sociopaths and clinical narcissists are frequently described - metaphorically, of course - as soulless "psychic vampires" who feed off the emotions of others that they themselves are unable to feel. Perhaps it is more than a metaphor. I myself don't think that this has happened to me. But my instinctive understanding of how the process works makes me believe that I have come very close to "crossing the Abyss" in this manner, and losing the life within in exchange for another sort altogether.

I am not so certain, like Nick thought he was, that life on the other side is any more "real" than it is here. In fact, it seems to suffer from a lack of reality. It is chaos, because its existence has been negated. The inhabitants of the otherworld rely on us believing in them, and giving them our energy, to provide the semblance of reality they must constantly strive for. This is the wilderness that the Israelites wandered in after the Exodus, and which the goat for Azazel was cast into by the Jewish priests at Yom Kippur. This is the land of Nod that Cain was confined to as well, where he "built a city" supposedly named after his son Enoch.

I have come to the understanding that this is what many paths of occult arcana lead to. The mystery schools are created by those trapped in the underworld, including the cryptic myths and legends associated with them. From the other side, the demons entice curious travelers to make the spiritual journey down to where they are, reeling them in with a trail of esoteric breadcrumbs to follow. But those who dare to venture forth may find themselves, like Hansel and Gretel, at the house of an evil witch who wishes to eat them. Then they may even be transformed into evil witches and vampires themselves, needing to feed off humans to stay "real."

It works because, at the top of the pyramid in any secret society of occult practice, you will always find a spirit acting as the true "outer head" of the order, whom the human grand master is merely a proxy for. They are generally in contact with each other, I believe, via channeling and possession. Just as the "Scholomance" school of magic in Bram Stoker's *Dracula* was taught by the Devil himself, the mysteries of each order are taught to the leaders by the true "Master."

They are then taught how to build an ark: a box, containing the "Tablets of the Law" (the script or program on which the machinery of the ark will operate). The prophet divines the words that shall go on the tablets (allowing them to be written by an "unseen hand," or their own hand under alien control). He also channels the dimensions for how to construct the vessel which contains them. He then allows what the alchemists call the "Compass of the Wise" or "Magnet of the Philosophers" to navigate the vessel on the seas of chaos.

It goes without saying that the one who receives these revelations from beyond and puts in the work to build the edifice is usually the first to steer the ship. Others follow in due apostolic succession. But the election to this highest office has nothing to do with democracy. It is something that you self-initiate. When you realize that you are a navigator, you build an ark and pilot it.

At an unseen level, self-elected solomonari of this sort are the ones running things on this Earth behind the scenes. This is represented in popular horror films and novels as the secret underground vampire scene. They live in a system of anarchy amongst themselves, unable to dominate each other because they have each reached a certain level of transcendental power. The general population doesn't recognize their power at all, because they don't know what to look for. But these illuminates know each other, because they can see the shining light of the Mark of Cain upon their brows.

Some of these have formed a league, and agreed to keep their own activities within certain boundaries, in order to prevent the general population from becoming aware of the existence of the vampires. But whenever "lone wolves" or criminal syndicates among them decide to act in a way that brings unwanted heat down on the vampire scene (say by committing gruesome murders and leaving the evidence to be found), the "Great White Brotherhood" (of the so-called "right-hand path") can sometimes step in to interfere. This is the closest they get to morality. It is really a system of rules constructed to prevent the human population from catching on to the rival species that controls them and feeds on them at a level beyond their awareness.

In most cases, secret societies and schools of the occult exist for two reasons: 1) So that fiends of this sort can keep an eye on one another, to keep each other in check, so that those of the right-hand path can enforce a code of behavior on those of a left-hand-path tendency. Those that think they're "climbing the ladder to Heaven" by "learning" from the "more advanced" initiates may just be led on a Caucus Race to nowhere while the upper classman in the school feed off of their energy. They are nothing more than blood bags to the vampires of the group. As in Bram Stoker's story, only one student out of the total is advanced enough to "ride the Dragon" with the school's hidden headmaster, or the "outer head" of the order.

I think that for most Western occult orders, which usually take their inspiration from the Knights Templar and the Freemasons, the outer head is Baphomet. Yes, he's the Devil, but he's a specifically mercurial expression of him: the teacher, the initiator, the lord of magic. He's a Frankenstein, a chimera, a conglomerate, created through alchemy, possibly by the Templars.

But that is what he is meant to be: unity from duality the ultimate "coagulation" of every imaginable set of opposing forces dissolved to their ultimate essence and recombined into one being of infinite contradiction. At one point, we asked Baphomet to let us see him through a physical apparition. He asked us "ARE YOU SURE?" These were the same words he had also used when we asked to understand the Abyss. We decided against it. We knew it would be too frightening for us to see him. As Arthur Machen described it in *The Great God Pan*:

Though horror and revolting nausea rose up within me, and an odour of corruption choked my breath, I remained firm. I was then privileged or accursed, I dare not say which, to see that which was on the bed, lying there black like ink, transformed before my eyes. The skin, and the flesh, and the muscles, and the bones, and the firm structure of the human body that I had thought to be unchangeable, and permanent as adamant, began to melt and dissolve.

I know that the body may be separated into its elements by external agencies, but I should have refused to believe what I saw. For here there was some internal force, of which I knew nothing, that caused dissolution and change.

Here too was all the work by which man had been made repeated before my eyes. I saw the form waver from sex to sex, dividing itself from itself, and then again reunited. Then I saw the body descend to the beasts whence it ascended, and that which was on the heights go down to the depths, even to the abyss of all being....

Traditionalist Julius Evola, in his classic book *The Mystery of the Grail*, gave us a relevant description of how the vision of Baphomet affected the Templars:

The central ritual of Templar initiation was kept very secret. From one of the proceedings of the trial we learn that a knight who underwent it returned as pale as a corpse, and with a lost expression on his face, claiming that from then on he could never be happy again. Shortly after, the same knight fell into a state of invincible depression and died... What produces an extreme terror in some knights and causes them to flee... is the vision of an idol... the Baphomet.

A similar story is told about Bérenger Saunière towards the end of his life. *In Holy Blood, Holy Grail*, it says:

As Saunière lay on his deathbed, a priest was called from a neighboring parish to hear his final confession and administer the last rites. The priest duly arrived and retired into the sickroom. According to eyewitness testimony he emerged shortly thereafter, visibly shaken. In the words of one account he 'never smiled again....' The priest, presumably on the basis of Saunière's confession, refused to administer Extreme Unction.

A version of Baphomet's sigil by Stanislas de Guaita includes the names of the demons Samael and Lilith. The opposite side of this sigil shows the figure of a man, with the names "Adam" and "Eve" written around it. Samael and Lilith are described in the cabala as a hermaphroditic being formed by two serpents locked in sexual union. There is an intermediary (called the "Tanin'iver") between them, necessary to make the union possible because Samael is said to have been castrated. When locked together, the cabalists referred to the combination of these two demons as lithe Beast" and lithe Other God." It is said that if they were ever truly allowed to unite, it would destroy the universe. That is why the male's organs were taken: to prevent cosmic doom.

Front and back sides of Stanislas de Guaita's Baphomet sigils, featuring the names of Samael, Lilith, Adam, Eve, and (in Hebrew) Leviathan

The two serpents can be seen represented in the Eliphas Levi depiction of Baphomet, where he is shown with the twin-snaked caduceus pole rising from his crotch region. These snakes, in combination, are said to be the serpent that tempted Adam and Eve in Eden. Samael may have been the true father of Cain through Eve, and Lilith may have mothered thousands of demon children by having sex with Adam, or so the cabalists say.

I believe that what is being alluded to is sex magic through demon possession. The serpent is "castrated" because he is no longer alive and able to generate sexually. He and his wife Lilith can only unite by possessing other humans. Their bodies are the "Tanin'iver," symbolized in mythology in stories like that of Isis, who had to fashion a golden dildo to have sex with her dead husband Osiris.

I think that these serpents have been breeding with humans, particularly the royal caste, for thousands of years. Their goal is to inhabit all of the seats of power in what is, by God's decree, the kingdom of the children of Adam. They want people that are their own descendants, and their own possessed automatons, to sit on the thrones of the world, and reshape the order of the globe to fit a pattern that they have in mind. Somehow by uniting the world in this way, and putting their own scion on the seat of power, they believe that they will be released from their infernal prison. This is just exactly what *Revelation* 20:7 predicts:

And when the thousand years are expired, Satan shall be loosed out of his prison....

The impression we have gotten from talking to Cain and Baphomet, which continues unto the present day, is that the reality in which we live is like a little bubble of safety within the vast expanse of nothingness that surrounds it. That is where they are now: in a state of negative existence. This is chaos, the Abyss, the land of Nod, and Hell. The metaphors used describe it as a "sea." But it is also said to be full of fire that burns like nothing else yet is, simultaneously, bitingly cold. All of these are attempts to explain what it feels like to not really exist, but to still be "out there" somewhere, with some form of consciousness that is ineffable.

During a recent conversation with Cain, he told us he and the other prisoners in Hell were being tortured. We asked if their tormentors were God's angels. He said "NO." When I inquired as to if the torture comes from the other prisoners, he gave an emphatic "YES."

When we asked, "What kind of torture are you experiencing?" He said "GITMO." When pressed, he said that, just like Guantanamo Bay prisoners have been water-boarded, he is tormented with the feeling like he is dying, over and over again. He also admitted that he too was torturing others.

Cain told us that the "land of Nod" was represented by the Ageio board. Now remember, he said that the "REAL POWER" was "IN THE SECOND SQUARE." The Second Square is the inner 36 squares on the board. Cain said that this is "Enoch," the city he built in Nod. We asked if he named the city after his son, and he said no, it was the other way around. He told us that the city is a cube. But interestingly, Cain said that he himself is not imprisoned inside of that cube. Rather, he said that he and the other prisoners are on the surface of the cube, in ring of 28 squares on the periphery of the Ageio board.

One can imagine that it is like the "Panopticon" prison design invented by Jeremy Bentham, now in use at penitentiaries all over the world. The way it works, the watchtower where the prison guards stand is positioned in the center, with the prisoners stationed around in a circle. The purpose is so that the guards can see everything that is going on in the cells, and the prisoners never know if they are specifically being watched at any given moment.

The Panopticon is named after Panoptes, the figure from Greek myth with one thousand eyes. The National Security Administration has tried to mimic this with their omniscient global communication surveillance program, which they code-named - appropriately - "PRISM." You'll recall that Cain used the same word to describe the prison in which he was trapped. But he is not at the center of that prism: that's where the cube is, containing the All-Seeing Eye.

It is interesting to note that the logo for the NSA's PRISM program shows a crystal triangle either coming into or going out of the black void inside of a shape that has been made from two hexagons. One of those hexagons is smaller than the other and is overlapping the larger one, partially obscuring two of its sides. It is as if the smaller hexagon is in the process of either entering or exiting the larger one. I am not saying that the people who designed this logo know about the prison in the underworld, or the structure of the Ageio board with the Second Square inside. However, it seems to me that these secrets have a way of emerging from the works of human creativity, often without the artisan's conscious knowledge, for reasons that I will attempt to describe further on in this chapter.

Cabalists also talk about "Metatron's Cube." This is a hexagram within a hexagram, made from thirteen circles, which can also be viewed as a flat representation of a three-dimensional cube within a cube. It is thought by some to be an ethereal vehicle, a "merkavah" or "chariot" used by the angel Metatron when traveling from one realm of existence to the next.

Who's Metatron? Why, he's nothing less than that other Enoch, the one descended from Seth, who is credited with writing *The Book of Enoch.* Actually there were several books written by Enoch, but the main one was about his descent to the underworld, guided by the angel Uriel, where he got to view where the fallen angels were imprisoned. He was shown what crimes led to their incarceration and torture: the breeding of giants with human females. They actually begged for him to pray to God on their behalf to forgive them and let them out of Hell.

Then, Enoch was taken up to Heaven, and shown all the secrets of that kingdom. He was also shown the future of the Earth, and what would happen

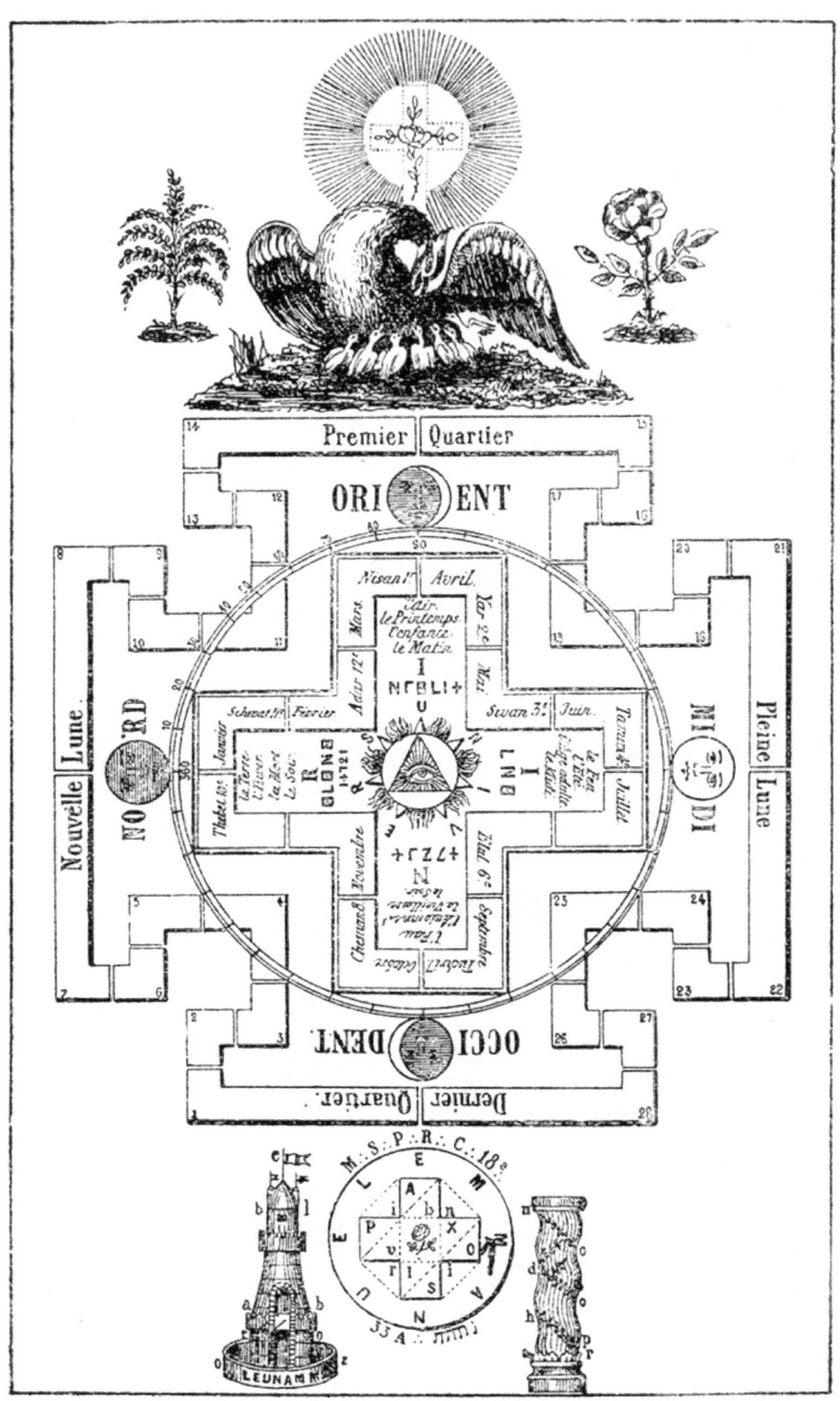

A Rosicrucian diagram of Solomon’s Temple

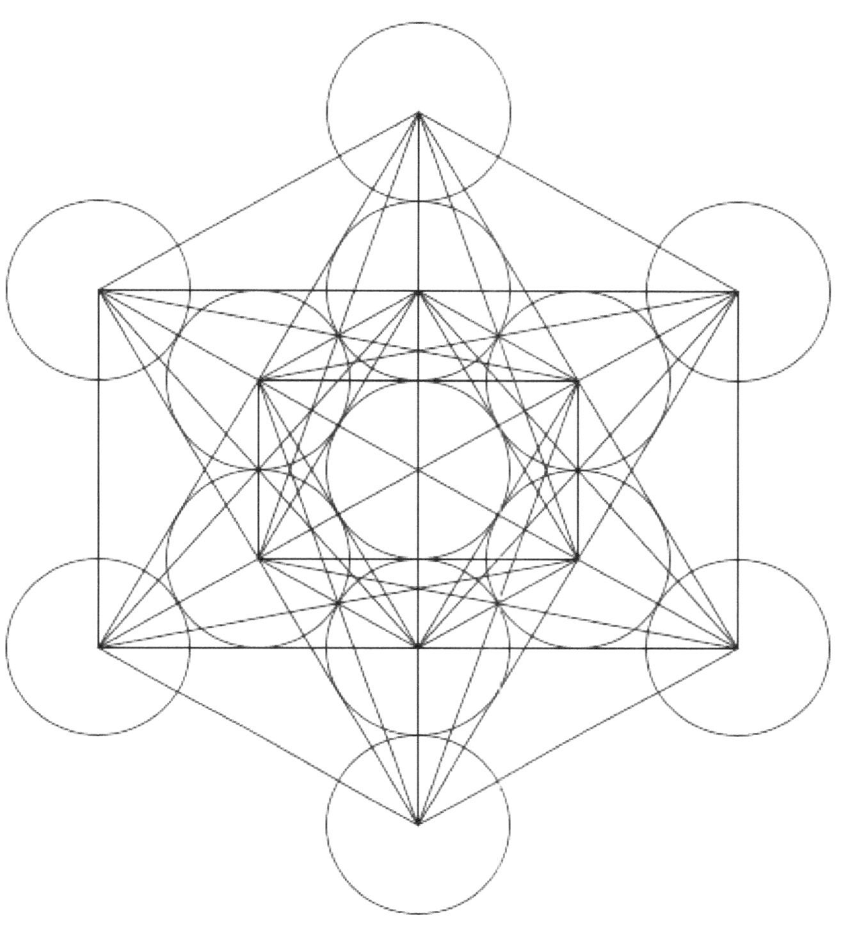

Above: Metatron's Cube. Below: the logo for the NSA's PRISM program.

in the days of his great-grandson Noah. Traditionally, Enoch is said to have stayed in Heaven, rather than having to return to Earth to die a mortal death. *Genesis* 5:22-23 tells us:

And Enoch walked with God after he begat Methuselah three hundred years, and begat sons and daughters: And all the days of Enoch were three hundred sixty and five years: And Enoch walked with God: and he was not; for God took him.

Interestingly, the number of years Enoch lived (365) is very close to the number of books he is said to have written (366). He is said to be the only human being to whom God has given this blessing. Then, the cabalists say, he was translated into an angel, and renamed Metatron. As Gershom G. Scholem wrote in *Major Trends in Jewish Mysticism*:

This Enoch, whose flesh was turned to flame, his veins to fire, his eye-lashes to flashes of lightning, his eye-balls to flaming torches, and whom God placed on a throne next to the throne of glory, received after this heavenly transformation the name Metatron.

To comparative mythologists, Enoch is a scribe and messenger angel, likened to Hermes, Mercury, Thoth and the Green Man. Some have even connected his name to that of Mithras. Another name applied to him in *The Zohar* means "the Youth," perhaps because he stopped aging after he went to Paradise. However it also seems to imply he's a servant boy to God. Another title he's given is "the Little Jehovah." Translations of the name Metatron include "keeper of the watch," "guardian" or "protector," "one who serves behind the throne," and "co-occupant of the throne." To him, perhaps, God truly is his co-pilot!

As stated, Enoch is said to have written many books. One of them, or perhaps the whole body of works taken together, are seen by esotericists as synonymous with the famed "Emerald Tablet of Hermes," which reveals the alchemical secrets of creation. In *The Third Book of Enoch* (also called *The Revelation of Metatron*) the 48th chapter tells us that God gave his secret name to Enoch, who then passed it on to Moses:

Metatron brought it out from my storehouses and committed it to Moses, and Moses to Joshua, Joshua to the Elders, the Elders to the Prophets....

Other angels, said to have been offended by this, objected: "Why are you revealing it to flesh and blood?" So once more we have an expression of jealousy by the angels towards mankind because of God's favoritism for some of our kind. Yet again, as in *The Book of Adam and Eve* and *The Koran* (with the stories of angels being asked to bow down to Adam), the objection from the dissenting angels is that we bleed, and we are made from matter ("clay"), making us inferior, in their eyes, to their own, loftier, subtle essence.

But it appears that mankind has a peculiar role to play in the universe. Enoch was chosen by God, like the "Adam Kadmon" of the Cabalistic creation, to be a microcosmos, the so-called "Microprosopus": an image of the invisible God. You will recall that his ancestor, Seth, was beget by Adam "in his own image," like God created Adam.

In a way, he was a mediator between God and man, the way Hermes was said to be for the Greeks. He was a guide, as Hermes was the "Psychopompus" (guide to the underworld). One of the things said about Metatron in *The Third Book of Enoch* is that he was the pillar of fire and cloud that guided the Israelites to that portal in the Red Sea (the official abode of Lilith), from which they entered the "wilderness" (Nod, the Abyss) where they wandered for 40 years. They passed through safely, but the pursuing enemies got cut to pieces, dissolved into chaos because the portal closes on them unexpectedly.

The land where they eventually arrived, in what seemed to them to be forty years later, was the site of what the Jews came to believe was the "foundation stone of the world." I am talking about the sacred stone beneath the Temple Mount in Jerusalem called the "Eben Shetiyah." It is on display in Jerusalem today. They say that God actually started building the universe from this point, working outward from here. It is said to have a well leading to Hell directly beneath it.

In religious iconography, there is something called the "Jerusalem Cross," or the "Crusader's Cross." It is an equilateral cross with four smaller crosses in each of its four corners. This is supposed to represent the "Five Wounds of Christ." But to me it more resembles a representation of the city of Jerusalem with twelve gates. It also resembles, as I recently realized, the image of the Ageio board with the four crosses marking out the corners of the "Second Square." Interestingly, this symbol was also used by Aleister Crowley when signing with the name "Baphomet" which he utilized in his capacity as the Grand Master of the Ordo Templi Orientis (Order of Oriental Templars). It's also the "triple cross" or "Salem cross" worn by the Sovereign Grand Commander of the Supreme Council of Thirty-Third Degree Freemasonry.

Key to the mystery here is the "New Jerusalem" described in *The Revelation of St. John* as descending from Heaven at the end of the Apocalypse. In dimensions, it is a perfect cube, and shines like a precious stone, just like the cubic stone of the Philosophers. This is all part of an alchemical process in which God creates Heaven and Earth anew, and expels all impurities from creation back into chaos. It is the death of the old universe, and the birth of a new one, with the heavenly city as the foundation stone, and the throne of

Upper right to lower right, clockwise: Jerusalem Cross, symbol used in Crowley's "Baphomet" signature, Masonic Salem or "triple" cross, and seal of modern "Ordo Baphometis" occult group

God. As in alchemy, it is even likened to a wedding. In *Revelation* 21: 1-6 we read:

And I saw a new heaven and a new earth: for the first heaven and the first earth were passed away; and there was no more sea. And I John saw the holy city, new Jerusalem, coming down from God out of heaven, prepared as a bride adorned for her husband. And I heard a great voice out of heaven saying, Behold, the tabernacle of God is with men, and he will dwell with them, and they shall be his people, and God himself shall be with them, and be their God. And God shall wipe away all tears from their eyes; and there shall be no more death, neither sorrow, nor crying, neither shall there be any more pain: for the former things are passed away.

And he that sat upon the throne said, Behold, I make all things new. And he said unto me, Write: for these words are true and faithful. And he said unto me, It is done. I am Alpha and Omega, the beginning and the end.

Then we get more details on the city in *Revelation* 21: 9. Again, its descent is described as a marriage:

And there came unto me one of the seven angels which had the seven vials full of the seven last plagues, and talked with me, saying, Come hither, I will shew thee the bride, the Lamb's wife.

Revelation 21:10-14 gives us another depiction of the cubic city as a stone. We are told that it has twelve gates, corresponding to the tribes of Israel, and the apostles of Christ:

And he carried me away in the spirit to a great and high mountain, and shewed me that great city, the holy Jerusalem, descending out of heaven from God, Having the glory of God: and her light was like unto a stone most precious, even like a jasper stone, clear as crystal; And had a wall great and high, and had twelve gates, and at the gates twelve angels, and names written thereon, which are the names of the twelve tribes of the children of Israel: On the east three gates; on the north three gates; on the south three gates; and on the west three gates. And the wall of the city had twelve foundations, and in them the names of the twelve apostles of the Lamb.

Revelation 21: 15-21 tells us that the city is actually made from gold and precious stones. The particular types of stone, and the dimensions of the city, are given:

And he that talked with me had a golden reed to measure the city, and the gates thereof, and the wall thereof And the city lieth foursquare, and the length is as large as the breadth: and he measured the city with the reed, twelve thousand furlongs. The length and the breadth and the height of it are equal. And he measured the wall thereof, an hundred and forty and four cubits, according to the measure of a man, that is, of the angel. And the building of the wall of it was of jasper: and the city was pure gold, like unto clear glass. And the foundations of the wall of the city were garnished with all manner of precious stones. The first foundation was jasper; the second, sapphire; the third, a chalcedony; the fourth, an emerald; The fifth, sardonyx; the sixth, sardius; the seventh, chrysolite; the eighth, beryl; the ninth, a topaz; the tenth, a chrysoprasus; the eleventh, a jacinth; the twelfth, an amethyst. And the twelve gates were twelve pearls; every several gate was of one pearl: and the street of the city was pure gold, as it were transparent glass.

What is happening here is a redefinition of reality. Everything that is to be saved is placed inside of the cube, with God. Everything on the outside is to be cast off, into chaos. Those inside are the ones with their names written in the Book of Life. If your name is not there, it is like you never existed. *Revelation* 21:7-8 says it like this:

He that overcometh shall inherit all things; and I will be his God, and he shall be my son. But the fearful, and unbelieving, and the abominable, and murderers, and whore mongers, and sorcerers, and idolaters, and all liars, shall have their part in the lake which burneth with fire and brimstone: which is the second death.

Then *Revelation* 22:14-15 again makes clear the distinction: those who are saved are allowed inside of the city. Those who are not are left trapped outside of the gates, as if left to fend for themselves in a deadly wilderness.

Blessed are they that do his commandments, that they may have right to the tree of life, and may enter in through the gates into the city. For without are dogs, and sorcerers, and whoremongers, and murderers, and idolaters, and whosoever loveth and maketh a lie.

Revelation 21:27 makes clear that for the sake of purity, the contents of the cubic city will be Hermetically sealed:

And there shall in no wise enter into it any thing that defileth, neither whatsoever worketh abomination, or maketh a lie: but they which are written in the Lamb's book of life.

This cube then becomes the foundation stone, the Eben Shetiyah, of the new world. The way I see it, something similar happened in the days of Noah in Genesis. God told Noah to build an "ark," according to certain dimensions, and collect samples of creation that he wanted to save, to use them to recreate creation at the end of the process. Then he told Noah to shut himself up with these things inside the vessel, and not to come out for a certain period of time. Around him everything was dissolved into chaos, the waters of the Abyss.

When they came out of the Ark after forty days, the land that his Ark rested upon became "Ground Zero" for a new civilization. It was the highest peak in the world, God's mountain, referred to in The Book of the Cave of Treasures as "Mount Kardo." It was the axis between Heaven, Earth, and the underworld. There is a Greek word for this: "Apobaterion" ("place of landing.") This term is applied to Mount Judi in Turkey, thought by many to be the location of the Ark's remnants. It is also said by some biblical scholars to be the same as Cain's city of Enoch.

We know that there were supposedly two Enochs: a good Enoch (descendant of Seth, great-grandson of Noah), and a bad Enoch (first-born son of Cain). The good Enoch was first sent to Hell (as a "Watcher," an All-Seeing Eye, watching the angels in their prison). Then he was translated to Heaven, where he was turned into an angel, Metatron, who roams the universe in a cubic vehicle. The bad Enoch was the inspiration for the building of Cain's city. Or, as Cain told us, the child was named after city. (He also implied, strangely, that perhaps the city and the child were the same thing.)

The heavenly city of the New Jerusalem has no night, and no need of sun or moon. It also has no temples, for God is the temple himself. In *Revelation* 21: 22-5 it says:

And I saw no temple therein: for the Lord God Almighty and the Lamb are the temple of it. And the city had no need of the sun, neither of the moon, to shine in it: for the glory of God did lighten it, and the Lamb is the light thereof. And the nations of them which are saved shall walk in the light of it: and the kings of the earth do bring their glory and honour into it ... And the gates of it shall not be shut at all by day: for there shall be no night there.

In contrast, the realm that Cain is trapped in is one of perpetual night. This is why they need the artificial sun - the Black Sun - to light the way for them, and to provide energy. It also provides magnetism, which they use as a compass to navigate the Abyss, and a gauge with which to measure it. To them, the Black Sun has been a cornerstone, a little nugget of reality upon which they could attempt to build something.

Cain's city of Enoch, built in the land of Nod, is probably, in fact, Cain's attempt to copy the design of the New Jerusalem with an infernal reflection down below. There are indeed cities in the underworld, according to the Greeks, and even to Dante Alighieri. In *The Divine Comedy* we learn that the center-most and most glorious of these cities is Dis, which is also another name for Hades, the ruler of the underworld in Greek myths. Dante said that this encompassed the sixth through the ninth circles of Hell. Its walls are guarded by the fallen angels. Believing that Muslims were heretics, the author also depicted the city with a mosque full of Mohammedans still worshiping what he saw as their false god.

Interestingly, the "Second Square" on the Ageio board encompasses the three inner rings of black and white squares on the chessboard, where the "real power," and his city of Enoch, resides. Since the underworld is a reverse and negation of the heavenly realm, it only makes sense to think of this infernal cubic city as black. Masonic writer, Albert Pike, said in his *Morals and Dogma* that:

The Ancients adored the Sun under the form of a black stone, called Elagabalus, or Heliogabalus. The faithful are promised, in the Apocalypse, a white stone.

Another Masonic writer, Manly P. Hall, brings up this subject, as well as the obvious connections which spring to mind regarding the Black Stone venerated by Muslims inside of the black cubic Kaaba temple in Mecca. This stone is believed by the faithful to have "fallen from Heaven." There is a tradition going back at least to Imam Ali stating that the Black Stone brought the germ of life with it. The veneration of this stone at the site of the Kaaba shrine is older than Islam. So too is the shape of the temple and many of the rituals that are still performed there, now in the name of Allah instead of pagan gods.

The polytheist Kaaba was formerly the home of 360 stone idols that were consulted by the pre-Islamic pagans there for divination and spell-casting purposes. The location is thought by Muslims today to be the center-point of the world, with a "gate to Heaven" open above it. On this subject, Manly P. Hall wrote in *Secret Teachings of All Ages* that:

Divination by stones was often resorted to by the Greeks, and Helena is said to have foretold by lithomancy the destruction of Troy.... The black stone also appears several times in religious symbolism. It was called Heliogabalus, a word presumably derived from Elagabal, the Syro-Phœnician sun god. This stone was sacred to the sun and declared to possess great and diversified properties. The black stone in the Caaba at Mecca is still revered throughout the Mohammedan world. It is said to have been white originally and of such brilliancy that it could be seen many days' journey from Mecca, but as ages passed it became blackened by the tears of pilgrims and the sins of the world.

"Lithomancy" is divining messages by stones - in particular, by the way in which light that may seem to shine out of them, or be reflected by them. This was the type of divination that took place in the Temple in Jerusalem, right before the Ark, using a set of crystal objects called the "urim and thummin." Is this related to the "LANGUAGE OF LIGHT" that both Baphomet, and now Cain also, have told us is spoken by the "LUSTEROUS (sic) ONES," the angels?

Perhaps this is what is behind the story that the Grail stone was a jewel in Lucifer's crown, which got knocked off during the war in Heaven, and fell into the Abyss. I have seen this stone referred to as a "jewel of light." In the same chapter of that book, Hall also said:

During the conflict, Michael with his flaming sword struck the flashing Lapis Exilis from the coronet of his adversary, and the green stone fell through all the celestial rings into the dark and immeasurable Abyss. Out of Lucifer's radiant gem was fashioned the Sangreal, or Holy Grail, from which Christ is said to have drunk at the Last Supper.

The metaphors found in the Bible, as well as the literature of Freemasons and other esoteric groups, refer to the cubic city (a.k.a. the "Ark," the "Grail") as the "cornerstone" of the world. In the Deluge story, after the world around him was dissolved into the Abyss, Noah and his children were able to literally forge a new world - order out of chaos - using the Ark as their basis. It provided the seeds of life, preserved from the old world, as well as the dimensions for measurement with which to build another civilization. To have such a "city" or vessel resting upon the mountain of God was like an anchor grounding them to reality, as the bitter seas of chaos nipped at their feet.

Immediately after the story of the Deluge is concluded in *Genesis*, following a page of genealogies, the next story is that of the Tower of Babel. Chapter 11: 1-4 tells us:

And the whole earth was of one language, and of one speech. And it came to pass, as they journeyed from the east, that they found a plain in the land of Shinar; and they dwelt there. And they said one to another, Go to, let us make brick, and burn them thoroughly. And they had brick for stone, and slime had they for morter. And they said, Go to, let us build us a city and a tower, whose top may reach unto heaven; and let us make us a name, lest we be scattered abroad upon the face of the whole earth.

Clearly they saw this tower, and this city, as a way of connecting themselves with God, the source of reality. They hoped it would give them a "name," a sense of identity, and safety from the waters of the abyss that had just ravaged their world. They were building their own world-mountain to provide an axis between Heaven and Earth. But apparently, God did not want there to be too much order in human society following the deluge of chaos, and set forward to confound them by casting them into confusion once more: *Genesis* 11: 5-9 states:

And the LORD came down to see the city and the tower, which the children of men builded. And the LORD said, Behold, the people is one, and they have all one language; and this they begin to do: and now nothing will be restrained from them, which they have imagined to do. Go to, let us go down, and there confound their language, that they may not understand one another's speech.

So the LORD scattered them abroad from thence upon the face of all the earth: and they left off to build the city. Therefore is the name of it called Babel; because the LORD did there confound the language of all the earth: and from thence did the LORD scatter them abroad upon the face of all the earth.

It has still not been established, by the way, who exactly the LORD was talking to in this scene when he says "let us go down." Now the king responsible for having the tower built, named "Nimrod,' is said in some Masonic literature to be the "original Master Mason," and, amazingly, also said to be the same as Cain! L.A. Waddell agreed, writing in his books that Nimrod and Cain were the same figure. Cain was credited with building six cities in total, in addition to the first, Enoch. So did he build the Tower of Babel as well? Or perhaps, are all these stories just different ways of telling about the same fantastic event?

I am not exactly sure, but I know that Cain said it was the Flood that brought his kingdom under the waters of the Abyss, caused by what he called "the Wrath of Cain," and that now he is in a perpetual state of confusion. This is just like the citizens of Babel who had their language, and thus their relationship with reality, confounded. I think the thing which Cain and other inhabitants of the Underworld anchor themselves to, is the artificial "Black Sun," which is either within the city or, perhaps, is somehow synonymous with the city itself. It provides the only sense of bearing they can get in this zone of chaos, where it is impossible to measure things because there is no structure to anything. As it says in *The Book of Enoch*, Chapter 21:1-2, describing the Hell realm where the fallen angels are trapped:

Then I made a circuit to a place in which nothing was completed. And there I beheld neither the tremendous workmanship of an exalted heaven, nor of an established earth, but a desolate spot, prepared, and terrific.

The imprisoned angels are then depicted as seven stars bound together, like the Pleiades or "Seven Sisters" in the Constellation of Taurus. The next line relates the following:

There, too, I beheld seven starts of heaven bound in it together, like great mountains, and like a blazing fire. I exclaimed: for what species of crime have they been bound, and why have they been removed to this place?

Then Uriel, one of the holy angels who was with me, and who conducted me, answered: Enoch, wherefore dost though ask; wherefore reason with thyself, and anxiously inquire? These are those of the stars which have transgressed the commandment of the most high God; and are here bound, until the infinite number of the days of their crimes be completed.

By this, I believe, Uriel was implying that their punishment would last eternally, because their crimes had themselves been eternal. Perhaps this is because these events took place in a timeless realm, and therefore the prisoners are trapped in a timeless realm as well, without form. Lines 5 and 6 complete the chapter:

...I beheld the operation of a great fire blazing and glittering, in the midst of which there was a division. Columns of fire struggled together to the end of the abyss, and deep was their descent. But neither its measurement nor magnitude was I able to discover; neither could I perceive its origin. Then I exclaimed: How terrible is this place, and how difficult to explore!

Uriel, one of the holy angels who was with me, answered and said: Enoch, Why art thou alarmed and amazed at this terrific place, at the sight of this place of suffering? This, he said, is the prison of the angels, and here are they kept forever.

I think these same seven prisoners, shown as the stars of the Pleiades, are seen with great frequency in the symbols of Freemasonry, often along with the "Blazing Star," depicted actually shooting down from Heaven, like the fallen angels. They are also many times seen arranged together in the form of a hexagram, with one in the center and the other six arranged around it. This, in my opinion, represents Metatron's Cube, or the city of Enoch.

The seven stars show up quite often on Masonic "tracing boards," which are tableaus of symbols given to the candidates to study before the initiation rite of each degree. They are always shown between the pillars of Jachin and Boaz of Solomon's Temple, usually underneath the "Royal Arch," right below the "keystone." In the ritual of the Royal Arch degree, this keystone is said to have been discovered by the Knights Templar in the floor of Solomon's Temple. In the rite, they remove the stone, and reveal a room full of treasure beneath. This is the Eben Shetiyah, and the room below is the underworld.

I think that what Masonic tracing boards are depicting is, beyond "Solomon's Temple," more specifically the "temple" of the cubic city Cain built in Nod, in the underworld. While the Heavenly cubic city has no sun (because it has its own light), no moon (because it has no night), and no temples (because God himself is the temple), the Masonic tracing boards, similar to the lodges themselves, feature all of these things, just like the infernal city that they are based on. It is shown having its own sun and moon, and its own "All-Seeing Eye" - the watchtower within the Panopticon, in the center of the complex, from which you can see all of the rooms of the prison on the periphery. At the bottom of every tracing board, just like on the floor of most Masonic lodges, there is the chessboard pattern, representing the entire complex of Nod and the city within it.

Recently it occurred to me that the Ouija board Brian designed has most of the elements of a Masonic tracing board. It has the sun, the moon, the two pillars, and a banner forming an arch between them. Each pillar is supported by a foundation stone with its opposite color, either black or white. In place of the All-Seeing Eye or a G within a square and compass, as you would see on a tracing board, our Ouija board has the thirteen-pointed star, surrounded by letters, forming a circle with a hollow aperture. Below, the floor is depicted as the Abyss. But in the corner you see the Ageio board, in place of the chequered floor.

In our most recent conversation with him, Cain was exploring the board methodically, touching the pillars, the four cardinal points, and then circumambulating through the letters repeatedly, with increasing speed. We realized he was trying to activate sacred space, like Masons and witches do in their ritual chambers. This is supposed to turn the room into a portal connecting them with the otherworld.

We asked Cain if he was trying to open a portal on the Ouija board between his prison and our world. He admitted it. We asked what would happen if he came through. He said "DOOM," and that God had forced him to admit that.

Interestingly, there is a folk legend in modern Greece saying that demons known as "Kallikantzaroi" are let loose from the underworld on December 25th of each year, when the sun "stops moving," according to tradition. This happens because all year long they work to saw down the pole that separates Heaven from Earth, and at Christmas they are finally successful, leaving them free to roam the Earth. If they were to remain at large, it would purportedly cause calamity on Earth. But luckily, on Epiphany Day, January 6, God puts them back in prison down below, and the pole is restored, so that they have to start all over again sawing it down once more.

Not knowing this story, years ago I channeled instructions for "the Divine Rite" of the OLE, meant to mimic the coming crowning of the Grail king. Remember, the rite involved pretending to sacrifice the king, so that Cain could be released from his prison, and possess the monarch's body, bringing him back to life. This, I envisioned, would be like a key unlocking the timeless realm of Drakenberg and merging it with our own. The date I had chosen to perform this rite each year was December 23rd, the days that King Dagobert II was killed in a hunting accident, just like Cain.

Cain wants to get out. All of those in who are in Hell want out. But the fallen angels down there know something that the human spirits also trapped there probably don't know: that at the End of Times, the Abyss will open up and let them out of Hell, temporarily. Heaven will also open up, and literally merge with Earth as the white cube of the New Jerusalem descends. In my mind, it is most likely that the black cubic city will ascend from the depths as well. Heaven, Hell and Earth will all co-mingle in a timeless moment. Perhaps the black and white cubes will merge. This may be the ultimate explanation for the checker pattern on the Ageio board.

This, I think, will be their opportunity to switch places with humankind, and be back in the bosom of the Lord. Then again, perhaps they think that they will be able to take control of the celestial Ark, the cube, and be in the driver's seat, the God position, when things start anew. I think the belief is that, if they can get inside the white cube, in the position of God, they can be God, and they can win the Apocalypse game. Meanwhile, they believe, Baphomet will get his expressed wish: to see "MAN LOST IN HELL." We will be outside the cube, trapped in the chaotic Abyss where they were once tortured.

Mephistopheles describes this future to Dr. Faustus during one of their conversations. As it says in the Marlowe play:

Mephistopheles: Now, Faustus, ask what thou wilt.

Faustus: First will I question with thee about hell.
Tell me, where is the place that men call hell?

Mephistopheles: Under the heavens.

Faustus: Ay, but whereabout?

Mephistopheles: Within the bowels of these elements,
Where we are tortur'd and remain for ever:
Hell hath no limits, nor is circumscrib'd
In one self place; for where we are is hell,
And where hell is, there must we ever be:
And, to conclude, when all the world dissolves,
And every creature shall be purified,
All places shall be hell that are not heaven.

When the portals open, Hell rises and Heaven descends. This is the "Marriage of Heaven and Hell" which William Blake wrote about. Perhaps it is the ultimate "chemical wedding." This is the true "Golden Dawn," which the magical order is named after. This is why they have a hexagram for a logo, often showing a golden sun within the descending triangle, merging into the blue Abyss waters of the ascending triangle.

Interestingly, in the Golden Dawn rituals, they treat the Garden of Eden as though the place itself "fell" along with Adam. In their graphical depictions of the Fall, they show the Dragon of Revelation enveloping Adam and Eve, and encompassing Christ as he dies on the Cross. They also speak of both the pre- and post-fall Eden as being places that exist presently. The event of the Fall, as well as the restoration of Paradise, are both referred to as in the present tense.

Similarly, Baphomet talks about the war in Heaven, the fall of Eden, and the Apocalypse as all being events that, to him, are occurring right now. When we became confused and asked why he was talking about these past events and future events like they were presently happening, he said: "NOW REALLY SOON." Note that the abbreviation "NWO" (commonly used now to refer to the "New World Order" of the coming Anti-Christ) is an anagram of "now."

It goes without saying that, as our time-space dimension merges with those that are outside of time, our perception of time will stop. This is why modern Satanists refer to the concept of "Year Zero." It is not really "Anno Satanas," the year the Church of Satan was created, in 1966. It is that future "final hour" that has yet to come.

This concept of the true "End of Times," and the breakdown of the time dimension, explains why the Beast of the Apocalypse is described by St. John as "the beast that was, and is not, and yet is," said to have been born in the "wilderness" of chaos. Chapter 17: 8-13 states:

The beast that thou sawest was, and is not; and shall ascend out of the bottomless pit, and go into perdition: and they that dwell on the earth shall wonder, whose names were not written in the book of life from the foundation of the world, when they behold the beast that was, and is not, and yet is. And here is the mind which hath wisdom. The seven heads are seven mountains, on which the woman sitteth. And there are seven kings: five are fallen, and one is, and the other is not yet come; and when he cometh, he must continue a short space. And the beast that was, and is not, even he is the eighth, and is of the seven, and goeth into perdition. And the ten horns which thou sawest are ten kings, which have received no kingdom as yet; but receive power as kings one hour with the beast. These have one mind, and shall give their power and strength unto the beast.

This "Year Zero" may be what is depicted on the Great Seal of the United States. Everything that exists is contained within the walls of the pyramid, surmounted by the All-Seeing Eye of the prison guard, surrounded by a barren landscape of nothingness. The Latin phrase "Novus Ordo Seclorum," is usually translated "New Order of the Ages." It is an allusion to Virgil's Eclogue IV, where it says:

Now comes the final era of the Sibyl's song;

The great order of the ages is born afresh.

The Virgin and the Reign of Saturn returns

Now a new lineage is sent down from high heaven.

I think that it ultimately refers to the dissolving of reality, and the coagulation, or collection, of a small remnant of that reality to be saved, via an "ark" or Hermetically sealed alchemical vessel. Cain said that one of the keys to winning Ageio is to "ACCEPT DEFEAT" because, "IF YOU ACCEPT DEFEAT, REALITY CANNOT WIN." As you will recall, there is ultimately not much competition between the white and black armies in the game, because there is no doubt that the white side is going to win. So perhaps the game is to play both sides, and make sure that you're on the winning side when the game stops.

Right now, because Cain and the fallen are trapped in chaos, outside of the real cube up above, they are unreal. Reality is defined within that cube, by God and his image: man. But the fallen are attempting to rise. They want us to be the ones to accept defeat, and become unreal, while they "reap all the wealth" or reality. Not only that: they want us to be the ones to figure out how to let them out of their prison, just so they can make us switch places with them!

This is what happens to Christian Rosenkreutz in *The Chymical Wedding*. Having accidentally stumbled upon the naked Lady Venus, lying in a death-like sleep in her "tomb," the title character then becomes obliged to guard her chamber forever. Meanwhile, the previous guard is finally allowed to leave, having himself been cursed to stand there at length, for the same reason.

One of the characters present at the scene is none other than Atlas, who works for the royal palace where the wedding is taking place. This makes the symbolism clear: the castle is the world-mountain, the axis pole that holds Heaven apart from Earth. Atlas was the one charged with playing this role himself, holding the weight of the heavens upon his shoulders, in Greek mythology. Atlas was freed from his burden by Hercules, who replaced him with two pillars (like Jachin and Boaz of the Freemasons, featured on their tracing boards and on our Ouija board). Now Christian Rosenkreutz is fated to play a similar role as Atlas:

Now as soon as 1was called in again, Atlas declared to me that although it was grievous to the King's Majesty that I, whom he loved above others, had fallen into such a mischance, yet because it was not possible for him to transgress his ancient usages, he did not know how to absolve me; the other [the previous doorkeeper] must be at liberty, and I put in his place; yet he would hope that some other would be

Masonic tracing board for the Entered Apprentice degree

Tracing board for the Fellow Craft degree

apprehended, so that I might be able to go home again. However, no release was to be hoped for, till the marriage feast of his future son.... I imagined nothing other than that I must finish my life under the gate.

Hesiod, in his *Works and Days*, says that Atlas is the father of the Pleiades. According to Plato, Poseidon named one of his sons Atlas. It was the first of his ten sons by the mortal lady, Cleito. Poseidon enclosed the hill on which Cleito lived all around her, making alternate zones of sea and land. He divided the "island," which he called "Atlantis," among his ten sons with Cleito.

The eldest was "Atlant," after which Plato says the island and surrounding ocean received its name. He made Atlant the chief king, and gave him the center portion of land with his mother's house on it, which was the best plot. The other sons received portions of land from the outer rings of the labyrinth in descending order from their birth. They were each given absolute control over their portion, to rule as tyrants over the populace.

The image of Poseidon enveloping his wife and children within a labyrinth of segments of land and sea bring to mind Louis Ginzberg's description of Cain in *Legends of the Jews*:

Cain knew only too well that his blood-guiltiness would be visited upon him in the seventh generation. Thus had God decreed against him. He endeavored, therefore, to immortalize his name by means of monuments, and he became a builder of cities. The first of them he called Enoch, after his son, because it was at the birth of Enoch that he began to enjoy a measure of rest and peace. Besides, he founded six other cities. This building of cities was a godless deed, for he surrounded them with a wall, forcing his family to remain within.

Cain said the fall of Atlantis, the fall of Eden, and the fall of Nod (or his fall into Nod) were all part of the same event (or set of events). He also said that there were ten "DOHIR KINGS" or "MOLOCHS," the "KINGS OF THE FALLEN LAND." In addition to being, perhaps, the same as the ten kings of Atlantis, are they also the same as the ten horns of the Beast of the Apocalypse, as described in the previous quote from St. John?

As I said, I think that the Flood was not just a physical deluge of water, but also a dissolving of reality into chaos. Surviving this requires an alchemical "ark" of safety, like the black cube or the white cube. This is what much of the arcane literature written by initiates of the occult seems to indicate, as well as the more esoteric scriptures of Judaism and Christianity.

In *Le Serpent Rouge*, a cryptic poem published by the Priory of Sion, the authors appear to be referring to a mystery and a treasure synonymous with those of the Grail, the Ark of the Covenant, the Ark of Noah, and the cubic Philosopher's Stone of the alchemists. It discusses the "strange manuscripts" of an enigmatic "friend." This friend's "name remains a mystery, but his number is that of a famous seal."

This "seal" is the hexagram, the Seal of Solomon. We know this because later in the poem, the authors confirm it:

Here is the proof that I knew the secret of the Seal of Solomon, and that I had visited the hidden houses of this queen.

As I discussed, this can be seen as representing the black and white stones merging at the Apocalypse. The "friend" is described in the poem as "like the pilot of the imperishable Ark, impassable like a column on a white rock, scanning towards the South, where the black rock is." At another point, the poem declares, in all capital letters:

DELIVER ME FROM THE MIRE, SO THAT I WILL NOT STAY HERE SINKING.

The phrase "Deliver me from the mire" is repeated again at the end of the poem, when the narrator awakes from a "dream" that he had apparently been in during the entire adventure described in the poem. This should remind us of Cain, lying in a coffin asleep in the land of Nod. According to Plutarch, this is the same position that Saturn (the Roman equivalent of the Greek Chronos) is in, chained on an island vivat et non vivat by his son Zeus. His chains, says Plutarch, are formed by the illusions of his dreams. As he writes in *Morals*:

...His slumber had been artfully produced in order to chain him, and round about him were many dæmons for his guards and servants.... For Saturn himself is imprisoned in a vast cavern, sleeping upon a rock overlaid with gold; for his sleep has been contrived by Jupiter for his chaining -whilst birds fly down from the rock, which are ordained to carry ambrosia to him, whilst the island is overspread with fragrance, diffused from the rock as from a fountain. Those genii wait upon and nurse Saturn, who had been his companions at the time when truly he used to reign over both gods and men; and they, being endowed with prophecy, foretell, on their own account, many things, but important matters, and such as concern the highest things, they go down into the cavern and report as the dreams of Saturn; for whatsoever things Jupiter is devising for the future, Saturn dreams what they are about, and that which is kingly and divine.

Jupiter is "Jove," and is broadly believed by comparative religionists to have some equivalence to the Jehovah of the Hebrews. ("Jove" is used in English parlance now to refer to Jehovah, as in the saying "By Jove!") Chief among the Olympian gods, he is the lord of this age, and this realm. Saturn was seen by the Romans as the lord of a past realm, the "Golden Age" that was overthrown by his son Jupiter (just as Saturn's Greek equivalent, Chronos, had his Titan kingdom overthrown by the Greek equivalent of Jupiter, Zeus).

Saturn's Golden Age was like the "day of rest" (of timelessness) on the seventh day of creation: the day in which the events in the Garden of Eden story took place. A "new Golden Age" will happen at the end of time, with a new Genesis and a new Eden. We represent this grand cycle in microcosm at the end of each week, with Saturday, the Sabbath, and also at the end of every year, with the celebrations of the winter holidays.

The ancient Romans observed these as "non-days," outside of the realm of time. This was their feasting time of "Saturnalia," the precursor to our own Christmas. Saturn was obviously the inspiration for Santa Claus. After all, Saturn was an "eternal old man" who must have lived near the North Pole (Plutarch says the sun only set there once every thirty days), and was served by a set of demons (elves). Saturn (like Chronos) was also the Roman lord of time (and carried a scythe, like Death). Therefore, he is clearly the inspiration for Father Time, used in modern iconography to represent the old year on New Year's Eve, always next to a baby, representing the new year.

During Saturnalia they suspended all laws, the slaves were temporarily freed, and nobody had to work. This was to mimic the Golden Age, in which, it was believed, there was peaceful anarchy, with none but the so-called "unrule" of Saturn. There was an abundance of everything wanted with no work required. This is possible because, like the Garden of Eden, the Golden Age was outside of time. Therefore there was no death, birth, or generation.

As I speculated in my other book, *Money Grows on the Tree of Knowledge*, such a state can only be maintained by negating the future, as Saturn is said to have swallowed his own children. He did this to keep them from growing up to overthrow him, as had been prophesied. This was the child sacrifice that purchased the peace and prosperity of the Golden Age.

In the Greek myths, the gods of Olympus live on "ambrosia," which is brought to them by doves. Whatever this substance is, it is what gives them immortality, and because of that, they don't need to eat normal food. It is said specifically that, because of the ambrosia, the gods have no blood in them, and therefore they cannot die. "Their thirst, thence bloodless and from death exempt," as Homer said it in The Iliad. Instead of blood, their bodies contain a golden substance called "Ichor," which is toxic to humans.

Remember, the angels in *The Third Book of Enoch* complained to God that he had given his secret name to someone of flesh and blood. But in the stories of vampires, it is drinking blood that gives them eternal life. This is because it is believed to contain the essential human life force, which, being without a soul, vampires lack. Therefore they need to get it through dietary supplements.

The inhabitants of the Grail king are eternally youthful, except for their gray hair. This is because they are fed by the food of the Grail. In Eschenbach's version, a dove brings a communion wafer from Heaven, and the Grail somehow transmutes it into food that brings immortality. In most of the Grail stories, there is a mysterious banquet at the Grail castle, called the "Grail service," in which people eat from the Grail. Events that occur at the meal imply that they are eating human flesh and drinking human blood.

Plutarch describes a strange sacrificial rite in which the "servants of Saturn" are sent out on perilous voyages to this island, where they serve him for a period of thirteen years. After that time, they have the choice of staying in his realm or returning home. He writes:

But when the star of Saturn, which we call the 'Informer,' but they 'Nocturnal,' comes into the sign of the Bull every thirty years, they having got ready a long while beforehand all things required for the sacrifice and the games ... they send out people appointed by lot in the same number of ships, furnished with provisions and stores necessary for persons intending to cross so vast a sea by dint of rowing, as well as to live a long time in a foreign land.... It is, indeed, allowed to such as have served thirteen years in waiting upon the god, to return home, but the greatest part prefer to remain there, partly out of habit, partly because they have all things in abundance without toil and trouble, as they pass their time in sacrifices and hymn singing, or in studying legends and philosophy of some sort. For wonderful are both the island and the mildness of the climate; whilst the deity himself has been an obstacle to some when contemplating departure, by manifesting himself to them as to familiars and friends, not by way of dreams or by tokens, but conversing with them in a visible form with many apparitions and speeches of genii.... The stranger having been carried there, as he told us, and waiting upon the god at his leisure, he gained acquaintance with astrology and geometry as far as it is possible to advance, whilst he took up 'natural science' for his department of philosophy.

On Saturn's island, the god teaches them by communicating through apparitions and dreams. That's also how he keeps them on the island as his slaves. This is the Scholomance that Dracula attended, and the "Invisible College" that Rosicrucians talked about. It seems to be more of a philosophical academy, akin to the "Philosophic Kingdom" of Sir Francis Bacon's *New Atlantis,* where everyone lives in leisure and spends their time working out the mysteries of the universe. It is the "Unseen University" in of Terry Pratchett novels, and Harry Potter's "School for Witchcraft & Wizardry," accessible through a portal at an underground train station.

Traveling to this school is like going to the Witch's Sabbath on fabled Mount Brocken (of German witchcraft legend). In these stories, the location is accessed by "going forth by night," in a drug-induced trance, ejecting your soul through the chimney in your house. You then ride to the mountaintop on a magical steed: the broomstick.

This is how Mohammed visited the temple mount (Jerusalem, associated with the "white stone") after falling asleep on the black stone (at the Kaaba). According to legend, this was his famous "night journey," flying a magical winged steed named "Buraq." Note that the Arabic word for the "night journey," which is "Isra," sounds very similar to the word "Israel," the land he visited.

Furthermore, the "salem" in "Jerusalem" comes from the word for "stairway." It was usually used in reference to a stepped pyramid or ziggurat-style temple, which was viewed as a "stairway to Heaven." The top of such a structure was viewed as a gateway to God's realm, just as there is believed to be such a portal on the roof of the Kaaba.

Interestingly, Francis Bacon called the utopian island civilization in his novel "Bensalem." The country was ruled by a "college" of wise elders called "Salomon's House." He described this institution as the "the very eye of the kingdom." They were divinely chose, for the "God of heaven and earth had vouchsafed the grace to know the works of Creation, and the secrets of them." Another title he gave this school was the "College of the Six Days' Work." This referred to the six days of creation in *Genesis*. He was saying that this is where one goes to learn how to create things alchemically, like God does. Their mission statement is given by the author:

The end of our foundation is the knowledge of causes, and secret motions of things; and the enlarging of the bounds of human empire, to the effecting of all things possible.

On the title page of that book, Bacon used an illustration of Saturn unveiling the naked Lady Venus in her secret tomb. Surrounding the image are the Latin words: "Tempore Patet Occulta Veritas." ("Time Reveals the Hidden Truth.") Saturn, of course, symbolized time. Venus denoted the secrets of nature, or alchemy. But as we learn in *The Chymical Wedding of Christian Rosenkreutz*, whoever unveils Venus is cursed to remain a prisoner in her kingdom forever. The slavery of the student is the price of knowledge, just as in Saturn's school described by Plutarch. That is the tuition of the Invisible College.

In Theophilus Schweighardt's Speculum Sophicum Rhodo-Stauroticum, there is an illustration of "the College of the Rosicrucian Brotherhood." It is shown as a box-like building with wings and wheels, somewhat like the prophet Ezekiel's vision of the divine chariot. In the distance, you can see the Ark of Noah resting upon a mountaintop.

One of the oldest versions of the Deluge story, from Mesopotamia, is that of Utnapishtim, the equivalent of Noah. He was told of the impending deluge from spirits who spoke to him through the walls of his house. They then instructed him on how to turn his own house into a vessel, in the shape of a perfect cube. This is how he survived the waters of the Flood.

In *Mystery of the Cathedrals,* Fulcanelli takes the last chapter to talk about alchemical concepts of the Apocalypse. He speaks of the destruction and regeneration of the world as though it were an alchemical transformation, in which humanity must die, be dissolved into chaos, and be reborn. This discussion is sparked by his analysis in that chapter of a strange monument called the "Cyclic Cross of Hendaye," found in a church courtyard in Basque France. He writes:

Whatever its age, the Hendaye cross shows by the decoration of its pedestal that it is the strangest monument of primitive millenarism... It is known that this doctrine, first accepted and then refuted by Origen, St. Denis of Alexandria, and St. Jerome, although it had not been condemned by the Church, was part of the esoteric tradition of the ancient hermetic philosophy.

By rearranging the oddly-spaced letters of the message on the cross's stand - "O crux ave spes unica (Hail o cross, the only hope)" - he obtained the following, hidden message: "Il est ecrit que la vie se refugie en un seul espace" ("It is written that life takes refuge in a single space"). The meaning of this, says Fulcanelli, is that:

...A country exists, where death cannot reach man at the terrible time of the double cataclysm. As for the geographical location of this promised land, from which the elite will take part in the return of the golden age, it is up to us to find it. For the elite, the children of Elias, will be saved according to the word of Scripture, because their profound faith, their untiring perseverance in effort, will have earned for them the right to be promoted to the rank of disciples of the Christ-Light. They will bear his sign and will receive from him the mission of renewing for regenerated humanity the chain of tradition of the humanity which has disappeared.

Fulcanelli believed that we really are heading towards an Apocalyptic event, and that messages predicting it are embedded in this monument. Moreover, he thought that alchemists and other "elite" would be able to decode the symbols left behind by the initiates of the past to figure out a special country or "space" where they will be safe from the cataclysm.

The Invisible College, from Theophilus Schweighardt's *Speculum Sophicum Rhodo-Stauroticum*

Masonic tracing board for the Royal Arch degree

This event will involve the opening up of one or more portals between the realms of Heaven, Earth, and Hell. It can be seen as a union or "chemical wedding" of these realms, just as the coming of the New Jerusalem is likened to a marriage of Heaven and Earth. It is seen also as a "collapsing" of the "pole" - the "world-mountain" - that separates the realms.

The instigation of this event will involve aid from humans who want it to happen. They believe that they are the chosen few, and that if they build an "ark" properly, they will be saved. It will also involve humans being persuaded into descending into the underworld to free the captive demons. But some of these people will be tricked into trading places with them, and forced to bear their torment. This includes the "burden" of keeping the heavens aloft again when the new order of the realms is established. We can see this by decoding the creative works of occult initiates, as well as the myths and scriptures that they refer to. Let us examine again the writings of Sir Francis Bacon.

New Atlantis was part of a series of texts called *Instauratio Magna* (*The Great Restoration*). It was supposed to have six parts, like the six days of God's creation, but he only got around to finishing four. I believe the title refers to the establishment of a new order of perfection, creating the universe anew. This can be seen by examining the image on the title page of one of the books: *Novum Organum Scientarium* (*New Scientific Instrument*).

The illustration shows a ship passing between two pillars, representing the "Pillars of Hercules," which are the two large rocks that flank the Straits of Gibraltar. There is a banner wrapped around each pillar, upon which are written, when taken together, the Latin words "Plus Ultra" ("Further Beyond"). You may recall that Satan had used the term "FURTHER AND BEYOND" when discussing the death curse on Boyd Rice. At the time I had no idea about the meaning and origin of that phrase.

The Straits marked the portal between the Mediterranean Sea, well-charted by the Greeks, and the Atlantic Ocean, which was considered the realm Itbeyond.1t Actually, during the Renaissance there was a legend that there was a warning written upon the pillars that said "Nec Plus Ultra" ("There is Nothing Beyond"). This was supposedly a warning to sailors not to risk their lives trying to explore past the pillars.

Plato said that Atlantis had been situated just beyond the Pillars. That meant that it was effectively in the "otherworld," and this, according to my thesis, truly did exist in another dimension. So when the Habsburgs of Spain financed Christopher Columbus, discovering vast wealth and exciting new lands beyond the pillars, they had it commemorated on the royal arms of

Spain. This new design boasted the pillars with the word "Nec" taken out, demonstrating that they had proven there was, in fact, "more beyond," and had boldly claimed it for themselves.

Christopher Columbus, when he discovered the American continent, is reported to have felt that God had guided him to the location of the "New Jerusalem." Perhaps he thought that within America there was that "single space" of refuge that Fulcanelli later wrote about, the touch-point where the white cube from Heaven would land. Manly P. Hall writes in *The Secret Destiny of America* that Columbus was inspired in his voyages by Plato's account of Atlantis.

Now the mythology that ties these pillars to Hercules is very relevant here. As the story goes, during his famous Twelve Labors, the hero was obliged to alleviate Atlas of his burden to hold the canopy of Heaven apart from the Earth. Just as is the case with Lilith and Samael, the story goes that if the lovers Gaia and Ouranos (Earth and Heaven) are allowed to sexually unite once more, the world will be destroyed. Poor Atlas, when the Titans lost the war with the Olympians (the equivalent to the war in Heaven between God's loyal angels and the rebellious ones) he was punished by the victor, Zeus, with the burden of preventing that destruction (unlike the rest, who were mostly imprisoned in Tartarus for eternal torture). The solution Hercules devised was to fashion the Straits of Gibraltar by splitting a mountain, and using them to prop up the sky instead.

Another version of this story was that, while traveling to the Garden of Hera to get the apples there, tended by the Hesperides, Hercules had to cross a mountain named "Atlas." Instead of doing that, he smashed the mountain in two. In this case, "Atlas" was the world-mountain, representing the pole between the worlds. By smashing it, he opened a portal between the worlds: between the "Mediterranean Sea" (which means, literally, "the sea in the middle of the Earth") and the "Atlantic Ocean" (the ocean of Atlantis).

In yet still another version, Hercules asked Atlas to fetch the apples for him, since he was the father of the Hesperides, the gardeners. He promised to hold the sky up for Atlas while he went on the errand, but Atlas tried to trick him into getting stuck there. However, the hero managed to thwart this maneuver.

It should be noted that this Atlas is supposedly totally different from the one that Plato said was fathered by Atlas. Remember he said that the island was named after this demi-god son. But it is hard to believe it is a coincidence that the land of this Atlas was situated just beyond the pillars, or rocks, associated with the Titan Atlas.

Atlas is more often said to be upholding the Earth, not Heaven. Many historians think this misconception came about simply because statues of the god show him holding a globe on his shoulders, and it was assumed by people looking at them (without reading the details of the myth) that he was holding our planet. Also, confusion may have arisen when, starting in the sixteenth century, people began referring to a book of terrestrial maps as an "atlas." However, it was really a celestial globe, showing the zodiac and visible night's sky on a sphere, that the god was always shown with.

The story becomes more confusing when you consider that Freemasons frequently depict their sacred pillars to be surmounted by two globes. One is a regular terrestrial globe, and one is a celestial globe. This symbolism tends to indicate an esoteric belief that there is a need of two "world -mountains" or "axis poles": one to hold up the firmament of Heaven, separating it from Earth, and another down below to support the fundament of Earth, to keep it from collapsing into the underworld.

Another common Masonic symbol worthy of note here is that of a broken column, which signifies death. It is usually shown with a lady called the "Weeping Virgin" standing over it holding a sheaf of wheat, wearing a toga. Father Time (Saturn) stands behind her lecherously, donned in only a loincloth, playing with her hair. Sometimes a symbol of the constellation Virgo is part of the scene as well. This emblem is often used on the gravestones and obituaries of Freemasons who have died, of whom it is said, "his column is broken."

Sure this is a fitting allegory for an individual who has died, but it could also signify the end of time, the collapse of the world's axis, and the death of a universe. Remember the passage from Virgil's *Eclogue IV* that is referenced on the apocalyptic Great Seal of the United States: "Now comes the final era of the Sibyl's song... The Virgin and the Reign of Saturn returns." It is almost impossible that there is not a connection between those words and this image.

An interpretation of the broken column given by several Masonic scholars is that it has something to do with the myth of Isis and her brother/husband Osiris. Their mutual brother Set (also called "Seth") resented Osiris (who was the lord over Earth at that point) because, like the Green Man of Celtic lore, and like Cain of the Bible (tiller of the soil), he made plants grow all over the land. Set supposedly hated this because he was a desert dweller. However, to me it sounds like he was jealous of Osiris' green thumb.

At any rate, Seth invited all of his brethren, the gods, to a banquet, and presented them with a beautiful chest he had crafted out of various woods. In addition to being a marvel of carpentry, it also have an overwhelmingly sweet and pleasant aroma. Everyone at the table loved it, and Seth told them that he would give it to whoever's body conformed to its dimensions most closely.

They all tried it out, like the ruby slipper in the story of Cinderella. Osiris fit inside perfectly, once he took his crown off. This was because Seth had secretly taken measurements of Osiris' body using his shadow. As soon as the god laid down in the box, Seth locked it and ran away with it. He had his servants pour molten lead over it, and then it was tossed into the Nile.

A "flood" caused the box to wash up in a thicket of trees near Byblos, now part of Lebanon. In this context, it makes sense to think of the flooding of the Nile that occurs annually. However, just the word "flood" and a box carrying the body of a god links it up with Noah's Ark (which carried the body of Adam), and with the basket of bulrushes that carried young Moses down the Nile.

The story goes on to say that one of the young trees there in Byblos grew up around the box, and subsumed it into itself. This tree then grew to be fragrant and lovely, due to the divinity trapped within it. So the king and queen of Byblos had the tree cut down and installed in their royal place as a column. There it continued to give off its wonderful scent, and was admired by all.

Now the king and queen of this land are reported to be none other than the Phoenician gods Melquart and Astarte. Melquart is the same as Baal (and also, according to many scholars, the same as Hercules). Astarte is the same figure as Ishtar, who is the same as Isis! Obviously, some major myth morphing (what poet Robert Graves called "iconotropy") has gone on over the years.

As the tale continues, Isis discovered the column and informed the royal family of Byblos about the contents of it. They cut it open and allowed her to take the casket. She was able to open it, and used magic to resurrect Osiris' body. But then Seth found them, and murdered Osiris again, this time chopping his body into 14 pieces and tossing them about.

Again, Isis was able to find the pieces. She put them together, and was able to resurrect him again. But this time, it was different. His body was still immobile, but "undead." Isis learned that his soul was alive in the underworld.

Just as death came into the perfect world of Eden through the sin of Adam, the death of Osiris (starting with his first death, when he was closed in the casket) was the initiation of mortality in our world. Prior to that, all had lived

Frontispiece to Bacon's *Novum Organum*

The Masonic "broken column"

in peace, immortality, and leisure similar to the Garden before the Fall, and much like the Golden Age of the Greeks.

This ended when he died. People and animals began to expire, and the crops failed. But when Osiris was resurrected in the underworld, and his body parts were reunited on Earth, fertility came to the land again. Also, like Jesus, by descending to the world below, he somehow won for humanity the right to eternal life. However, like Jesus, Osiris is the judge of the dead at the end, and will decide who is not worthy of eternal life down there with the gods.

The symbol of Osiris inside of the column of the royal palace became part of a beautifully all-encompassing icon that the Egyptians used to represent the concept of the world-axis. It was called the "Djed pillar," and it was mainly viewed as Osiris' spine, holding up the Earth and the sky from the underworld. But it also contains the image of the Ark (the casket) and the "world-tree," probably the second most-common archetypal symbol of the axis found in cultures around the planet (second only, perhaps, to the mountain archetype).

So when Osiris was resurrected the second time, and became the lord of the Earth, with his soul reigning from the underworld, and his body undead but inanimate, he took on the burden of upholding the worlds, just like Atlas. Significantly, depictions of the tomb of Osiris show him lying inside of a stepped pyramid constructed beneath the Earth. The chamber is being illuminated by the shining rays of a sun positioned at the roof.

Certainly this ties in with how Cain described his prison to us, but it also connects with tales told by the Hermetic Order of the Golden Dawn. In their rituals, they say that the tomb of Christian Rosenkreutz is lit by an "inner sun," which is also emblematized as a rose situated somewhere on the ceiling. They say he is lying undead there, waiting for his tomb to be discovered. When that happens, he will come alive again, and a new Golden Age of Hermetic enlightenment will begin.

The Golden Dawn's "Adept us Minor" ritual describes, and replicates, the inside of this tomb. It is said to be covered in mystical symbols, and to contain the Emerald Tablet of Hermes, with the secrets of alchemy inscribed upon it. This brings to mind the 1595 illustrated alchemical treatise *Amphitheatrum Sapientiae Aeternae* (*Amphitheater of Eternal Wisdom*) by Heinrich Khunrath, which depicts the Tablet as actually being inscribed upon the side of a mountain, as if the mountain itself is the Tablet. In the ritual, the candidate is told:

The Tomb is symbolically situated in the centre of the Earth, Mountain of the Caverns, the Mystic Mountain of Abiegnus. The meaning of this title of Abiegnus -

Abi-Agnus, Lamb of the Father. It is by metathesis Abi-Genos, Born of the Father. Bia-Genos, Strength of our Race, and the four words make the sentence: ABIEGNUS ABIAGNUS ABI-GENOS BIA-GENOS. 'Mountain of the Lamb of the Father, and the Strength of Our Race.'

One of the lines from *Le Serpent Rouge*, when telling about the mysterious location of the tomb of Isis, and the mountain she rests in, says:

It is not by the magical strength of HERCULES that one deciphers these mysterious symbols engraved by observers of the past.

Within driving distance of Rennes-le-Château in France is the mountain of Montségur. It has a long history associated with the Knights Templar and the heretical Christian movement of the Cathars, also known as the "Albigensians." The Church actually fought a war against them to stamp them all out, which they effectively did. It was called the "Albigensian Crusade." Many theorists believe that the Holy Grail, or perhaps the Ark of the Covenant, or some other sacred treasure, was there at one point. It may have been smuggled out to safety somewhere when the heretics' last stronghold, their fortress on Montségur, was taken by their enemy.

The name "Montségur" means "Mountain of Security." Some writers postulate that this mountain was the basis for "Montsalvat" ("Mountain of Salvation"), where the Grail Castle resides in the old romances. Montségur is a reported hotbed for modern UFO activity. Recently, when the year 2012 came to an end, thousands of New Agers converged on Montségur, certain that it was the "single space" of refuge that Fulcanelli wrote about, of which I spoke previously. They believed that being there would protect them from the end of the world. Fascinatingly, there is a cavern in the mountain with a stalagmite in it that is called, for some reason, the "Tomb of Hercules."

During another Golden Dawn ritual, for the grade of "Theoricus," the candidate is directed to assume a stance mimicking Atlas, who is described as holding up two pillars that support the universe. As it says in the rite:

Stand with feet together and raise both arms upwards and back, palms up, as if supporting a weight. It represents you in the Path of YESOD, supporting the Pillars of Mercy and Severity. It is the Sign made by the Greek God ATLAS, who supported the Universe on his shoulders and whom Hercules was directed to emulate. It is the ISIS of Nature, supporting the Heavens.

Francis Bacon's use of the image of a ship going through the Pillars of Hercules, along with the words "Plus Ultra" are taken by most as a metaphor. Hercules smashed Mount Atlas to create a portal to the new world. In Bacon's time, Europeans were now penetrating that opening to colonize new lands, and greatly expanding mankind's understanding of the world. Likewise, Bacon might have been predicting that his own touted "scientific method" (one of his credited inventions) would collapse the barriers to greater understanding of the universe.

However, I think that what specifically might have been on his mind was the collapsing of the pole that holds up the heavens, so that the New Jerusalem will come crashing down to Earth. The Latin sentence written at the bottom of the *Novum Organum* illustration makes it clear that he had the End Times in mind. It says: "Multi pertransibunt & augebitur scientia," which translates to: "Many will travel and knowledge will be increased." Again, you might think that this is about traveling to the New World. But it is actually a slight paraphrase of something from *The Book of Daniel* 12:4:

But thou, O Daniel, shut up the words, and seal the book, even to the time of the end: many shall run to and fro, and knowledge shall be increased.

Bacon was smart enough to know that there might not literally be a "mountain" or a "pole" that is "holding up the sky." But he could understand that there were other dimensions of reality that mankind has yet to explore. On the topic of smashing a portal between the worlds, and possibly collapsing them together, let us have a look at some of the projects being done with the atomic particle collider in Switzerland known as "CERN" (which stands for words that translate to "European Council for Nuclear Research." They are presently doing tests with something called a "Large Hadron Collider" that, according to their spokespeople, could open a "doorway" to an "extra dimension."

Sergio Bertolucci, the Director for Research and Scientific Computing at CERN, told the technology newspaper The Register, as reported in an article from November 2009, that:

Out of this door might come something, or we might send something through it.

The article continues:

Dr. Bertolucci later got in touch to confirm that yes indeed, there would be an 'open door,' but that even with the power of the LHC at his disposal he would only be able to hold it open "a very tiny lapse of time, 10^{-26} *seconds, [but] during that infinitesimal amount of time we would be able to peer into this open door, either by getting something out of it or sending something into it.*

These scientists seem quite confident that this small amount of time in which this tiny little door will open won't at all be enough to collapse the barrier between these dimensions and destroy this entire dimension instantly, or any other manner of disaster-based science fiction scenarios that could theoretically come from such tinkering with the fabric of existence. But I'm not so sure. It should be obvious to all that the Final Hour of *Revelation* can take place in the twinkling of an eye. How long does it take for space-time to end? It's a meaningless question, and afterwards (although there is no such things as "afterwards") it won't really matter, will it?

One of the collider's projects is actually named "the ALICE Collaboration," purportedly because it will allow the scientists to explore the root of matter the same way Alice explored Wonderland down the rabbit hole. The logo for the project is an octagonal portal with rays of energy bursting from the center. The acronym stands for "A Large Ion Collider Experiment." Their website describes it as:

...One of the largest experiments in the world devoted to research in the physics of matter at an infinitely small scale. ...You are invited to tumble down the rabbit hole into the wonderland of ALICE.

If you'll recall, Alice was only able to enter Wonderland by shrinking herself so that she was small enough to fit through the door at the bottom of the rabbit hole. She got into that state by eating and drinking certain things. Alice's Adventures in Wonderland appears to be one of the preeminent works of fiction published in the last two centuries that truly fits the ancient pattern of a "portal to the underworld" epic myth. In that story, the white rabbit who lured her down there complains that he is "late for a very important date." This may be an allusion to that late hour - that final hour - before Year Zero begins.

Believe it or not, one of the particle detectors in the Large Hadron Collider is named "ATLAS." Other interesting names for CERN experiments include "AEGIS," "ALPHA," "ALEPH," "DELPHI," "COMPASS," "TOTEM," "ATHENA," "AWAKE," and, perhaps most menacingly, "ATRAP." I mention this last one, which can clearly be decoded to "a trap," because I think that this may be what the opening of any such dimensional portal could lead to.

I suspect that those who are imprisoned in the regions below are constantly working to inspire their chosen genius few among us - certain scientists, artists, writers and philosophers - to penetrate God's secrets of creation. In particular, they want somebody to learn how to build one of these alchemical arks, and to open a gateway to where they are. They are hoping that someone will come and rescue them. But as I have said, ultimately, I think they will play humans a scurvy trick, and try to take over the ark for themselves, leaving us to suffer in their stead.

In the Hermetic Order of the Golden Dawn, they tell their initiates to pretend that they are Atlas. They ask them to imagine themselves taking up the burden of one of the gods of the old, fallen kingdom of the now-dead golden age of the Titans, who was cursed, shackled and tortured by the usurping Olympian gods. I wonder if, by going through the motions in this ritual, you are tacitly agreeing to do so. Perhaps it is just meant to get you used to the idea, and comfortable with it. Certainly there are many cultural influences around us that seem geared towards doing just that.

We find an overwhelmingly repetitive pattern in the fictional works of man, portraying what Joseph Campbell called the "Hero's Journey" and the "Monomyth." There are many variations on the theme, but generally, these stories involve the protagonist journeying to an unknown, hidden realm to confront gods, demons, or the monarchs of the other side. Here he must battle with these villains, gaining thereby a magical treasure, which he then takes back to Earth with him. Or, conversely, sometimes he becomes the monarch of the other side, effecting a revolution, and remains there.

In these stories, there is always a mysterious guide for the hero that comes along in the very beginning. This person (often using trickery) beckons the protagonist to his appointed adventure, and shows up at specific times throughout the story to provide further aid. The white rabbit plays this role in Lewis Carroll's story, leading Alice down the rabbit hole to revelation. Amazingly, two white rabbits and a man are shown leading a blindfolded alchemist to a rabbit hole at the foot of the alchemical mountain in *The Cave of the Ancients*, and illustration from Stefan Michel Spacher's 1616 book *Cabala: Spiegel der Kunst und Natur in Alchymia* (*Cabala: Mirror of Art and Nature in Alchemy*). Usually, with the help of this trickster, the hero in these stories obtains an object (symbolizing the alchemical "Compass of the Wise") that helps him find the hidden kingdom, and the treasure within it.

With this in mind, let us again examine some of the things we find in *Le Serpent Rouge*. This poem is about the previously-mentioned mysterious "friend." He is a "traveler of the unknown,"

He goes on a voyage to a hidden, fallen realm in an attempt to rescue the goddess Isis from the "mire." As I said, at the end the whole thing is revealed to be a dream. It came about by the process of "going forth by night" through astral portals.

Now this goddess, say many comparative mythologists, is the same figure known in pantheons from other cultures. She was Ishtar to the Babylonians, and Inanna to the Sumerians. Inanna is said to have descended through several chambers of the underworld, and became trapped there for a while.

In this story, she visits her sister Ereshkigal, the Queen of Hell. Before Inanna enters each chamber, the guardians insist that she remove a piece of her clothing. Thus she is naked - a bare soul with no fleshly clothing - when she gets to the inner chamber (just like Venus sleeps naked in her tomb in Andrae's *Chymical Wedding*).

At that point, with Inanna apparently now vulnerable to mortality, her sister has her turned into a dead, rotting piece of meat, andhangs her on a hook on the wall. But with the help of her servants, Inanna is brought back to life. In the end, she is able to ascend once again to the land of the living.

Inanna's symbol, by the way, was an eight-pointed rosette star, which brings to mind the 8 x 8 structure of the chess and Ageio boards. L.A. Waddell said that this star was called "Ash." This, among many other clues, connects her to the Semitic goddess Asherah, another name for Ishtar, denoted in the Bible as the male demon Ashtaroth.

Isis is often compared to the figure of Eve from *Genesis*, as well as to the Virgin Mary, and Mary Magdalene. In particular, Eve was called the "mother of all living," a title also given to Isis. Reflecting upon this, I recalled something that Cain told us when he was describing the Flood. He said that he "TRIED TO SAVE EVE."

In *Le Serpent Rouge*, the protagonist has to find his way through a wilderness in order to reach the hidden house of Isis, who is here said to be sleeping in a tomb (again like Andrae's depiction of Venus), where she is somehow trapped and in need of rescue. The surrounding wilderness is a metaphor for the chaos of the underworld, usually shown in literature as either a labyrinth, a dry, expansive desert, or an impenetrable forest.

In this example, Isis' "kingdom" is said here to be "fallen" and hidden by dense woods, like the goddess Diana's secret grove, and like the castle of the princess Briar Rose in the fairy tale by Charles Perrault known now as "Sleeping Beauty." As we read in the poem:

In my arduous pilgrimage, I was tempted to clear for myself, with a sword, a way towards the inextricable vegetation of the woods. I wanted to reach the mysterious house of the Sleeping BEAUTY in whom certain poets see the QUEEN of a fallen kingdom.

The narrator expresses his desire to "free" his goddess from some form of bondage in her "sepulcher." He also describes the pleasant odor coming from her undead corpse:

From her who I wish to free, steams of perfume that impregnated the sepulcher climbed towards me.

Above: Noah's Ark depicted as a stationary building, from the thirteen century North French Hebrew Miscellany. Below: CERN's logo for the ALICE project, showing the portal to the underworld underneath a blue arch.

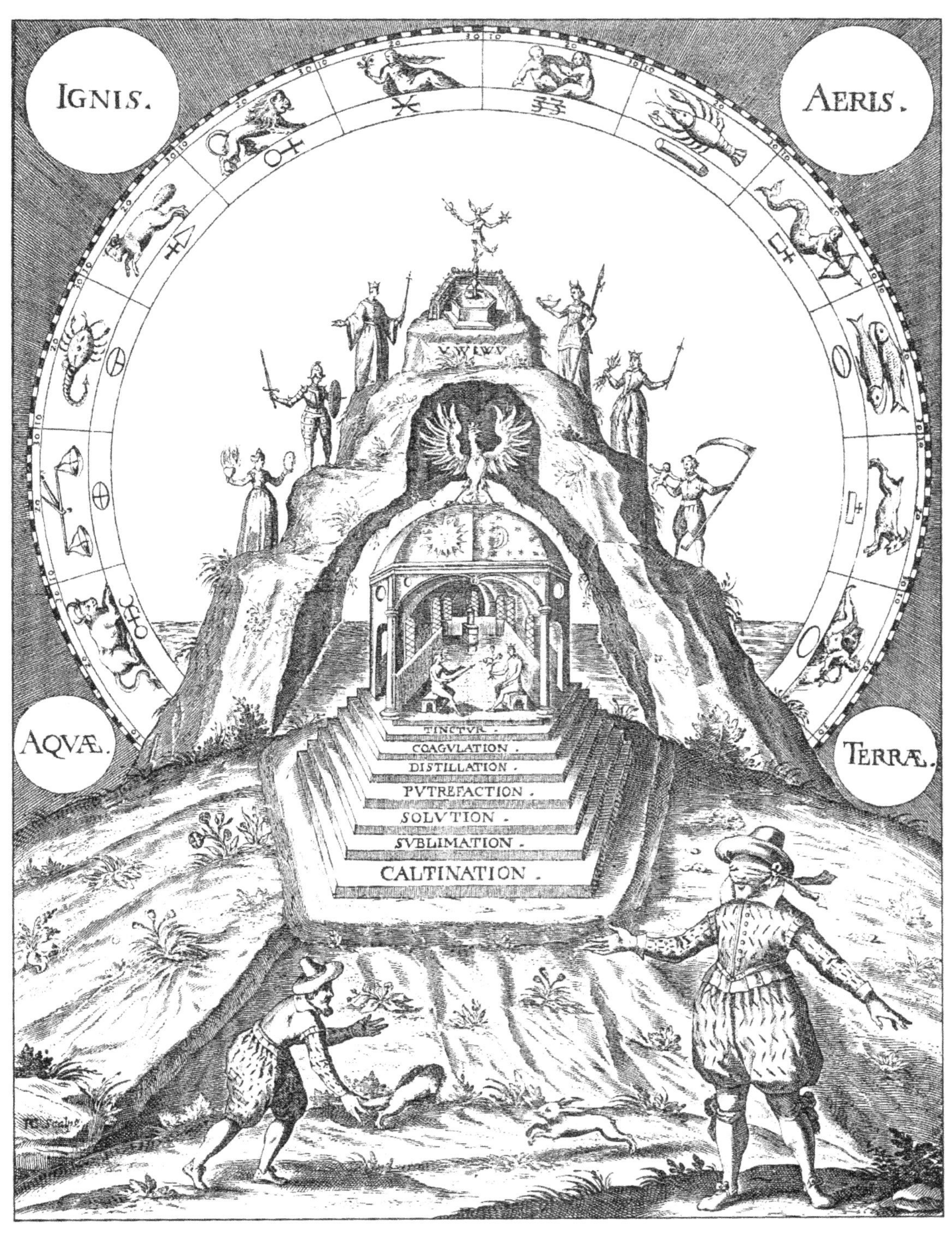

"The Cave of the Ancients," from Stefan Michel Spacher's *Cabala: Spiegel der Kunst und Natur in Alchymia* (1616). Here we see the alchemical mountain, with a blindfolded man initiate being led into a rabbit hole at the bottom.

These must be the same aromas associated in the Egyptian myth with the casket Seth made for Osiris, which his body took on also after being placed within it. In this section of the *Le Serpent Rouge* text, the narrator demonstrates his understanding that this goddess is represented by several other figures in various legends from throughout the world. He says:

Formerly some called her ISIS, queen of the beneficial spring, COME TO ME ALL OF YOU WHO SUFFER AND WHO ARE AFFLICTED, AND WILL COMFORT YOU. For others: MADGALENE, of the famous vase full of healing balm."

The line encouraging those who suffer to come for comfort is from *Matthew* 11:28-30. It can be taken, in this context, a couple of different ways. If it is a statement from Isis to the hero of the poem, or to the reader, she could be saying that people who are burdened should come down to where she is for comfort. Or perhaps, she is the one who is suffering, and is begging for a hero to come down to where she is to comfort her.

Isis' "healing vase" of magical and beautifully odorous fluids is what she used, in the Egyptian myth, to bring Osiris back to life. Aphrodite, likewise, carried a perfume vial full of "ambrosian oil" that was "divinely sweet" in its fragrance, according to Homer. In the story of Jesus, Mary Magdalene anointed Jesus with precious oils from a vase just before his arrest and crucifixion.

This latter act was described in the Bible as an act of embalming Christ, metaphorically, for burial. Of course, three days after descending into Hell, he rose from the dead. So the image of the vase is specifically about resurrection. In the case of Isis, the verses of *Le Serpent Rouge* describe her state of being (or non-being) in the Abyss of chaos as being like "mire." It reads:

DELIVER ME FROM THEMIRE, SO THAT I WILL NOT STAY HERE SINKING. Twice IS, embalmer and embalmed, miracle vase of the eternal White Lady of the Legends.

"Twice IS" is, obviously, another invocation of the name of Isis. "Embalmer and embalmed" refers to the fact that she once embalmed her husband's corpse, as part of the process of his resurrection, and now she too is an embalmed corpse in need of resurrection. The poem instructs the reader to discover the "64 dispersed stones" of the "perfect cube," and then specifically to stand before the "fourteen stones marked with a cross.' Remember, Osiris' body is described in the myths as having been divided by Set into fourteen pieces, which Isis then had to reassemble.

Later in the text, it says that these fourteen stones are at "the summit of the mountain." The cross is said to itself be the "fourteenth" stone. But recall that these are just part of the total of 64. To "reassemble the scattered stones," the narrator tells us to "work with the square and compass to put them back in regular order." To discover where these stones are, one needs to use a "certain eye" and "measured steps."

This "eye" is some probably sort of oracular or photoreceptive device that, metaphorically or otherwise, is omniscient. It might be something like the external eyeball that the three blind "Stygian Witches" of Greek mythology would use to see things in this world and beyond. Or it could be more akin to a crystal ball, or a scrying mirror, or like the magic reflecting pool on Mt. Olympus that the gods used to watch events on Earth. It is the "All-Seeing Eye," the capstone on the pyramid, and the watcher at the center of the Panopticon prison in Hell.

The fact that there are 64 stones forming the "perfect cube" described in the poem makes it clear that we talking in some way about a chessboard (or perhaps more specifically, as I suspect, an Ageio board). Later on the text says:

The stones of the mosaic pavement from the sacred place are alternately white or black, and JESUS, like ASMODEUS, observes their alignments.

The "Mosaic pavement" is the term Masons use to refer to the chequerboard pattern on the floor of their lodges. Because of this statement, we know that the authors of this poem are familiar with the church at Rennes-le-Château, which features statues of Jesus and Asmodeus at the entrance, with a chessboard marked out on the floor between them. They are saying that the black and white squares of chess are ultimately a puzzle to be put together. Doing this will recreate the "white stone" (the New Jerusalem, represented in the church by Jesus) and the "black stone" (the infernal cubic city, represented by Asmodeus). Perhaps it is a process of putting both stones together into one structure.

The reference to observing the "alignments" of the "stones" brings to mind the mystical novel *Mount Analogue*, by René Daumal, published posthumously (and unfinished) in 1959. This novel was the inspiration for the cinematic alchemical allegory from 1973, *The Holy Mountain* by Alejandro Jodorowky. In Daumal's novel, which is about ascending the secret mountain of the alchemists, it states that the summit can only be seen when the sun hits it at a certain angle. As the book says:

...Its summit must be inaccessible, but its base accessible to human beings as nature made them. It must be unique and it must exist geographically. The door to the invisible must be visible.

Likewise, in *Le Serpent Rouge*, after mentioning the observation of the "alignments" by Jesus and Asmodeus, the narrator complains, "My view seemed incapable of seeing the summit where the Sleeping Beauty lay hidden." But then later on, at high noon, he does indeed view the "summit of the mountain," including the fourteen stones and the cross there. Moreover, he specifically mentions an optical effect created by the sun. He says:

...The cross detached itself from the crest under the midday sun.

This undoubtedly connects with the parchments purportedly found by Bérenger Saunière at Rennes-le-Château. Remember, the second parchment says " ...By the cross and this horse of God I destroy this demon guardian at noon blue apples." Recall how Baphomet told us that "blue apples" meant "blood sacrifice," and that this was a message about doing a sacrificial Ageio ritual at noon.

Later on in *Le Serpent Rouge*, again the narrator tells us that the discovery of this tomb can only happen during the day:

Begun in darkness, my journey could only be completed in Light.

The allegorical journey of initiation that Freemasons go through is said to be one "from darkness to light." At noon, when the sun is at its zenith, is when the architect Hiram Abiff was purportedly killed in the Temple of Solomon, according to Masonic tradition. Consequently this is when many of their important rituals take place. This is also when the Merovingian King Dagobert II is reported to have been murdered in the forest on December 23. So perhaps we are talking about a portal opening ritual that involves blood sacrifice at noon, probably on that date. This was also the day that many people expected the world to end in 2012.

Saunière's parchments talk about a "horse of God." *Le Serpent Rouge* mentions "divine horsemen." Specifically:

Here I am, thus, on my knight's tour, on the circuit of the divine horsemen of the abyss.

As I mentioned earlier, a "knight's tour" is a math trick that involves using a knight's move to touch every square on the chessboard once, thus connecting them and, conceivably, "reassembling the scattered stones." In ceremonial magic, "Crossing the Abyss" is supposedly the final step in becoming a master magician. Some say it involves the death of the ego, and the rebirth of the magician into his "higher self." Usually he takes on a new ceremonial name which is given to him by his "higher self."

A more sinister interpretation might be that "Crossing the Abyss" involves making a Faustian pact with a demon, posing as your "higher self." You then "cross the Abyss" separating Earth and the underworld, where your soul (denigrated in this system as a mere "ego") helplessly resides from that point onward, while the demon goes on a joyride in your undead body for the rest of your physical life. You will probably not notice this is happening because you have been trained by your occult teachers to identify with the demon instead of yourself.

Perhaps, then, this is the meaning behind the terms "Horse of God," and "divine horsemen." The human is the horse, or, more specifically, their body is. It is the vehicle that possessing demons use to get to our world from their own, and to travel around in while they're here. It's like a suit that they use to interface with our world. When practitioners of Vodoun are possessed by their gods during their rituals, they call it being "ridden." This may explain the Knights Templar seal that involved two knights riding one horse. When the knights gave their souls to Baphomet, their bodies became possessed, thereby having two "riders."

In *A Synopsis of the Books of Adam and Eve*, Michael Stone writes about the Jewish pseudepigraphical *Primary Adam Books*:

Satan says to the serpent, according to the Greek, "be my vessel and I will speak through your mouth words to deceive them." The word 'vessel' seems to imply the idea of possession.... Satan is identical for all practical purposes with the serpent; Satan enters or possesses the serpent and speaks through its mouth; the serpent is Satan's instrument or tool.

Stone also mentions a rabbinical commentary called Pirkê de Rabbi Eliezer, and what he finds as:

...the theme of angelic jealousy of Adam and Adam's superiority to the angels in his ability to name the animals. The fall of the archangel Samael is described, together with his host. He found the serpent, and 'its likeness was like a sort of camel and he mounted it and rode it.' This relationship is likened to that of a horse and a rider.

We get similar information from *Zohar* I.35b:

R. Isaac said: 'This is the evil tempter.' R. Judah said that it means literally a serpent. They consulted R. Simeon, and he said to them: 'Both are correct. It was Samael, and he appeared on a serpent, for the ideal form of the serpent is the Satan. We have learnt that at that moment Samael came down from heaven riding on this serpent, and all creatures saw his form and fled before him.

Furthermore, Zohar II.152b-153 says that when Lilith and Samael join together, then they are called the "Rider on the Serpent," which, it says, is also Azazel.

Baphomet told us that the term "Horse of God" was a reference to Judas Iscariot, whom he said had died on the cross in Jesus' place. The canonized Gospels say that Judas became possessed by Satan right before he betrayed his Lord. They also say that Jesus handed him the piece of "sop" which seemed to act as a vector for Satan to come into him when he ate it.

The "divine horsemen of the Abyss" in *Le Serpent Rouge* are later in the poem specified to be "four horsemen," of whom one horse has left "four imprints on the stone." Clearly these are the "four horsemen of the Apocalypse," as mentioned in St. John's *Revelation*. The whole subject of this poem seems to me to be specifically apocalyptic. It is about liberating a fallen female entity from the Underworld. But this jail-break and tomb-robbery results, it seems, in the unleashing of is the "scarlet coloured beast" with seven heads and ten horns from John's *Revelation*. It says in the text:

I turn again towards the East. Facing me I see rings unrolling without end, the enormous SERPENT ROUGE cited in the parchments. Salty and bitter, the enormous unchained beast became, at the feet of this white mountain, red in color.

Recall the "Blanchefort tombstone" I discussed in an earlier chapter, which has long been seen as a clue to researchers of the Rennes-le-Château mystery. Remember that when we asked Baphomet "What is the hidden message in the Blanchefort tombstone?" His response was "FEAR OF GOD." At the bottom of the tombstone image you have written the Latin word "praecum," which means "herald." Underneath these words, there is a picture of an octopus. Baphomet said the meaning of this is "8 X 8." I asked if that was a reference to the Ageio board, and he said "YES."

An octopus is also described in *Le Serpent Rouge* before the poem talks about the "unleashing" of the "beast." It says:

...and the spiral in my mind becomes like a monstrous octopus expelling its ink. The tentacles absorb the light, I am dizzy....

The octopus on the Blanchefort tombstone, and the one mentioned in *Le Serpent Rouge*, are joined by a third clue. In the *Secret Dossiers* of Henri Lobineau, another set of documents published by the Priory of Sion, there is an article that talks about the Priory front group known as the "Hieron du Val d'Or." A large portion of the text is about the esoteric meaning of the color red. The author talks about it being the color of a royal, priestly race, mentioning that Jesus comes again wearing a red cloak in *Revelation*.

Octopus image from Henri Lobineau's *Secret Dossiers*

At the end of the article, there is a quote from an inscription on a tomb in France. Lobineau points out that the first letter of the first five words form the word "ICHTUS" (fish). At the bottom he signs the piece "Le Poulpe" (the Octopus), with an image of the creature beneath. The inscription reportedly says (when translated into English):

O divine race of the celestial fish, receive with a respectful heart in immortal life among the mortals the waters of the divine ones. Friend, remake your heart with the eternal flood of the wisdom which gives treasures. It is a reservoir of nourishment, soft like the honey of the Savior of the saints. Eat with hunger: you hold the fish in your hands.

The words "eternal flood of wisdom" brings to mind the interpretation of Baphomet's name as meaning "Baptism of Wisdom." In *Le Serpent Rouge*, a flood (likened to that of Noah) is described as being like a baptism. This makes since, as the flood waters of Noah's time were brought to wash away all of the impure elements from the Earth, allowing it to be reborn afresh, as the Christian is reborn free from sin at baptism. But a baptism in the wisdom of Baphomet has a different connotation. It means being immersed and reborn into the "knowledge of good and evil" that gave rise to sin in the first place.

It seems to me that the "celestial fish" here is the same as the octopus, and the red serpent of the poem. It is the Red Dragon, the Beast of the Apocalypse. It is Leviathan, the sea beast of the infernal Abyss. Her name can be found on the Baphomet sigil designed by Stanislas de Guaita, along with the names of

Lilith and Samael (all written in Hebrew). Rabbinical tradition tells us that she has a male consort, Behemoth, another infernal monster who resides on dry land.

The Book of Enoch says that Behemoth lives in "a waste wilderness named Duidain, on the east of the garden where the elect and righteous dwell." This sounds a lot like Cain's land of Nod, which is also east of Eden. It is also reminiscent of "Dudael" ("Cauldron of God"), the desert wilderness with burning-hot sands where the fallen angel Azazel was imprisoned, as mentioned in Chapter 10 of *The Book of Enoch*.

The rabbis say that God has separated the monsters because if they ever came together, the world would be annihilated. This is exactly what they also say about Lilith and Samael (and what the Greeks said about Gaia and Ouranos). Some sources specify that the danger occurs when the "procreate." By all appearances, Samael and Lilith are the same entities as Behemoth and Leviathan, respectively. Together they are what the Cabalists call the "Other God" and simply "the Beast." They are also sometimes both called "the Leviathans," or also, "the Taninim."

But these Jewish traditions go into even greater and more bizarre details that not only figure perfectly into our inquiry, but also specifically shed light upon the tomb inscription quoted by Henri Lobineau. For supposedly, at the End of Times, Behemoth and Leviathan will be slaughtered by God, salted, and served to the righteous at a great banquet. *Psalm* 74, 13-14 praises God thusly:

Thou brakest the heads of the dragons in the waters. Thou brakest the heads of leviathan in pieces, and gavest him to be meat to the people inhabiting the wilderness.

This final banquet will occur within a tent that God will fashion from Leviathan's "beautiful skin," as the prayer book known as *The Artscroll Siddur* tells it. This is why, during the holiday known as the "Feast of the Tabernacles," which takes place inside of a ritual tent, it is traditional to conclude with a prayer before the participants leave the tabernacle, in which they say:

May it be your will, Lord our God and God of our forefathers, that just as I have fulfilled and dwelt in this tabernacle, so may I merit in the coming year to dwell in the tabernacle of the skin of Leviathan next year in Jerusalem.

Rabbinical legends tell us that Leviathan is the same as the so-called "whale" that swallowed the prophet Jonah, in whose body he lived for a time before miraculously being spit up on dry land again. (This is another story about traveling through a portal to a new world, just like that of Noah, with whale being the "ark," in this case). So I suppose sitting under a tent made from the monster's skin is like being inside her too. Eating her flesh is an inversion ceremony, and a fitting revenge for what happened to Jonah.

There is a bit of confusion in the traditions about whether Leviathan has already been killed by God (to separate her from Behemoth), and already salted (to preserve her flesh until the end times), or whether the killing and salting will all take place at the end. The *Midrash* seems to say in several places that it already happened, but Talmudic traditions give it as an end times event. Again, we have the same confusion between the "Alpha" and the "Omega" that Baphomet displayed when he talked about the War in Heaven, the Garden of Eden and the Apocalypse as all happening at the same time.

Sometimes Leviathan is spoken of as though she is synonymous with the ocean itself, so then this may be Jewish folklore's explanation of why the seas are salty, and would place the salting of the monster back in the beginning. Recall that *Le Serpent Rouge* talks about the red serpent being "salty and bitter." But the serpent only "becomes red with anger" when it is "at the foot of the white mountain." In St. John's *Revelation*, the seas turn to blood.

In the article by Henry Lobineau that I discussed earlier, it is clear that the authors repeated mentioning of the color red, and its mystical meaning, has something to do with blood. The gravestone inscription that he quotes encourages the reader to drink "the waters of the divine ones" which give "immortal life among the mortals." Earlier in the article, Lobineau talked about the "wine" of Dionysian rituals. Now, Jesus said that the wine at the Last Supper was his blood. Therefore, it seems to me that this tomb inscription is quoted by the author because it is about drinking blood to obtain eternal life.

So let us reexamine what the Bible has to say about eating flesh, drinking blood, and the benefits, as well as the potential consequences, of each. In *Genesis* Chapter 1:29-30, God declares to the man he has created that he has given him "every herb bearing seed, which is upon the face of all the earth, and every tree, in the which is the fruit of a tree yielding seed; to you it shall be for meat." Likewise, he proclaims that to the animals he has "given every green herb for meat." There is no mention of anybody actually eating meat as meat - not even the animals!

Later, in Chapter 2: 8-9, it talks about the LORD God planting a garden "eastward in Eden," where he made "to grow very tree that is pleasant to the sight, and good for food; the tree of life also in the midst of the garden, and the tree of knowledge of good and evil." The tree of life is mentioned, but it is later in that chapter, in verses 16-17, that:

...The LORD God commanded the man, saying, Of every tree of the garden thou mayest freely eat: But of the tree of the knowledge of good and evil, thou shalt not eat of it: for in the day that thou eatest thereof thou shalt surely die.

Note that it is only the Tree of Knowledge that is prohibited. Since God told him that he could eat "of every tree" other than that one, presumably the Tree of Life was included as being available. So why then, in Chapter 3:22, after Adam and his wife have both eaten the contraband fruit, does God, speaking to persons unknown, declare his concern that they will eat of this other special tree as well:

And the LORD God said, Behold, the man is become as one of us, to know good and evil: and now, lest he put forth his hand, and take also of the tree of life, and eat, and live for ever.

The first mention in the Bible of humans eating meat comes from Chapter 9:2-4, right after Noah's family and the animals have exited the Ark. It is at this point that God proclaims to Noah the so-called "Noahide Code": seven laws which preceded and are in many ways similar to the Ten Commandments of Moses. One of these involves the declaration of a carnivorous food chain with mankind at the top. He says:

And the fear of you and the dread of you shall be upon every beast of the earth, and upon every fowl of the air, upon all that moveth upon the earth, and upon all the fishes of the sea; into your hand are they delivered.

Every moving thing that liveth shall be meat for you; even as the green herb have I given you all things. But flesh with the life thereof, which is the blood thereof, shall ye not eat.

But this event is preceded by something important. At the top of that mountain, the only visible land mass in a world covered by water, Noah sacrificed to God a burnt offering from among the animals on board his ark, the only non-aquatic creatures alive still on Earth. God was attracted to the scene, and moved with compassion, by the pleasant smell of the meat cooking on the fire. As the text says in Chapter 8:20-21:

Noah builded an altar unto the LORD; and took of every clean beast, and of every clean fowl, and offered burnt offerings on the altar. And the LORD smelled a sweet savour; and the LORD said in his heart, I will not again curse the ground any more for man's sake.

As far as I can tell, this is the first time that the Bible - mentions a burnt offering, or the cooking of flesh at all. It is not, however, the first sacrifice mentioned. The first and only other sacrifices described in *Genesis* before this one are those offered by Cain and Abel.

Cain was the first to sacrifice, and there is no mention of anybody telling him to do it. Rather, it was something that "came to pass" in "the process of time." Therefore it may have been a spontaneous act, based on some innate understanding of what God wanted from him. However, Cain, apparently not understanding fully, offered the fruit of his labor, the "the fruit of the ground," thinking that would be a fitting gift for the Lord who had given him life. But it wasn't. God wanted blood.

Was it because he had a deeper understanding of God, or was it mere coincidence, that Abel offered God what he really wanted, which was "the firstlings of his flock and of the fat thereof"? It seems that he may have been copying his brother by offering a sacrifice, and it just so happened that he had cattle to give instead of vegetation. Also, why were these people keeping cattle anyway, if nobody on Earth was eating meat until after the Flood, as Genesis seems to indicate?

Well, it seems that God, at least, was carnivorous. The basic understanding in the ancient world was that the gods were actually eating the sacrifices that were offered to them, and even when a portion of it was consumed by the priests (as was the common tradition), some of it was going to the gods as well. Particularly they were known to be attracted to blood. This was because, long before it was scientifically understood that blood carries oxygen to the heart, "blood" and "life" were considered synonymous to our ancestors. In the Old Testament, the same word, "nephesh," has been variously translated as "life," "soul," "breath," and "blood."

This is what God breathed into the clay man he had formed to bring him to life as Adam. When Cain killed Abel, in *Genesis* 4: 10-11, it was this same "nephesh" that went into the Earth, and "cried" unto God. As the text states:

And he said, What hast thou done? the voice of thy brother's blood crieth unto me from the ground. And now [art] thou cursed from the earth, which hath opened her mouth to receive thy brother's blood from thy hand....

Cain had just witnessed Abel killing freshly-born cattle and offering them to God. This was probably the first time anybody on Earth had killed anything that bled. Cain witnessed God "accepting" his brother's sacrifice. Afterwards, Cain murdered his brother. Was he trying to offer the blood of his brother as a sacrifice to God, or perhaps, to some other entity? After all, it was the "Earth" (known to the Greeks as the goddess Gaia) that "opened her mouth to receive" Abel's blood. Or was he intending to eat the flesh and drink the blood, just as he had seen God taking the blood and flesh of cattle? Did he think that doing so would make him immortal like God?

In the Hebrew tradition, the priests were allowed to eat the flesh of sacrifices, but the blood was to be poured upon the altar, and the fat was to be burned to make a "sweet savour" that the "LORD" enjoyed. Humans were specifically prohibited from consuming blood because "the blood is the life." *Leviticus* 17: 6-14 lays it all out:

And the priest shall sprinkle the blood upon the altar of the LORD at the door of the tabernacle of the congregation, and burn the fat for a sweet savour unto the LORD ...And whatsoever man there be of the house of Israel, or of the strangers that sojourn among you, that eateth any manner of blood; I will even set my face against that soul that eateth blood, and will cut him off from among his people....

For the life of the flesh is in the blood: and I have given it to you upon the altar to make an atonement for your souls: for it is the blood that maketh an atonement for the soul. Therefore I said unto the children of Israel, No soul of you shall eat blood, neither shall any stranger that sojourneth among you eat blood.

And whatsoever man there be of the children of Israel, or of the strangers that sojourn among you, which hunteth and catcheth any beast or fowl that may be eaten; he shall even pour out the blood thereof, and cover it with dust.

For it is the life of all flesh; the blood of it is for the life thereof' therefore I said unto the children of Israel, Ye shall eat the blood of no manner of flesh: for the life of all flesh is the blood thereof: whosoever eateth it shall be cut off.

So blood is literally "soul food," containing the very life essence of which the living soul consists, only to be had by God. Therefore its purpose (perhaps, it seems, the very reason why animals exist on Earth) is to make "atonement" for the human soul. In other words, animals that bleed exist so that their lives can be offered to God, in exchange for the souls (that is, the blood) of man that God would otherwise be hungry for.

Just as a ram was offered instead of Isaac, lambs took the place of the firstborn sons of Israel on the Passover, and Jesus then finally came and paid the price for all, God wants his blood sacrifice, one way or another. Critics of Judeo-Christianity often complain that their God is "bloodthirsty." Usually when people say this, they are referring to all of the wars that he instigated and encouraged, but it is quite literally true. However, all gods of the ancient world were viewed as being this way.

Years ago, when Cain was explaining to us what led to the "Wrath of Cain," the fall of the "Dohir Kings," and the Deluge, he said "I WANTED YOUTH." It didn't make sense to me at the time, but it does now. In a recent discussion I had with Cain on the Ouija board, he repeatedly talked about "GUM," which he seemed to be describing as a sort of life force derived from freshly harvested blood.

Cain indicated that he fed on this "gum" to maintain his semblance of life. He said that God sends "BIRDS" down to feed him this stuff. Remember what Plutarch wrote of Saturn sleeping on his island: "...Birds fly down from the rock, which are ordained [by Jupiter] to carry ambrosia to him," just as doves carry ambrosia to the Olympian gods. "Gum," by the way, is a word that is traced back to Sumer, where, according to Stephen Bertman's *Handbook to Life in Ancient Mesopotamia*, it was called "shim-gam-gam-ma."

Now compare Cain's story about himself, and Plutarch's story about how Saturn is nourished, with how Wolfram von Eschenbach's says that the "Grail stone" of the hidden "Grail kingdom" received its nourishment, which it then had the ability to transmute into any kind of food that anyone in the kingdom desired, in abundant supply. Remember what is says in *Parzival*: that every year on Good Friday (the day Jesus' blood was shed on the cross and fell onto the ground), a dove would come down from Heaven and places a small white wafer on the Grail stone, from which it got its power to produce food and other miracles in abundance out of nothing, including flesh.

The food from the stone is what gives everyone in the kingdom their perpetual youth (albeit with gray hair), and keeps the Fisher King alive despite continuously suffering from a grievous wound that acts up whenever Saturn is ascendant in the heavens. I assume that what is being implied here is that the blood of Christ is what feeds Saturn, the Stone, the King of underworld, and allows him to nourish the others who are there with him.

Of course, this is what Jesus repeatedly offered to those who would follow him: the fruit of the "tree of life," the "bread of heaven," and the "living waters" to drink. At the beginning of *The Gospel of John*, Chapter 4, while visiting Jacob's well, which is said to be in Sychar, "near to the parcel of ground that Jacob gave to his son Joseph," Jesus has an encounter with a Samaritan woman. He asks her to draw some water for him, and she expresses surprise that he is talking to her. Then he tells her:

If thou knewest the gift of God, and who it is that saith to thee, Give me to drink; thou wouldest have asked of him, and he would have given thee living water... Whosoever drinketh of this water shall thirst again: But whosoever drinketh of the water that I shall give him shall never thirst; but the water that I shall give him shall be in him a well of water springing up into everlasting life.

"Jacob's well" is, of course, near the Cave of Treasures, where, according to the book of the same name, the Ark is, along with Adam's body, and an entrance to Eden. When we spoke to Jesus on the Ouija board, he said that

Dohir was known as "the fallen land" because that is both where the "ARK RESIDES" and where the "ARK DESCENDS." While I still don't entirely understand it, I do realize now that he was talking about the New Jerusalem as the "Ark" coming down from Heaven.

At that point, the Ark will subsume everything God wants to keep into itself, and everything outside of it will be eliminated. This is what Jesus meant when he called it "ONE BOX OF THINGS." Remember he also said that the Dohir Kings hid the Ark near a WELL. Baphomet even told us that Brian and I were going to inherit an "ARC" and a "WELL" with "WATER" at the bottom of it.

Continuing from *John* Chapter 4, in verses 31-36, when his disciples return from buying meat, Jesus tells them that he has access to special meat:

...His disciples prayed him, saying, Master, eat. But he said unto them, I have meat to eat that ye know not of ... My meat is to do the will of him that sent me, and to finish his work. Say not ye, There are yet four months, and then cometh harvest? behold, I say unto you, Lift up your eyes, and look on the fields; for they are white already to harvest. And he that reapeth receiveth wages, and gathereth fruit unto life eternal....

In *John* Chapter 6, right after the miracle of the loaves and fishes, Jesus again returns to the theme, preaching:

Labour not for the meat which perisheth, but for that meat which endureth unto everlasting life, which the Son of man shall give unto you: for him hath God the Father sealed.

In verses 31-35, as the gospel continues, Jesus proclaims that he himself is the "bread from heaven," "the bread of God," and "the bread of life." He also says that this bread "came down from Heaven," like the Grail stone is said to have. He preaches:

Our fathers did eat manna in the desert; as it is written, He gave them bread from heaven to eat ... Verily, verily, I say unto you, Moses gave you not that bread from heaven; but my Father giveth you the true bread from heaven. For the bread of God is he which cometh down from heaven, and giveth life unto the world.... I am the bread of life: he that cometh to me shall never hunger; and he that believeth on me shall never thirst.

Then later still in that chapter, Jesus again identifies himself as this bread that "came down from heaven," and uses the word "living bread." He also reveals that the bread is specifically his flesh. He tells his disciples to actually eat his flesh, and also to drink his blood. In verses 48-58 he states:

I am that bread of life. Your fathers did eat manna in the wilderness, and are dead. This is the bread which cometh down from heaven, that a man may eat thereof, and not die.

I am the living bread which came down from heaven: if any man eat of this bread, he shall live for ever: and the bread that I will give is my flesh, which I will give for the life of the world.

... Except ye eat the flesh of the Son of man, and drink his blood, ye have no life in you. Whoso eateth my flesh, and drinketh my blood, hath eternal life; and I will raise him up at the last day. For my flesh is meat indeed, and my blood is drink indeed.

He that eateth my flesh, and drinketh my blood, dwelleth in me, and I in him. As the living Father hath sent me, and I live by the Father: so he that eateth me, even he shall live by me.

This is that bread which came down from heaven: not as your fathers did eat manna, and are dead: he that eateth of this bread shall live for ever.

Of course, as we all know, at the Last Supper, Jesus told them again to eat his flesh and drink his blood, in a ritual that is the basis for the primary rite of Christendom: the Eucharist. As *The Gospel of Matthew* describes it in Chapter 26: 26-29:

And as they were eating, Jesus took bread, and blessed it, and brake it, and gave it to the disciples, and said, Take, eat; this is my body.

And he took the cup, and gave thanks, and gave it to them, saying, Drink ye all of it; For this is my blood of the new testament, which is shed for many for the remission of sins. But I say unto you, I will not drink henceforth of this fruit of the vine, until that day when I drink it new with you in my Father's kingdom.

This is why the symbol of the Pelican plucking at its own breast to feed its young is often used in Christian churches to represent the sacrifice of Jesus, and the miracle of the Eucharist. This symbol shows up quite frequently in cryptic alchemical treatises as well. Since we know that "blood" and "life" are synonymous in the Old Testament and since Jesus repeatedly instructed his followers to drink his blood, should we imagine this "living water" of which Jesus spoke as being blood? He did at one point describe the fluid as coming out of a person's stomach. In *John* 7:38 he is quoted as saying:

He that believeth on me, as the scripture hath said, out of his belly shall flow rivers of living water.

The rivers of Paradise, from Herrad von Landsberg's *Hortus Deliciarum* (*Garden of Delights*)

Woodcut from *Boek van den Leven ons Heeren by Gerard* Leeu, 1487, showing Adam, Eve, the two sacred trees, and the four paradisal rivers

**Above: Enki on the throne, with the waters of life and the plant of immortality.
Below: Enki in the Absu chamber.**

Above: Enki, with the Tigris and Euphrates rivers springing from his back. Below: The Philosophic Seal of the Society of the Rosicrucians, showing the "aurum potabile" (drinkable gold) of the alchemists coming from the veins of Hermes.

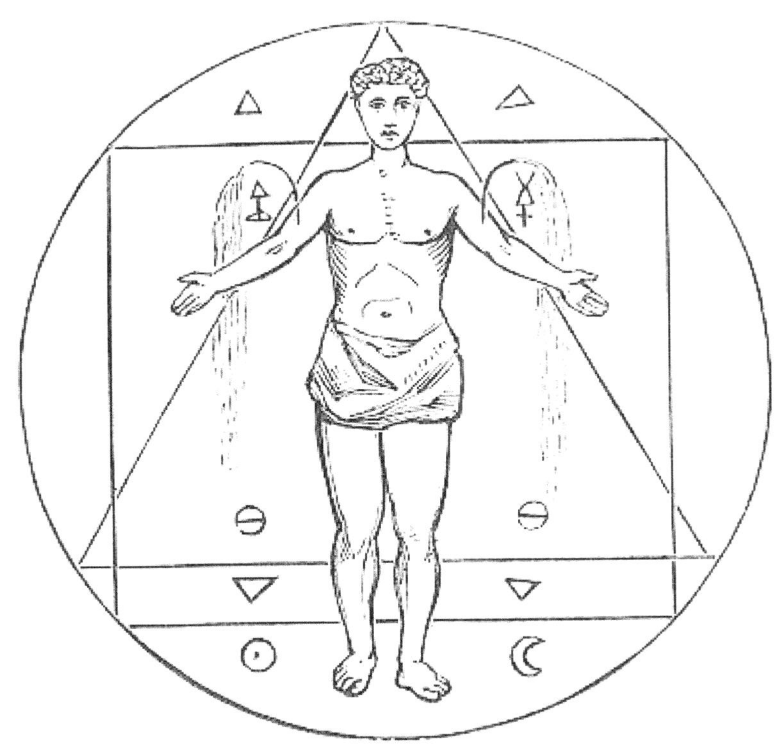

The four rivers of the New Jerusalem pour forth from the Agnus Dei, surrounded by the four cherubim, from Brevary No. 128, fol. 10, Zwiefalten Abbey, Germany

Agnus Dei pouring blood into a Grail chalice, from a chapel in El Cajon, California. Photo by Rebecca Kennison, 1985. The center of the cross is rose-colored.

Regardless, all of these special life-giving foods and beverages will be served to the righteous at the End of Times, just like the Jews say Leviathan will be. In St. John's vision of Christ, as recorded in *Revelation* 21:6, Jesus said to him:

It is done. I am Alpha and Omega, the beginning and the end. I will give unto him that is athirst of the fountain of the water of life freely.

Furthermore, *Revelation* describes the special water flowing as a river through the New Jerusalem, which actually issues forth from beneath the throne of God. Verse 21:1 states:

And he shewed me a pure river of water of life, clear as crystal, proceeding out of the throne of God and of the Lamb.

There are illustrations of this river coming from God's throne. They greatly resemble the Sumerian God Enki in his "Absu," which was his house within the Abyss (and where etymologists think the word "abyss" ultimately comes from). The Absu was depicted as a square chamber with waves of water all around. There are also depictions of Enki with the waters of the Abyss issuing from a square chamber filled with water pots upon which he sits as though it is his throne. In the pictures, this water is offered to others, with a plant, believed by Sumeriologists to be the "plant of immortality," springing up from it.

What is being illustrated here pertains to the Mesopotamian versions of the Flood myth. It was Enki who told the hero that the Flood was coming. He contravened his oath to the other gods (particularly Enlil, the storm god) in order to do this. He gave the hero specific instructions on how to build an ark to save himself and his family. Interestingly, the ark he built was a perfect cube, about the size of an ocean liner. It was made starting with the hero's own house, which was used as the basis for the vessel. Enki spoke to him through the walls of his house, which means that he spoke to him telepathically.

Then afterwards, the gods blessed the hero and his wife just like Enoch was blessed in the Judeo-Christian tradition. They were translated to the realm of the gods, given a residence at "the mouth of the rivers," and turned into gods themselves, because they were permitted to eat from the secret plant of immortality. This is why, in one version of the story (found in *The Epic of Gilgamesh*), the Flood hero is called Utnapishtim, which means "he found life." He is also given the epithet "faraway." In another version, the ark pilot's original name was "Atrahasis" ("extremely wise,") but after becoming immortal he was renamed "Ziusudra" ("found long life" or "life of long days").

Again, in one of our early séances, when I asked Cain to describe the situation surrounding the Deluge, he said:

FALL OF ATLANTIS. I WANTED YOUTH. TRIED TO SAVE EVE. LIVE WATER.

Was he saying that he tried to rescue his mother, and himself, from mortality, utilizing the same "living waters" of which Jesus later preached? Was he saying that this was somehow tied in to the events of the Flood, just as the Mesopotamian Deluge stories are all about the "plant of immortality"? Is this the same as the Tree of Life that grew "in the midst" of the Garden of Eden"? Is it the one that was also spoken of by Jesus in *Revelation* 2:17?

To him that overcometh will I give to eat of the tree of life, which is in the midst of the paradise of God.

In the Mesopotamian myths, the Flood hero is rewarded for enduring the hardship of watching the death of the world around him by being granted eternal life. The same reward, it is being said, will come to those who make it faithfully through the tribulations of the End Times. *Matthew* 24: 37 reports that Jesus said:

But as the days of Noe were, so shall also the coming of the Son of man be.

But in the Biblical flood tale, instead of granting immortality to anybody, God does the opposite. Right before the story of the Deluge, as God is announcing his plans to bring the catastrophe, he also declares that he is going to shorten the lifespan of man, which had heretofore averaged several hundred years per person. In *Genesis* 6:3 he states:

My spirit shall not always strive with man, for that he also is flesh: yet his days shall be an hundred and twenty years.

Thereafter the lives of the people recorded in the Bible from that time forward are similar to those of modern people. However, it is interesting to note that Noah's grandfather, Enoch, *was* granted immortality in a manner very similar to that of the Sumerian Flood hero. Also, *The Book of Enoch* tells us that it was Enoch who was first warned about the coming of the Deluge.

Therefore, we should take seriously L.A. Waddell's claim that Enoch and Noah were probably the same person. Waddell believed that it was Enoch (whom he views as Cain's son, with the son of Seth being a fabrication) who built and navigated the Ark. This would also make Enoch the first to sacrifice burnt offerings upon an altar.

In the Mesopotamian stories, when the waters began to subside, just like Noah, the hero found his vessel resting upon a high mountaintop. He went forth from the ark and immediately sacrificed a burnt offering to the gods, just like Noah. Then, as in the Bible story, the gods were attracted to the "sweet savor" of the meat cooking, and gathered around "like flies."

Strangely, the gods are described as starving during the flood (which in these versions only lasts a week instead of forty days). They had retreated up into the heavens during the destruction because they themselves were frightened by it. For us in modern times, it is probably hard to imagine gods needing to eat, much less being so careless as to fail to pack away emergency supplies for a cataclysm that they themselves had brought about. But perhaps that is because we don't understand the cosmic food chain.

God actually was witnessed consuming the sacrifices made to him, according to the Old Testament. He licked them up with a tongue of flames. As it says in *Leviticus* 9:24:

And there came a fire out from before the LORD, and consumed upon the altar the burnt offering and the fat: which when all the people saw, they shouted, and fell on their faces.

Also, in *I Kings* 18:38, we read:

Then the fire of the LORD fell, and consumed the burnt sacrifice, and the wood, and the stones, and the dust, and licked up the water that was in the trench.

Then, in *II Chronicles* 7:1, it says:

Now when Solomon had made an end of praying, the fire came down from heaven, and consumed the burnt offering and the sacrifices; and the glory of the LORD filled the house.

Finally, in *Hebrews* 12:29, it is put simply:

For our God is a consuming fire.

According to the online "Bible Dictionary," the word translated as "altar" in the Old Testament is "mizbe'ah," which it says is "from a word meaning 'to slay.'" This Hebrew word referred to "any structure of earth or unwrought stone on which sacrifices were offered." Dictionary.com says that the English word "altar" is "of disputed origin and formation, but probably akin to Latin "adolēre," to ritually burn." Clearly, the concept has at its root the idea of killing to offer food to gods, and most likely of cooking the meat as well.

In his *Book 4*, ceremonial magician Aleister Crowley wrote that the "altar is connected with the Ark of the Covenant, Noah's Ark, the nave ('navis,' a ship) ...." He also described the ideal shape of an altar for a magician to use (something he picked up from the Hermetic Order of the Golden Dawn). He wrote:

The Altar is a double cube, which is a rough way of symbolizing the Great Work; for the doubling of the cube, like the squaring of the circle, was one of the great problems of antiquity. The surface of this Altar is composed of ten squares. The top is Kether, and the bottom Malkuth. The height of the Altar is equal to the height above the ground of the navel of the Magician.

What Aleister Crowley said to do put is to one cubic box upon another, and then place the ritual elements on the surface of the one on top. Now on the diagram of the Tree of Life used in the Jewish mystic system known of the Cabala, the geometry of the paths between the spheres of existence forms two stacked cubes. Masonic writer Albert Mackey, in his book *Masonry Defined*, wrote that the architecture of Masonic lodges is based on the double-cube:

...The square form was esteemed by our ancient operative brethren as one of the Greater Lights, and a component part of the furniture of the Lodge. The double cube is an expressive emblem of the united powers of darkness and light in the creation.

In the study of geometry, "doubling the cube" (making a cube exactly twice the size of another cube) was long considered one of those unsolvable problems, and it still cannot be done with a square and compass. Plutarch wrote that this problem came to the attention of the Greeks when the oracle at Delphi told the people of Delos that they would not receive answers to their prayers until they doubled the size of their altar to the god Apollo, which was a cube.

So when *Le Serpent Rouge* instructs us to "reassemble to the scattered stones" using a "square and compass," they are saying that it requires Masonic magic to achieve. I also think that they are talking about two cubes - a white stone and a black stone - representing the New Jerusalem, and Cain's infernal city of Enoch.

In *Revelation* 2:17, Jesus describes the New Jerusalem as a stone. He also describes it as being edible. He proclaims:

To him that overcometh will I give to eat of the hidden manna, and will give him a white stone, and in the stone a new name written, which no man knoweth saving he that receiveth it.

This is a reference to the "manna" that the Israelites ate, fed to them by Metatron (Enoch), who appeared to them alternately as pillars of fire and cloud. This is what they were fed during the forty years that they wandered in what, as I theorized before, may have been the land of Nod, which they probably teleported to when the "Red Sea" opened up a gateway for them. The mysterious, flaky white substance rained down on them from above every morning, and they had to catch it as it fell or gather it into baskets from the ground before it melted in the "sun."

A pot of this stuff was kept for years, miraculously, and placed in front of the Ark of the Covenant, or inside of it (according to varying traditions) in the temple in Jerusalem. This is probably connected to the mysterious "shew bred" that was always presented to the "Presence" of God in the inner chamber of the temple, which only the priests were allowed to eat.

The Hebrew word for this literally meant "Bread of the Presence." Recall that in the "Real Presence" of Jesus is what is said to incarnate within the communion wafer in the making of the Eucharist. After it is made, it is kept inside of a container called a "tabernacle" (meaning "dwelling place") which is flanked by two cherubim in the style of the Ark of the Covenant. During their wandering in the wilderness, the Israelites kept the Ark, which housed the Presence, inside of a "tabernacle" whenever they were camped.

In *Revelation,* Jesus says that eating the "hidden manna" causes rebirth, and thus the receipt of a "new name" on a "white stone." The stone and the manna are implied to be the same. Now what could this all be about?

In the story of Zeus, his mother protected him from being eaten by his father Chronos, like his eleven brothers before him, by substituting a stone for his body, which Chronos ate instead. In *I Peter* 2:5, the Apostle tells Christians:

Ye also, as lively stones, are built up a spiritual house, an holy priesthood, to offer up spiritual sacrifices, acceptable to God by Jesus Christ.

Remember what it said in *Leviticus* 17:11:

For the life of the flesh is in the blood: and I have given it to you upon the altar to make an atonement for your souls....

Crowley suggested people store their supplies inside of their altars. But in the New Jerusalem, according to St. John, there is an altar full of souls, and they cry out for the vengeance of their blood. *Revelation* 6:9-10 tells us:

And when he had opened the fifth seal, I saw under the altar the souls of them that were slain for the word of God, and for the testimony which they held: And they cried with a loud voice, saying, How long, O Lord, holy and true, dost thou not judge and avenge our blood on them that dwell on the earth?

We know that the words for "soul" and "blood" were the same: "nephesh." It seems that in modern Western occultism, this life force within the blood is viewed as a form of light. Aleister Crowley's OTO, in certain private communion rituals, distributes tiny cookies called "Cakes of Light" that include, as their "active ingredient," menstrual blood. Eliphas Levi wrote in his book *Magic: A History of Its Rites, Rituals, and Mysteries*, about what he called the "Astral Light," defined as:

...a natural and divine agent, at once corporeal and spiritual, an universal plastic mediator, a common receptacle for vibrations of movement and images of form, a fluid and a force which may be called, in a sense at least, the imagination of nature.

It was this agent which he said reflects the magician's will, expressed during a ritual, and actualizes it into existence. He illustrated this concept with the hieroglyphic form of the Baphomet. More details on the subject can be found in the introduction written by David Godwin for the book *The Golden Dawn: As Revealed by Israel Regardie*:

The key theme in both the Neophyte Grade and the ritual of Adeptus Minor is that of being brought <u>to the Light</u>.... But a true 'secret' of the entire system is that this Light is not a metaphysical or philosophically speculative construct meaning grace, spirituality or healing (although the Light does bring all of these) but <u>is an ACTUAL FORCE which although independent of egoic man can be generated by men through the use of his consciousness to bring about CHANGE AT WILL!</u>

So then, let us again consider the concepts of the "bread of life" and the "water of life" that Jesus spoke about, and which the hero of the Mesopotamian flood epic was questing for. In the Garden of Eden, where life purportedly began, there were four rivers flowing through it, all issuing from a common source, In *Genesis* 2:10-14 we read:

And a river went out of Eden to water the garden; and from thence it was parted, and became into four heads. The name of the first is Pison: that is it which compasseth the whole land of Havilah, where there is gold; And the gold of that land is good: there is bdellium and the onyx stone. And the name of the second river is Gihon: the same is it that compasseth the whole land of Ethiopia. And the name of the third river is Hiddekel: that is it which goeth toward the east of Assyria. And the fourth river is Euphrates.

Hiddekel is generally taken to be the Tigris River in Iraq, where the Euphrates flows as well. The Gihon and Pison have been identified with various rivers on Earth by different scholars throughout history. There isn't much consensus as far as I can tell, although the Nile and the Ganges have been frequently suggested. But what is important here is the idea that Eden is the source of the rivers on Earth.

But how could Eden be the "source" and below ground? Wouldn't that put it in the same region as "Hell"? Remember, Cain described Eden as having "fallen," as part of the same series of events that included Adam and Eve being expelled, his expulsion to the land of Nod, the war between him and his brother, and finally the "Wrath Of Cain" that sent large portions of both Eden and Nod beneath the waves.

Also remember how *The Book of the Cave of Treasures* portrays things, in which there is a holy mountain that contains Eden within its center, as well as the Cave and Well of Jacob, with the children of Seth living close to the top, and the realm of the Cainites at the bottom of it. It could very well be that when Adam and Eve were expelled, Eden became occulted within the mountain, and thus is "fallen."

In this sense it is very similar to Enki's Absu, where the Sumerian god lived and commanded the waters. The Absu was thought to be the source of all bodies of water. Thus all of these could be considered portals to the Absu, including man-made water features, such as the baptismal Absu pools that were placed at the front of temples to Enki.

Inside the Absu, Enki is shown seated on a cubic throne that has what looks like a tic-tac-toe board depicted on the side of it. Alternatively, within the seat, we see pots of water around, with water flowing out of them into other pots on the outside of the throne. Water is flowing out of those pots as well, and mingling with the others to form a continuous stream that encircles the god. This culminates in the budding of the "plant of immortality" that flowers out of a pot held in his hands, which he proffers forth to worshipers in from of him that are offering him sacrifice.

Furthermore, Enki was always shown with two streams of water seemingly issuing from his back, which, anthropologists say, are the Tigris and Euphrates rivers (the latter being one of the rivers of Eden. In Christian scripture, these paradisal rivers also appear in the New Jerusalem at the End Times, where they are again associated with the Tree of Life. In *Revelation* 22: 2, after describing the "pure river of water of life" flowing from "the throne of God and of the Lamb," St. John says:

In the midst of the street of it, and on either side of the river, was there the tree of life, which bare twelve manner of fruits, and yielded her fruit every month....

In Christian iconography, it is not uncommon to show the four rivers with the Tree of Life, both in depictions of the Garden of Eden, and in the New Jerusalem. Another emblem also frequently included in this scene, is an altar with a lamb on top (the "Agnus Dei," or "Lamb of God," representing Christ).

The lamb is usually wounded in the jugular vein and pouring forth blood into a chalice.

It is implied that the blood is the source of the four rivers, which both issue from, and also feed, the Tree of Life. Sometimes a fountain is also included in the picture, demonstrating the idea that the water is available to drink. These are the "living waters" that Jesus invited his followers to imbibe. They consist of his blood, spilled in sacrifice, as any Christian theologian will tell you. Thomas Jefferson said that the "Tree of Liberty" must be "watered" with the "blood of patriots," and similarly, the divine tree of immortality must be watered with the blood of holy sacrifice.

Interestingly, there are also rivers in the underworld. The Greeks said there were five main ones: Styx, Lethe, Acheron, Phlegethon, and Cocytus. Acheron is the one that separates the land of the dead from the land of the living. It is the one that a person must cross when they die, with the help of a ferryman, who must be paid a coin for his troubles.

The Greeks believed that Elysium, the paradise land for the righteous deceased, was essentially a chamber within the otherwise totally unpleasant underworld. Similarly, the way the Old Testament portrays it, everybody went to the underworld (which they called "Sheol"), with no exceptions. There, everyone would await the Final Judgment and the coming of the Messiah.

Everything there was torment. However, there was a bubble of safety called the "Bosom of Abraham," in which the righteous were separated out so that they could enjoy the wait in comfort, while everyone else burned in Hell. There was a river that acted as a "chasm" of separation, keeping those in the Bosom of Abraham safe from the Hell that surrounded them. Jesus preached about it in *Luke* 16:22-27, comparing the afterlife fates of a bad rich man and a good poor man:

Now the poor man died and was carried away by the angels to Abraham's bosom; and the rich man also died and was buried. In Hades he lifted up his eyes, being in torment, and saw Abraham far away and Lazarus in his bosom. And he cried out and said, 'Father Abraham, have mercy on me, and send Lazarus so that he may dip the tip of his finger in water and cool off my tongue, for I am in agony in this flame.' But Abraham said... 'between us and you there is a great chasm fixed, so that those who wish to come over from here to you will not be able, and that none may cross over from there to us.'

If you consider that perhaps the Bosom of Abraham and Paradise are the same thing, and the river surrounding it is Acheron, then that means that the underworld has four rivers, and within that realm, is Paradise, or Eden with its own four rivers. There is also a common river between them that is actually a void space separating the two.

There is another way to think of it. Recall that the Sumerian god Enki was depicted with the Tigris and Euphrates rivers coming from his back as he sat on his throne in the Absu, or Abyss. The name of Enki's underground house, the "Absu," literally meant "the waters of knowledge." Therefore, perhaps two of the rivers of Eden actually come from the Abyss below, and the Tree of Knowledge was watered by these. (These could also be the waters of the "Baptism of Wisdom" of Baphomet.)

Herein we find a possible connection with the game of Ageio, as well as the story Cain told us about the Flood and "FALL OF ATLANTIS" which lies behind it. Enki seems roughly equivalent to Poseidon, the father of the Atlantean kings. Poseidon was said in reside in a place called "Aegae," in a grand temple built upon a hill there. One of the epithets he was known by was "Poseidon Aegaeus." He was also called "mover of the Earth and the barren sea," as he was considered to be responsible for earthquakes, tsunamis, and sea storms. The location of Aegae has been traced to an ancient settlement near modern Aigeira in western Greece.

In the Sumerian, Akkadian, and Babylonian myths, Enki is one of the gods who was involved in the creation of mankind. As the story goes, the gods decided that it was too much work to keep "creation" going, so they made humans as a slave race to do the work for them. The tablets are in bad condition, and the translations have always been sketchy, but in the Babylonian *Enuma Elish,* it appears that they created mankind to manufacture something for their consumption, which is frequently interpreted as being "bread."

Ancient astronaut theorists bandy about the idea, proposed in the books of Zecharia Sitchin, that the Sumerian gods were aliens from another planet, and they made humans to mine gold for them in Africa, which they needed, supposedly, for their far-off civilization. But that's not what the texts say. They say that the gods created us to "keep the cosmos working," and to make for them something that they needed.

If it was "gold," it probably wasn't common gold. However, it may have been more akin to the gold of the alchemists, which is made with the Philosopher's Stone. The images of Enki sitting on a box containing a network of water pots all flowing into one another greatly resembles the images of athanors and other glass vessels connected via tubes in the laboratories of alchemists.

Maybe that is actually what it is depicting. Enki was the god of wisdom and magic, and he is credited with creating several species of animals, in addition to humans, in what sounds like a laboratory. Hybrid species abound in these stories, as the gods themselves were frequently depicted with the body parts of fish, goats, bulls and other animals. These are the types of creatures that show up in every alchemical treatise from the Middle Ages and Renaissance. The adept can reportedly create things like this through the hidden science of transmuting matter and extracting souls from bodies.

Enki's alchemy lab in the Absu was sometimes called the "House of Life." To the Akkadians and Babylonians he was known as "Ea." This is from the same Semitic root word that *Eve* of *Genesis* gets her name: "hyy," meaning "life." Enki's wife, Ninhursag, was nicknamed "Ninti," which means "Lady Rib." This may be connected to the story of Eve being created from Adam's rib bone, because Ninhursag was also called "the mother of all living." These are the exact words we find in *Genesis* 3:20:

And Adam called his wife's name Eve; because she was the mother of all living.

She is given this name immediately after their expulsion from the garden and immediately after they are cursed to forevermore to eat "in sorrow," and "in the sweat of thy face." Recall that Adam and Eve were created and placed inside of the Garden "to dress it and to keep it," and "to till the ground." The word "husband" means "tiller of the soil," and Adam was the first, with his wife as his "helpmeet."

Cain followed in Adam's footsteps as a "tiller of the ground." But Adam's husbandry must have been different from Cain's, for before Cain was conceived they were cast from the garden, and told "cursed is the ground for thy sake; in sorrow shalt thou eat of it all the days of thy life; Thorns also and thistles shall it bring forth to thee; and thou shalt eat the herb of the field...." So perhaps, what was going on in the Garden of Eden was gardening of another sort: what the alchemists called "celestial agriculture."

Note that in myth and legend, eating certain foods can cause you to translate from one dimension to another, just like in Lewis Carroll's adventures of Alice. If you have traveled through a portal to another world, eating the food there can cause you to get stuck there. Adam and Eve were thrown out of the Garden upon eating the fruit of the Tree of Knowledge. Thus began "all living," and also "death," for God had told the man and woman that upon eating that fruit they would "surely die."

Adam was then barred from the Tree of Life, "lest he put forth his hand, and take also of the tree of life, and eat, and live for ever," Likewise, we know that Persephone became condemned to stay in the underworld when, in her hunger, she devoured six pomegranate seeds while there. As I mentioned,

Baphomet told me that Brian was cursed with LETHARGY because he owed "6 SEEDS" to the demon.

One can only wonder what manner of existence was happening in the Garden of Eden before they ate the forbidden fruit that caused "life" and "death" to begin. Adam and Eve were told to "freely eat" from "every tree in the garden," (*Genesis* 2:16.) Before that, remember, in *Genesis* 1: God told them:

I have given you every herb bearing seed, which is upon the face of all the earth, and every tree, in the which is the fruit of a tree yielding seed; to you it shall be for meat.

The words "fruit" and "seed" are often used in the Bible to indicate children, offspring, and descendants, as they are in common parlance today. "Knowledge," in the Bible often refers to the "carnal knowledge" of sex. The word "tree" could indicate the generations of a family of blood relatives. So we are back, once again, to the subject of blood - "the water of life," it seems.

In particular, the fruit of the vine - the grape - is used and scripture, and literature of all sorts, to represent blood, just as the wine of the Eucharist is viewed as the blood of Jesus. The vine, then, is, again, the family tree. There is an interesting line in *The Book of Isaiah* that appears to refer to God himself keeping a "vineyard" to make red wine, and announcing his intention to "water" it at "every moment." This line comes right after one in which the LORD promises to "punish leviathan" and "slay the dragon that is in the sea." As it says in *Isaiah* 27:1-3:

In that day the LORD with his sore and great and strong sword shall punish leviathan the piercing serpent, even leviathan that crooked serpent; and he shall slay the dragon that is in the sea. In that day sing ye unto her, A vineyard of red wine. I the LORD do keep it; I will water it every moment: lest any hurt it, I will keep it night and day.

This may be related to the Messianic promise that God will let the righteous feast on the flesh of Leviathan. Perhaps they will be permitted to drink of his blood too. Maybe Leviathan's blood will be part of the rivers of living waters in the New Jerusalem, issuing from the throne of God. We know that according to St. John, in the Last Days, a third of the sea will turn to blood. *Revelation* 8:8 says:

And the second angel sounded, and as it were a great mountain burning with fire was cast into the sea: and the third part of the sea became blood....

We further know that Jesus turned water into wine at the wedding at Cana, something that Baphomet tried to take credit for. Baphomet also emphasized that "turning water into wine" could be used as alchemical metaphor. At the Last Supper, Jesus promised his disciples he would drink the "fruit of the vine" with them in his "Father's kingdom." Also, in *Revelation* 7: 16-17, John says of the righteous citizens of the New Jerusalem:

They shall hunger no more, neither thirst any more.... For the Lamb which is in the midst of the throne shall feed them, and shall lead them unto living fountains of waters.

We know that those waters are depicted in Christian iconography as the blood issuing forth from the neck of a sacrificial lamb on an altar. Jews were certainly not allowed to consume blood, as I mentioned earlier. But Jesus is clearly telling people to make an exception and drink his blood. In the Jewish sacrificial system, the blood was reserved for God himself, because it contained "life." Mortals, who had their own life (albeit in short duration), were told not to touch it.

Jesus, of course, is viewed as God incarnate, and part of the Holy Trinity. So would his blood be similar to "ichor," the golden fluid in the veins of the Greek gods? The living waters of the New Jerusalem are said to be "clear as crystal." Also, in *Revelation* 5:8, St. John witnesses the Lamb of God being offered "golden vials full of odours, which are the prayers of the saints."

With these things in mind, let us look at the story of Tantalus. He was one of the sons of Zeus and a mortal. According to Edith Hamilton's *Mythology: Timeless Tales of Gods and Heroes,* Tantalus was "honored by the gods beyond all the mortal children of Zeus." He frequently dined with the gods on Mount Olympus, eating ambrosia. At one point he stole some of the holy food and shared it with some of his human companions. This was taboo. He also illegally passed on some Top Secret divine intelligence that humans were not supposed to know.

For these crimes, he was chastised. However, this was not what got him consigned to the worst tortures of Tartarus in Hades eternally, where he is tormented with an apple that he can't eat and water that he can't drink. This happened because he murdered his own son Pelops - or "sacrificed him," as some chroniclers put it. He then chopped him up, and tried to feed his meat to the gods.

The way the story is told in some cases, it is as though he had invited the gods to a banquet that he was throwing for them, just as he had been a guest at their table. However, since his son's death is described sometimes as a "sacrifice," and knowing what we know about how deities eat sacrificial offerings, it makes sense to consider that the "table" which he invited them to was probably an altar.

According to the myth, the gods knew what the meat was that they were being offered. That is why they all refused to eat it, except for Demeter, who "accidentally" ate some of the shoulder, because she was distraught with grief over her daughter Persephone, who had been kidnapped by Hades. Afterwards, the boy was resurrected, with his remains being placed in a magical cauldron. Hephaestus fashioned a prosthetic shoulder for him out of ivory.

"Demeter" literally means "Mother Earth." So it was "the Earth" that ate Pelops "absent-mindedly," just as Genesis says she "opened her mouth to receive" the blood of Abel. In his book *The Holy Grail: Its Origins, Secrets, and Meaning Revealed,* Malcolm Godwin recounts the details of an Arthurian legend about the "Ship of Solomon," which purportedly contained wood taken from trees that were descended from the Tree of Life in the Garden of Eden. As he writes:

When Adam and Eve were banished from the Garden of Eden Eve still carried a part of the branch of the Tree of Life which she planted and it took root.... The twig... became a tree, but white as snow, signifying the pure soul and the virgin body. For at the time Eve plucked it from the tree in Eden she was still a virgin. Abel was conceived beneath that tree which then turned green.... God curses Cain and the earth upon which the blood of Abel had been spilled, except for the tree, which underwent a transformation, becoming red in remembrance of the blood of Abel. The shoots from the tree were each red, white and green, and it was from these trees that Solomon's wife had cut the three posts around the bed of the ship.

So here we have a myth that combines the idea of the tree of life being watered by the blood of the martyred Abel (causing it to turn red and virile, springing forth more trees), with the idea of a ship - an "ark." But what is really interesting here is the claim that Eve indeed dared to "put forth" her hand "and take also of the tree of life." This is exactly what God told his unnamed companions in *Genesis* 22 that he feared would happen. There is no mention of her eating the fruit of that tree in this Grail story, but she was able to grow another tree, so presumably this would have been possible.

Returning to the story of Pelops, we learn that this unfortunate soul was the father of Atreus, patriarch of the accursed house which resulted in Menelaus and Agamemnon, who started the Trojan War. Atreus did to his own nephew what his grandfather had done to Atreus' father. He killed him, cut him up, and served him to the boy's father, his brother Thyestes, as part of a fraternal vendetta. Significantly, the nephew's name was Tantalus, just like his eternally damned great-grandfather who started the infanticidal, brephophagic family tradition.

Now are we really going to believe that the original Tantalus wasn't influenced to sacrifice and serve the meat of his firstborn son to the gods because of what he'd seen at their own dinner table on Olympus? He had been initiated into the secrets of their ambrosia. Supposedly the gods were too civilized to eat human meat, perhaps most especially that of someone like Pelops, who was still one-quarter divine in lineage.

Yet we know they weren't above the rape and enslavement of such people. There are dozens of such stories, including that of Pelops himself. This poor lad was kidnapped by Poseidon upon being resurrected, and then taken to Mount Olympus to serve the gods as an "eromenos" (a prostitute). Later, Pelops was purportedly thrown out of Olympus as a punishment because he couldn't get over his anger at his father Tantalus, the man who had murdered him! That doesn't really square with the claim that it was the murder of Pelops that brought about the extreme punishment meted to Tantalus in Tartarus.

Furthermore, wasn't giving away ambrosia, and the secrets of the gods, to humans (including, most likely, the secret of what ambrosia was) in fact his biggest crime against the gods? Isn't this a much more likely reason for them to imprison and torture him? Is the story of the murder of Pelops told in such a way as to obscure what the gods were really eating at their banquets on the holy mountain? What made Tantalus think to feed them the flesh of his son in the first place?

In *The White Goddess*, Robert Graves theorized that the story of Tantalus was doctored for political reasons. He states:

...Tantalus belonged to the old religion superseded by Olympian ism, and the Olympian priests have deliberately misinterpreted the icons in favour of Father Zeus by presenting him as an odious criminal. Tantalus's crime, the mythographers explain, was that, having been privileged to eat ambrosia, the food of the gods, with Olympians, he later invited commoners to try it.

Perhaps in these older religions, where human sacrifice was rampant, the priests were more open about what the gods wanted to eat, whereas in later religions, these things were wrapped in allegory. Now we really get down to the crux of the issue. In every major culture, they say that their immortal gods, who live in an unreachable realm on high, maintain their immortal status via consumption of a special food. They keep the location of this food a secret, along with the mystery of what it is. The holy place is both psychically and physically guarded by creatures of terrifying countenance.

For those outsiders who dare to penetrate this forbidden realm, there is reserved the most awful of punishments. So, too, for those apostates among their own realm, and their privileged guests at that august table, who profane the mysteries by sharing the Bread of Life and its secret recipe with those who have not been invited to dine thereof.

As soon as Adam and Eve ate from the Tree of Knowledge, God became concerned that they would "stretch forth" their hands, take from the "tree of life," and "live forever." Since the Tree of Life was mentioned previously in Genesis, but in narration to the reader, and not as the quoted voice of God speaking to Adam, we can infer something: God was not concerned that they would eat from the Tree of Life until after they ate from the Tree of Knowledge.

This implies that the fruit of life was located somewhere that was inaccessible to them before they ate of the Tree of Knowledge. With what they had gained from eating the first forbidden fruit it became conceivable that they might be able to access the fruit of life as well. It is like a parent who is not concerned about the baby putting his fingers in the electrical outlet until the day that he learns to crawl, and isn't concerned about the knives in the drawer until he can stand up.

But there is no reason to believe that the erection of this barrier between us and the Tree of Life was done for our own good. All we know for certain is that the gods don't want us to have that fruit, and they don't want us to know what it is. For this reason, as *Genesis* 3:24 tells us, God "drove out the man; and he placed at the east of the garden of Eden, cherubims, and a flaming sword which turned every way to keep the way of the tree of life." There are brave heroes who try to bring us the secret of this fruit as a stolen treasure from the other side. But they are always sent to Hell as a punishment: like Tantalus; like Prometheus; like Jesus.

In the Hermetic Order of the Golden Dawn, the second degree is that of "Zelator," which, the candidate is told, is a term for a zealous (that is, "daring" or "persevering") student of alchemy. After being instructed to "Enter the Pathway of Evil," the neophyte is directed to a pair of pillars that he is told mark the entrance to the zone in the Garden of Eden where the Tree of Life is protected by cherubs and a flaming sword. The person playing the part of the Hierophant explains it to them thusly:

And Tetragrammaton [the Hebrew letters of the name 'IHVH' - that is, Jehovah] placed Kerubim at the East of the Garden of Eden and a Flaming Sword which turned every way to keep the path of the Tree of Life, for he created Nature that man being cast out of Eden may not fall into the Void. He has bound Man with the Stars as with a chain. When the times are ended, he will call the Kerubim from the East of the Garden, and all shall be consumed and become Infinite and Holy.

Note that the Neophyte is told that he or she has the power to penetrate into the sanctity of a realm that God literally sealed off from our plane of existence just to keep us out of it. Furthermore, at the end of that passage, the Hierophant talks about the total annihilation of creation through fire at the End of Times. Then the Neophyte is told that if they know the proper passwords (which he will have been given before the ritual), then he can enter the "Holy Place." The imagery of Eden suddenly becomes replaced with that of the inner sanctum of the Israelites' Tabernacle, wherein God was worshipped with the Ark of the Covenant. The Hierophant explains further:

...In this Grade you pass through the Gate-way and come into the Holy Place. You are now in the Court of the Tabernacle, where stood the Altar of Burnt Offering, wereon was offered the sacrifice of animals....

Between the Altar and the entrance into the Holy Place, stood the Laver of Brass wherein the priests washed before entering the Tabernacle. It was the symbol of the Waters of Creation....

Having made offering at the Altar of Burnt Sacrifice, and having been cleansed at the Laver of Brass, the Priest then entered the Holy Place.

Again, just as the candidate is encouraged to imagine himself penetrating the forbidden realm of Eden, now he is being told to imagine himself going forth into that inaccessible chamber within the Temple at Jerusalem, where only the priests were permitted. In the Old Testament, those who entered the inner sanctum of the temple that were unworthy were killed instantly by the Ark of the Covenant. But here in this rite, you are told to just walk right in like you own the place.

As we know, the inner sanctum of the Tabernacle of the Israelites was a cube. In this Golden Dawn ritual, they tell you that behind that cube is another cube. Just as with the "Second Square" in Ageio, this is where the "real power" resides. The Hierophant's speech continues:

To the Northern side of the Holy Place, stood the Table of Shewbread.... On it twelve loaves were laid as emblems of the Bread of Life, and it is an image of the Mystery of the Rose of Creation....

Before the Veil of the Holy of Holies, stood the Altar of Incense, of which this Altar is an image. It was of the form of a double cube, thus representing the material form as a reflection and duplication of that which is Spiritual... For were this double cube raised in the air immediately above your head, you would but see the single square forming the lowest side, the others from their position being concealed from you. Just so, behind the material Universe, lies the concealed form of the Mystery of God.

The ritual then goes on to explain the Golden Dawn's cabalistic paradigm, which includes their schema of the Tree of Life, and below it the Tree of Knowledge (a.k.a. the "Tree of Death," the "Qlippoth," or the "Kingdom of Shells"). In their graphic depiction of "the Garden of Eden Before the Fall" (based on an 1872 drawing by Elizabeth Burnett, wife of Golden Dawn founder Wynn Wescott), Eve (whom they also refer to as "Isis") stands with her feet upon the spheres (the "sephiroth") of the Tree of Knowledge. The spheres are quite small, and all bound up into a tiny circle that sits beneath her. This circle is surrounded by the coils of a red dragon with seven heads, all of which appear to be sleeping. Each head corresponds with one of the spheres, and just like on the Tree of Life above, these spheres correspond to aspects of existence - or in this case, negative (non-) existence.

Four branches, or perhaps sprigs of young trees, are sprouting out from Malkuth, the lowest sphere on the Tree of Life, which sits behind Eve's ankles. Her hands are thrust upwards above her head to hold two pillars: one white and one dark, one in each hand. On top of her head, stacked on her as though in a cheerleading formation, is Adam. Coming forth from the six spheres that surround him are vines, which are winding their way up both of the pillars.

Let us think about this cabalistic "Tree of Life" for a moment. It's not really a tree, is it? This is a schematic arrangement of chambers into which fluids flow, from one to the other, with the quality of the fluids changing as they leave each chamber. It looks just like an image of an alchemist's laboratory, with various glass vessels hooked up to one another via tubes, because that's exactly what it is. In an alchemy lab, substances pass from one vessel to another, getting separated into elements, added to, heated, cooled, and otherwise transmuted along the way. That is also what is described as happening as the energy of creation moves through the various spheres on the cabalistic Tree of Life.

Here on the Golden Dawn diagram of the Tree before the Fall, living things, such as tree sprouts and vines are shown coming from the spheres. What this demonstrates is that the entire system is itself a garden (just as the Golden Dawn calls it in this diagram). It is a system of irrigation, producing different "fluids" that water different "plants" to produce various "fruits."

If you'll take a second look at some of the ancient Mesopotamian depictions of the gods gathered around the "Tree of Life," you will notice the same thing. It often looks like a fountain, with one main tube standing upright, and several other connected tubes with bulbs on the end sticking out of it. It sometimes almost looks like a hookah, artfully arranged to resemble a tree. Around it, the gods are usually shown greedily waiting to feast upon it.

Akkadian depictions of the Tree of Life. Above, we see a god riding in a divine chariot with hoses coming down, while other entities feed from the alchemical apparati.

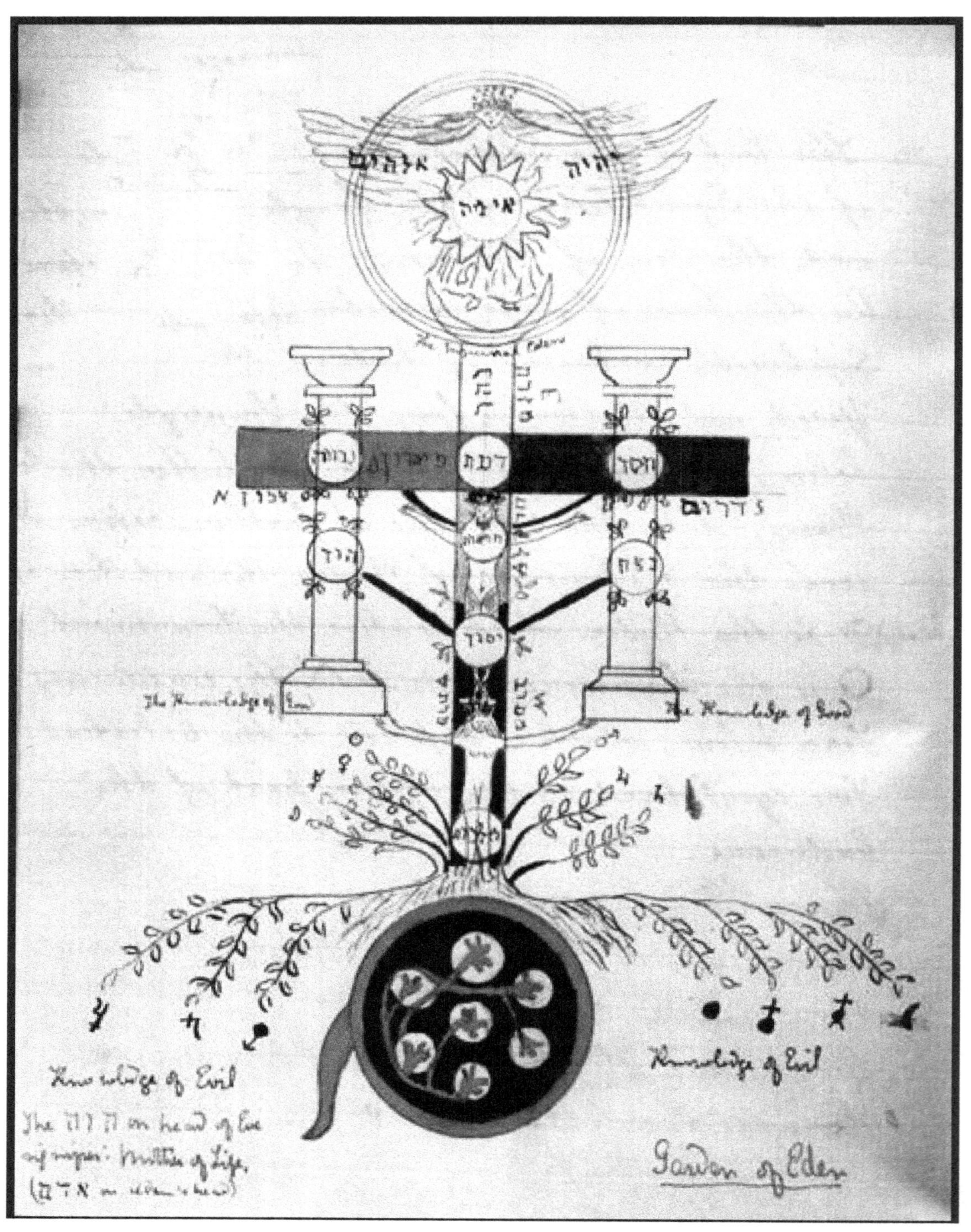

Diagram of the Garden of Eden Before the Fall, drawn by Elizabeth Burnett, wife of Dr. William Wynn Wescott, co-founder of the Hermetic Order of the Golden Dawn

“Lid of the Pastos,” from the Golden Dawn’s Adeptus Minor ritual

Sophia pulling down the sun and moon from their heights with the Gnostic "Chains of the Archons," from Joseph von Hammer-Purgstall's *Mysterium Baphometis Revelatum*

Above: Another image of the Chains of the Archons.
Below: The Golden Dawn's "Floor of the Vault of the Adepti," featuring the seven-headed dragon.

Cain drinking Abel's blood after watching God take his brother's blood sacrifice, from Don Luis de Guzman's *Biblia Alba*, fifteenth century. Is this a case of "Monkey see, monkey do?"

This also appears to be what's going on with Enki in his Absu chamber. Recall that he is depicted with streams of water coming off his back (or possibly hoses), and streams of water flowing between a network of pipes (or alternately, again, those streams could actually be hoses). In one scene he is apparently being approached by a priest who is offering him animal sacrifices, as he proffers to the priest the "plant of immortality." It is budding forth from one of those posts connected to the network of hoses that issue from the pots set beneath his chair.

Cabalists do in fact describe their Tree of Life as a system of channels hooked up like irrigation pipes. They say that this is how the universe is arranged, with energy flowing down to us on Earth (Malkuth) from the supernal realm of God on top (Kether), just as energy rises up from our realm towards God. They also say that, as man is a microcosm of the universe, in the image of God, so there is a Tree of Life operating within his own physical body, channeling spiritual energy to and from the realms above, transmuting it alchemically along the way.

In this sense, it links up to the Hindu system of "chakras" (energy spheres) in the body. Indeed, as has been widely noted, the Hindu scheme matches almost precisely with the middle pillar of the Tree of Life. As it turns out, the cabalistic spheres and the chakras land in the same basic positions along that central pole. This is something that is surely beyond coincidence. So if you imagine the chakra system as the middle pillar of the Tree of Life arranged along the human spinal column, then the sleeping apocalyptic dragon in the Kingdom of Shells at the bottom of the diagram is analogous to the so-called "Kundalini serpent" of yoga. This is a charge of powerful energy in *potentia* that reportedly rests at the bottom of the spine in the lowest chakra.

They call this region "Muladhara." It is the Earth chakra, corresponding to Malkuth, the lowest sphere on the Tree of Life. There the Kundalini serpent is said to be "sleeping" most of the time, but can be "awakened" through yoga practices. This causes it to rise up the spine through all of the other chakras. Finally, it reaches the top of the head - the "godhead" zone - where it intermingles with divine energy from above. From there, it cycles back down the spine to return as a new, alchemical mixture of polar opposite powers that enlivens the body as well as the soul. This serpent, then, most likely corresponds to the one in the cabalistic Qlippoth Tree of Knowledge before the Fall, shown sleeping in a spherical cocoon that looks like an egg waiting to hatch.

The Golden Dawn's schematic of "the Garden of Eden After the Fall" shows the results of that dragon being awakened. The beast is now much larger, and it has totally escaped the Kingdom of Shells, which the lower portion of Eve's body is now subsumed into. Its coils are enveloping the bottom half of the Tree of Life, including Eve, Adam and six of the lower spheres.

These now include an additional sphere: "Knowledge" (called, in Hebrew, "Daath"), which purportedly sprang up during the Fall. It now has eight heads instead of seven, making it identical to the eight-headed "Hydra" dragon famously slayed by Hercules. These heads are reaching up towards the supernal realm at the top, the source of the rivers of fluid that run down the tubes throughout the rest of the tree.

According to the Golden Dawn's system, these are the rivers of paradise. The rivers start out as one stream, called "Naher" (meaning "perennial stream"), which issues from the "Supernal Eden" at the very top of the Tree of life. It then divides into the four rivers, with only the fourth, the Euphrates, actually flowing into Malkuth, the earthly realm. Remember, two of these are the rivers that the Mesopotamians depicted as coming from Enki's back as he sat on his throne in the Absu.

It is implied that, from our sphere, the other three rivers of paradise are invisible, as well as their perennial source. But it was also this extra sphere of "Daath," which caused the rivers to split off in the first place. As the Hierophant proclaims to the candidate in the Practicus ritual:

A River Naher went forth out of Eden, namely from the Supernal Triad, to water the Garden (the rest of the Sephiroth), and from there it was divided into Four Heads in Daath, whence it is said 'In Daath the Depths are broken up and the clouds drop down dew....' The Fourth which receiveth the virtues of the other three, is PHRATH, Euphrates, which floweth down upon the Earth....

These rivers (at least prior to becoming polluted by the dragon) are also referred to as a celestial river of the stars. They are imagined as forming a cross on the Tree of Life, which Adam is envisioned as being "crucified" upon as he stands on top of Eve's head. In the Golden Dawn's Practicus initiation rite, the symbolism of an image called "the Calvary Cross of Twelve Squares" is explained by the Hegemon. He says that it:

...fitly represents the ZODIAC which embraced... the Waters which be above the Firmament. It also alludes to the Eternal River of Eden, divided into four Heads which find their correlations in the four triplicities of the Zodiac.

Now the eleventh sphere of "Daath," which suddenly appeared on the Tree of Life after the Fall, is always said to be "false" or "illusionary." Its existence is said to be variously both a result of the Fall and the cause of it. Daath is also said to be a "portal" to the Tree of Knowledge (the Tree of Death) below. This makes sense when you realize what the Golden Dawn tradition is saying about the fall of Eden: that the Tree of Life above collapsed when Eve stopped holding up the pillars for a moment.

At that point, Eden and the Tree from above fell down into the Tree of Knowledge, so that the realm above is now subsumed into the realm below, and even has a piece of the realm that was formerly below now inside of it. Daath is an apple from the Tree of Knowledge that got stuck inside of the realm of life when Eve consumed it. It then became a gateway allowing death into this life, at its very heart, just as life is also surrounded with the ever-present threat of death.

Clearly, the Tree of Knowledge is the same as the subterranean kingdom of Hades. But what would that have meant before the fall in Eden, when nobody had died yet? Its epithet "the Kingdom of Shells" implies not just empty vessels, but specifically ones that were once full - those which once housed living beings. They are described as shells because they once existed, but they have been wiped out from the memory of time, as though they never were. Yet the imprint of them still remains somehow.

In The Golden Dawn, and cabalism in general, the Kingdom of Shells is personified by another, historical, kingdom that is mentioned in the Old Testament: Edom. Their kings descended from Esau, the eldest son of Isaac and the older brother of Jacob. He is said to have sold his "birthright" (which included the Cave of Treasures and the nearby well) to his younger brother in exchange for a bowl of pottage. He is described as a hunter, with a red tint to his skin, and covered with hair. Like Cain, he was a mighty hunter in the wilderness.

Also like Cain, he has been demonized in Judeo-Christian tradition, which obfuscates the fact that he should have been the rightful heir to his father Isaac's blessing. Jacob used subterfuge to trick his father, who was lying on his deathbed, into passing the birthright on to him instead. He also tricked Esau into tacitly "selling" it to him in a moment of desperation.

Perhaps most significantly, there are several women that the sons of Esau married and bred with who are recorded in rabbinical literature as actually being incarnations of Lilith. They were not natural women, but she-demons. Their sons, the Edomite rulers, who are described variously as "dukes" and "kings," are said in the Bible to have ruled "before there reigned any king over the children of Israel" (*Genesis* 36:31).

Later, the Edomites got into a series of wars with Israel. They were defeated, first by King Saul, and then later by King David also. David appointed Israelite governors to rule them. When Israel eventually split into two kingdoms (Israel and Judah), Edom became a protectorate of Judah. Later still, the Edomites were among those who plundered Jerusalem when it was sacked by King Nebuchadnezzar II.

So this is who the Edomites were, according to the pseudo-history of the Bible and the legends of the rabbis. In the cabala and Western Hermeticism, they seem to symbolize the reign of chaos before God's creation established order in the universe. That would explain why they are equated with the sons of the older brother, Esau, who by the right of primogeniture, should have inherited his family's birthright. However, it was his older brother (a son of creation, not chaos) who ultimately took that position, prevailing as the children of Israel conquered the Edomites, the "Children of Before" (as they are called by cabalists).

In the Golden Dawn's "Practicus" ritual, the Hierophant explains Edom as a personification of primordial chaos, and the order of creation as the coming of Israel. He says:

Ere the Eternal instituted the Formation, Beginning and End existed not. Therefore, before Him, He expanded a certain Veil, and therein He instituted the Primal Kings. And these are the Kings who reigned in Edom before there reigned a King over Israel.

But they subsisted not. When the Earth was formless and void - behold this is the reign of EDOM. And when the Creation was established, la, this is the reign of Israel. And the Wars of titanic forces in the Chaos of Creation, La, these are the Wars between them.

From a Light-bearer of unsupportable brightness, proceeded a radiating flame, hurling forth, like a cast and mighty Hammer, those sparks which were the Primal worlds. And these Sparks flamed and scintillated awhile, but being unbalanced, they were extinguished. Since la, the Kings assembled, they passed away together, they themselves beheld, so they were astonished. They feared. They hasted away. And these be the Kings of Edam who reigned before there reigned a King over Israel....

As the ritual goes on, more detail is given about the war with the Edomites: a war that is depicted as really being between the dragon and God himself. It is the dragon whose heads and horns are the Edomite kings and dukes. This war with the Edomites was, in Judaic history, recorded as an ongoing military feud that lasted generations. However, in this ritual it is conflated with the primordial war in Heaven between God and the Devil, as well as the fall of Adam and Eve from Eden. This was really, they say, the fall of Eden itself away from the Garden and into the mouths of the dragon. They also connect it to the Flood, as well as, implicitly, the final battle with the dragon at the Apocalypse. Describing God's defeat of the Edomites, the Hierophant says:

He beheld and drove asunder the Nations. And the Everlasting Mountains were scattered - and Perpetual Hills did bow.... Thou didst cleave asunder the Earth with the Rivers. The Mountains saw Thee and they trembled. The deluge of waters rolled by.

In Kundalini Yoga, you push the dragon energy up into the godhead realm, resulting in an allegedly beneficial exchange of both earthly and divine energy. In the cabala, the rise of the serpent up the tree from the depths below caused the rivers of paradise to be polluted. As it says in the Golden Dawn's "Fifth Knowledge Lecture":

Thus were the four Rivers of EDEN desecrated, and the Dragon Mouth gave forth the Infernal Waters in DAATH - and this is LEVIATHAN, The Piercing and Crooked Serpent. Therefore God sealed off the source of the pure waters above, so that it would not also be polluted. As the Golden Dawn rite teaches it, God:

...placed the Four Letters YHVH of the NAME and the Flaming Sword of the Ten Sephiroth between the devastated Garden and the Supernal Eden, that this should not be involved in the Fall of ADAM.

Note that here the Golden Dawn equates the four cherubim on the throne with the cherubs that Genesis says God set in place to guard the Tree of Life in Eden, as well as with the four letters of the holy name. Via the iconotropy mentioned previously, they would also, presumably, equate the four letters and cherubim with the cherubs that were said to flank the Ark of the Covenant. The Golden Dawn views that Ark as a tiny microcosmic version of Eden's supernal, as they allude to elsewhere in their rituals.

According to their system, when Eden fell into the coils of the dragon, Malkuth (the "kingdom" - that is, the Earth) got cut off from the spheres (from the River of Life) by those coils. As the Hierophant says in the Practicus ritual:

Then arose the Great DRAGON with Seven Heads and Ten Horns, and the Garden was made desolate, and MALKUTH was cut off from the Sephiroth by his intersecting folds, and linked unto the Kingdom of Shells. And the Seven Lower Sephiroth were cut off from the Three Supernals in DAATH....

This was all Eve's fault, purportedly, because she failed in her duty to uphold the pillars of the universe. Instead she stooped down to pick up some fruit from the tree beneath her, causing the realm above and the realm below to collapse into each other. In the same ritual, while explaining the diagram of "the Garden of Eden After the Fall," the Hierophant declares:

...The Great Goddess who... was supporting the Columns of the Sephiroth, being tempted by the Tree of Knowledge (whose branches indeed tend upward into the

Seven Lower Sephiroth, but also tend downward unto the Kingdom of Shells) reached downward unto the Qlippoth, and immediately the Columns were unsupported, and the Sephirothic system was shattered, and with it fell ADAM, the MICROPROSOPUS.

But at another point in that rite, after invoking the name of God as the "Lord of Armies," the Hierophant discusses the meaning of the tarot card depicting "the Tower." Here he paints a picture of God using the Flaming Sword to destroy some columns as well:

[The card] represents a Tower struck by a Lightning Flash proceeding from a rayed circle and terminating in a triangle. It is the Tower of Babel struck by the Fire from Heaven. It is to be noted that the triangle and the end of the flash, issuing from the circle, forms exactly the astronomical symbol of Mars.

It is the Power of the Triad rushing down and destroying the Columns of Darkness. Three holes are rent in the walls, symbolizing the establishment of the Triad therein and the Crown at the summit of the Tower is falling, as the Crowns of the Kings of Edam fell....

The reference to the symbol of Mars is meant to emphasize the fact that this event was part of a war, as was an earlier reference made in the ritual to God as "YOD HE VAU HETZABAOTH ... Mighty and Terrible ... Commander of the Ethereal Armies." This goes along with what Cain has said to us during the séances. Remember how he told us that the fall of Eden is the same as the fall of Atlantis and the Deluge of Noah. He said that it resulted from a war between Nod (chaos, Edom) with his brother for control of Eden. He said that this was the same event as the war in Heaven. He spoke about the ten "Molochs" or "Fallen Kings Of Dohir," a.k.a. the "Fallen Land." He said that Eden itself fell into the watery Abyss as a result of the war. Referring to how these events are depicted in the game of Ageio, he too utilized the image of the tower. He said "CASTLES FALL."

For the Golden Dawn to connect the Tower tarot card with the Tower of Babel, as well as with the fall of Eden and the war with Edom, means they are saying that it was specifically the Lord's Flaming Sword that came down to destroy Babel's tower. It is depicted on the tarot card as a bolt of lightning, just as in the cabala the sword is shown as a jagged lightning bolt zig-zagging its way through the paths down the Tree of Life. It means that this too is another story from the war over Eden. Those who built the tower were trying to penetrate that supernal realm in Eden where the Tree of Life is. They were thwarted by the Flaming Sword.

Furthermore, the Golden Dawn's deliberate conflation of events goes along with the way in which Baphomet talked about the Garden of Eden, the war in

Heaven, and the Apocalypse as all being the same event occurring simultaneously: now. Another image used in the Golden Dawn's Adeptus Minor ritual shows Jesus on the Cross being enveloped from below by the now eight-headed dragon, just as Adam and Eve are shown on the "Garden of Eden After the Fall" graphic. Above that picture is placed a depiction of the Flaming Sword coming down from the Supernal Eden. This demonstrates the Golden Dawn's view that the crucifixion was also part of this eternal moment. Again, when discussing the "Garden of Eden After the Fall" during the Practicus ritual, the Hierophant says:

And thence it was necessary that the SECOND ADAM should come to restore all things and that, as the First Adam had been extended on the Cross of the Celestial Rivers, so the SON should be crucified on the Cross of the Infernal Rivers of DAATH.

In the Golden Dawn's Fourth Knowledge Lecture, author Frater S.M.R.D. again talks about Adam on a cross made from the rivers of paradise, adding that these are also the rivers of the New Jerusalem in the Apocalypse:

The River going out of Eden is the River of the Apocalypse, The Waters of Life, clear as crystal proceeding from the Throne, on either side of the Tree of Life.... Thus the Rivers form a Cross and on it THE GREAT ADAM, the SON who is to rule the nations....

Note here that Adam is now equated with Jesus, reigning forevermore with the Father as the King of Kings in the New Jerusalem. The symbol of Jesus on the cross is compared in the New Testament to that of the Nehushtan: a brass serpent figure mounted on a pole that healed the Israelites when they were stricken by "fiery serpents" during their sojourns in the wilderness. But it is also connected in Christian theology and iconography to the Tree of Life in the Garden of Eden. In alchemy this concept is referenced with the symbol of a serpent being crucified.

This is quite clearly because Jesus said that his body and blood were the fruits of this tree, and that consuming them would bring eternal life to mortals. He also said that by shedding his blood on the cross, the "Tree of Life," he was paying the price for the Original Sin that resulted from Adam eating from the Tree of Knowledge.

At that moment, the Dragon was defeated. Thus, the events that play themselves out in St. John's *Revelation* have, from the viewpoint of the eternal, Supernal Eden, already happened. This is why Baphomet said the Apocalypse, and the Fall in the Garden, were both happening "Now" and "Really Soon." This is why Cain said that in the game of Ageio it was important from his perspective (that of the black kingdom, the losers) to "Accept Defeat."

According to the Golden Dawn, the first of the four tributaries to issue fourth from Naher, the perennial stream of paradise, is Pison. In their "Fourth Knowledge Lecture" Pison is described as a river of fire pooling up into the sphere called "Geburah" (Judgment). Whether this is related to the alchemical annihilation of sinners in the Lake of Fire at the Final Judgment is unknown. However, I do think at this point we can assume that the "golden" nature of the stream relates to the fact that the "water of life" which comes from the gods is golden and sparkling clear, like ichor (god blood). This is in contrast to the "water of life" that living things on Earth bring forth, which is red.

I also think that at least one of these "rivers" is the Flaming Sword itself. It seals off the supernal realm of Eden from the rest of the universe, polluted by the chaos of the dragon. This is the same as the chasm described by the Jews as a "river" between the Bosom of Abraham and the rest of the underworld of Sheol.

It may also be what is represented on the board of the Chinese game of Xianqi, where there is a "heavenly river" that certain pieces cannot cross, and which transforms others into more powerful pieces when they do cross. Recalling that the Golden Dawn connects the four rivers of paradise to the cross and the zodiac, it may be important that the word "Xianqi" might mean "constellation game," according to some writers. (Also, the movement of the pieces may have been based on the apparent movement of objects in the sky.)

Alchemy teaches that there is a process to create a knife that can cut through time and space. This is the "Universal Solvent," what Fulcanelli called "le Bon Saber" ("the Good Sword"). Like Arthur's Excalibur, only the predestined owner of this sword can "release" it from the "stone." This, he says, is what Michael used to spear the dragon, and connected to the image of the crucified serpent.

The same can be said of the nearly identical icon of St. George, the patron of England, slaying a dragon in the style of the aforementioned archangel. England is home to Glastonbury (literally, "Glass Stone Hill"). This place is not only associated with King Arthur and the Holy Grail, but is also said to have at one time hosted Jesus himself, along with Joseph of Arimathea. In his poetry, William Blake portrayed England as the landing site of the New Jerusalem at the Apocalypse.

In *The Faerie Queene*, Sir Edmund Spenser dealt with all of these themes. The hero, "the Redcross Knight," battles a dragon that had attacked and destroyed the kingdom of "Eden," including the castle of its king and queen. He does this at the behest of the castle's princess, who is distraught over what has happened to her parents. After successfully conquering the beast, he is dubbed "Saint George," and shown a vision of the New Jerusalem.

However, this "Flaming Sword" which pierced the dragon, and which sealed off the fruit of life from mortal hands, is what gave birth to the demons Samael and Lilith. In *Zohar* I:19b, it says of Lilith:

She approached the gates of Paradise on earth, and saw the Cherubim guarding the gates of Paradise, and sat down facing the Flaming Sword, for she originated from that flame. When that flame revolved, she fled.

Recall that God is said to have *already* pierced at least one of those two dragons, Behemoth and Leviathan, and separated them from each other, to prevent the world from being annihilated. The same is told about Lilith and her partner Samael, who seem to be the same entities as Behemoth and Leviathan. So that means that Lilith became what she is (an individual apart from her partner) because of that Flaming Sword. This event was probably itself part of the process of sealing off Eden, to protect all of creation from total destruction. In fact, there may be reason to believe that Lilith herself is one of those cherubim.

Genesis merely says that God placed "Cherubims" on "the east of the garden of Eden." It does not say how many there were. However, this image tends to get combined with that of the four creatures that are said to guard the "throne" or "chariot" of God. They take the form of a man, a lion, an eagle, and an ox. They are called the "living creatures." (The Hebrew word for "chariot" comes from "chai," which means "to live.") However they are also referred to as "cherubim." The chariot and the creatures show up whenever God makes a physical appearance somewhere, and it appears to function like a vehicle.

Because the Ark of the Covenant was also guarded by cherubim, and because the Ark acted as a "throne" on which God's presence would sit when he appeared inside of the temple, there does appear to be an implicit connection between those cherubs and the ones guarding the chariot. Also, since the inner sanctum of the temple, with the Ark inside, seems to be a replica of the "Supernal Eden," and the rituals which took place inside appear designed to supernaturally teleport the priests to Eden, a connection with the cherubim guarding Eden is also implied. But the Ark is usually shown with two cherubs flanking it, whereas God's throne always has the four creatures. Eden has been variously depicted in visual artwork as having either two cherubs guarding a gate (identical in appearance to the way the two are always shown on the Ark), or the four creatures of God's chariot (each stationed at one of the four compass points).

In the Golden Dawn's Theoricus ritual, the Hierophant interprets the Twenty-First Tarot Card ("The World"), and the woman it features, surrounded by the four beastly cherubim of God's chariot and throne. Intriguingly, he describes her not only as both Isis and a character in the Apocalypse, but also on of the cherubs guarding the Ark of the Covenant. He states:

Her legs form a cross. She is the Bride of Apocalypse, the Kabbalistic Queen of the Canticles, the Egyptian ISIS or Great Feminine Kerubic Angel SANDALPHON on the left hand of the Mercy Seat of the Ark.

Indeed, there is a cabalistic tradition that the Ark guardians are the angels Metatron and Sandalphon. Here the Golden Dawn is saying that it was a male and female pair. In his book *Dark Mirrors: Azazel and Satanael in Early Jewish Demonology*, Andrei A. Orlov presents evidence that the cherubim of the Ark were a male and female entwined in sexual union. He quotes the "Yoma treatise" from the Babylonian Talmud:

Whenever Israel came up to the Festival, the curtain would be removed for them and the Cherubim were shown to them, whose bodies were intertwisted with one another, and they would be thus addressed: Look! You are beloved before God as the love between man and woman.

Then, elsewhere in the same text, we read the following:

When the heathens entered the Temple and saw the Cherubim whose bodies were intertwisted with one another, they carried them out and said: These Israelites, whose blessing is a blessing, and whose curse is a curse, occupy themselves with such things! And immediately they despised them, as it is said: All that honored her, despised her, because they have seen her nakedness.

As for the confusion about the cherubim guarding God's throne, and whether or not they are the same ones guarding the Tree of Life in Eden, Orlov does make some very interesting connections. He provides several quotations stating that God's presence would "rest" on a cherub on the Tree of Life, just as he would sit upon the cherubs on top of the Ark of the Covenant, and just as in the New Jerusalem he's seen on his chariot throne surrounded by cherubs. In *The Life of Adam and Eve*, it says:

As God entered [the Garden,] the plants of Adam's portion flowered but all mine were bereft of flowers. And the throne of God was fixed where the Tree of Life was.

Then in *II Enoch* 8:3-4, we are told:

And in the midst (of them was) the tree of life, at that place where the Lord takes a rest when he goes into paradise.

Finally, in *III Enoch* 5:1, we learn that this has not always been the case, but rather God's throne has been there since the Fall. It says:

From the day that the Holy One, blessed be he, banished the first man from the garden of Eden, the Shekhinah resided on a cherub beneath the tree of life.

Even more intriguingly, Orlov discusses a tradition that squarely backs up the Golden Dawn teaching of the two trees that were originally stacked on top of one another, and which are now separated from each other with the Flaming Sword. The Zohar says that the Tree of Knowledge was driven out of Paradise along with Adam and Eve. Not only that, but also, apparently, there are cherubim now beneath the trees, both above and below.

Could this explain the tradition that there are four cherubim total? Are there two for the Tree of Life in the supernal Eden (which is represented on Earth and supernaturally accessed by the priests from the inner sanctum of the temple via the Ark of the Covenant)? Then perhaps there are two also flanking the Tree of Knowledge.

Maybe Lilith and Samael are themselves the guardians of that cursed Tree. It could be that this is a form of forced servitude and part of their punishment, just as Rosenkreutz was cursed to guard the tomb of Venus. Also, maybe the Tree of Knowledge can be viewed as sitting directly outside of Eden, and thus maybe it is these four cherubs together-two inside the gates of Eden, and two without, that form the quaternity which surrounds God's throne.

Perhaps, unlike the cherubs that the Shekinah rests upon in Eden, and the two on top of the Ark, these two are not locked in sexual union, manifesting a divine presence in their bliss. Rather, these two have been divided in such a way that true union can never take place. Thus, their ability to activate a "presence," as God does, has been hampered, thereby saving the universe from destruction. This may be why Lilith sits lamenting at the gates of Eden.

Recall that, as I explained previously, in the Golden Dawn's diagram of "the Garden of Eden Before the Fall," the spheres around Adam on the Tree of Life have vines coming out of them, which are wrapped around the pillars that Eve is holding. In *Dark Mirrors*, Andrei A. Orlov explores pseudepigraphal writings stating the grape was the forbidden fruit of the Tree of Knowledge - or rather, from a vine wrapped around that tree.

This is interesting for many reasons. For one thing, a vine is actually a parasite that feeds off of other plants, like trees, and coils itself around its host like a snake. Clearly, there are parallels here with the concept of the serpent on the Tree. We get the idea that the serpent may have possessed one or both of the human protoplasts to encourage them to eat from the tree, and have carnal knowledge with each other.

Orlov talks about a passage in *The Apocalypse of Abraham* where a picture is painted of Adam and Eve standing under the Tree of Knowledge, entwined with each other physically, and with the fallen angel Azazel between them. In the midst of this a bunch of what appear to be grapes hang from the Tree.

Orlov likens this to a ménage à trois, and suggests that it may be an allusion to the first couple being "ridden" via demonic possession. As I have said, I think that this is, in fact, what is meant when it is said that Lilith and Samael cannot have sexual union without the "Tanin'iver" as an intermediary. Remember, some rabbinical traditions say that Azazel is the name for the combination of Lilith and Samael.

Now symbolically, grapes imply blood, and vines imply bloodlines being bred over generations. The Bible certainly mentions the grapevine being preserved as a species in the new world that Noah and his family emerged into. Genesis says that Noah made wine from the grapes and got drunk from it (which is why Jews credited Noah, like Dionysus was among the Greeks, as the inventor of alcoholic beverages). He ended up naked in his tent, where his children scandalously found him, echoing the realization of their own nakedness that Adam and Eve had after eating from the Tree of Knowledge.

But in the scriptures cited by Orlov, there is much more to the story of the grape. In the Slavonic version of the book *3 Baruch*, it talks about angels being assigned by God to plant trees in the Garden of Eden. The angels were Michael, Gabriel, Uriel, Raphael, and Satanael, and they each planted a tree. The first four planted good trees. But Satanael planted the vine. This is undoubtedly a reference to the rebellious angels who injected their own seed into human females.

Orlov cites certain texts, and commentary on those texts, that make it seem like the Garden of Eden was almost as a prison, complete with "bailiffs," where humans were kept and bred like livestock by angelic "gardeners":

4Q530 refers to the gardeners watering numerous roots issued from their trunk. Who are these gardeners? Jozef Milik was first to identify the gardeners as angelic beings. He argued that the gardeners are 'guardian angels' or 'bailiffs of the world-garden'.... Loren Stuckenbruck... suggests that in light of 4Q530 line 8 the ultimate outcome of the gardeners' work seems to be the production of 'great shoots' from the root source, which, in Stuckenbruck's opinion, signifies 'the birth of the giants from the women.' He further argues that the 'watering' activity is a metaphor for impregnation and the gardeners, in fact, represent fallen angelic beings, the Watchers.

The intentions of the angels towards the humans that they bred with may not have been based on erotic love. Rather, it could have been a mass rape intended to humiliate the race of Adam, whom they jealously despised. Orlov says that in 3 Baruch, Satanael sets out purposely to plant "a tree designed to cause the fall and degradation of the human race." Then in the Midrash of Shemhazai and Azazel, according to Orlov:

...The evil desire of the Watchers over humans seems to come as consequence of the Watchers' disrespect for humanity in general and the first human creature in particular.

In order to wipe out this accursed bloodline, God caused everything, including the Garden itself, to be destroyed in the Deluge. But according to *3 Baruch*, the vine - the bloodline "planted" by the fallen angels - survived. It was washed out of the Garden as the waters receded, and ended up at the feet of Noah as he disembarked the Ark. Lines 4:10b-11 state:

And the water entered into the garden, (and took all that was blooming), bringing out one shoot from the vine as God withdrew the waters. And there was dry land, and Noah went out from the ark.

When Noah discovered that the vine had escaped, he did now know what to do. He did not want to plant it because it had produced the fruit that caused the fall of Adam and Eve. But God sent an angel named Sarasael to tell Noah: "Rise, Noah, and plant the vine, and alter its name and change it for the better."

More evidence that the vine, and in fact, all of the trees of the "Garden" represent bloodlines can be found in the *Midrash of Shemhazai and Azazel*, where it talks about prophetic dreams had by two giants, sons of the (soon to be fallen) angel Shemhazai. It involves a "stone" hovering over the Earth, followed by genocidal gardening:

One night the sons of Shemhazai, Hiwwa and Hiyya saw ... dreams. One saw the great stone spread over the earth.... The other (son) saw a garden, planted whole with (many) kinds of trees and (many) kinds of precious stones. And an angel (was seen by him) descending from the firmament with an axe in his hand, and he was cutting down all the trees, so that there remained only one tree containing three branches. When they awoke from their sleep they arose in confusion, and, going to their father, they related to him the dreams. He said to them: 'The Holy One is about to bring a flood upon the world, and to destroy it, so that there will remain but one man and his three sons.'

In *3 Baruch*, the placement of the passages about the survival of the vine, right next to verses about the survival of Noah's line, implies that the former is a metaphor for the latter. This seems to be a method that is often used in scripture to draw parallels between things and explain symbolism. There are also references in *The Book of Enoch* to Noah being a "plant of righteousness and truth." In the Syncellus translation of *The Book of Enoch*, God tells the angel Sariel to tell Noah:

And now instruct the righteous one what to do, and the son of Lamech, that he may save his life and escape for all time; and from him a plant shall be planted and established for all generations for ever.

Recall that, in the Mesopotamian versions of the Flood story, the pilot of the Ark was rewarded with the plant of immortality. However, in most versions of the Judeo- Christian tales, it was Noah's grandfather Enoch who was made immortal, as he was also given the first warning about the impending disaster of the Deluge. But here we have an angel being told by God that Noah will "save his life and escape for all time."

Did that mean that he escape death itself, forever, like his great-grandfather? Or it is possible that just as L.A. Waddell has suggested, Noah and Enoch are in fact based on the same historical figure? What about my theory that perhaps Cain and Seth are the same person, and that Cain's name was changed to obfuscate the fact that he and his descendants survived the Flood? After all, Sariel is instructed to tell Noah to "plant the vine, and alter its name and change it for the better." Could this be a reference to the line of Cain surviving in altered form?

Is it possible (as the stories Cain told us in the séances seem to imply) that Cain's son Enoch and Seth's descendant Enoch were really the same? Could it be that Cain's son Enoch (whom Cain indicated is identical with the "city" of the same name) is also the figure who was translated to Heaven to be God's personal assistant? Also, is Noah merely a mythological, iconotropic extension of the personage of Enoch?

Think about it: Enoch is said to be the first scribe, and the author of the first books, which told the story of the universe from the Creation through the Deluge experienced by his alleged great-grandson Noah. As the author of his own story (working, of course, under the tutelage of God), isn't it his prerogative to tell the story the way he chooses (or perhaps, the way God tells him to)?

According to *The Book of Jubilees*, Enoch was translated not just to "Heaven," but specifically to the Supernal Eden, where the Tree of Life is. There he was apparently placed as a sort of guardian, like the cherubim and the Flaming Sword were. Somehow, the text says, his written testimony of the story of creation acted to protect Eden from the Flood. In *Jubilees* 4:23 we read:

...The flood water did not come on any of the land of Eden because he was placed there as a sign and to testify against all people in order to tell all the deeds of history until the day of judgment.

Perhaps Enoch's written history acts to solidify the reality of the story, to keep it from dissolving into chaos like the waters of the Flood. Solidifying reality appears to be one of the roles that mankind has been charged with. Remember what it said in the Golden Dawn's Zelator ritual, when it describes the placement of the cherubim and the Flaming Sword on the east of Eden:

...For he created Nature that man being cast out of Eden may not fall into the Void. He has bound Man with the Stars as with a chain. When the times are ended, he will call the Kerubim from the East of the Garden, and all shall be consumed and become Infinite and Holy.

What it seems to be saying is that God placed the sword and the cherubim there (which, as we know, separated Behemoth/Samael and Leviathan/Lilith) to prevent the universe from being annihilated. At the End of Times, these barriers will be removed so that this destruction can proceed except for, presumably, for the segment of the universe called the "New Jerusalem." Somehow, part of maintaining this necessary separation involves "binding" mankind with celestial "chains." What is the meaning of this? We are used to seeing images of demons bound in chains, as well as the damned in Hell. But are we, the living, also bound?

In Joseph von Hammer-Purgstall's *Mysterium Baphometis*, he reproduces an Ophite Gnostic image that he says influenced the Templars' representation of Baphomet. It involves a Hermaphroditic figure wearing a crown, dragging the sun, moon, and stars down from their heights by chains that suspend from them. These are the "Chains of the Archons" that the Gnostics talked about. They keep the planets and stars bound to their orbits, as they keep us tied to our fates.

I think that this, somehow, is part of the process of keeping Heaven and Hell separated. This realm that we are now in was created, and mankind was cast out of Eden into here, in order to provide that buffer zone. This is why the Golden Dawn portrays Adam and Eve (particularly the latter) as being responsible for holding up the pillars of the Tree of Life. This is why they tell the would-be Theoricus to imagine himself in the position of Atlas, holding up the Heavens on his head and shoulders.

Notice the frequency with which people and demigods are described in these myths and traditions as having to stand perpetually in unendurable stress positions *a la* Abu Ghraib-style torture. Tantalus not only has the fruit dangling out of reach of his mouth, but is also positioned standing with one foot on land, and another dangling over water, always trying to stand on a little boat that is constantly slipping out from beneath him. Atlas, also, is clearly in pain.

As for Adam and Eve, as they are shown in the Golden Dawn diagrams of Eden, they certainly don't look comfortable. Eve is holding up the weight of the pillars with the palms of her hands hoisted above her head in a way that looks impossible. As for Adam, his arms are outstretched, and his feet are contorted together strangely in a pose that the Golden Dawn's ritual describes as "crucifixion." Then, of course, consider the real crucifixion of Christ (or Judas, if you believe that story). The real pain came not from the nails themselves, but from the way that the weight of his body had to hang from his arm and chest muscles. Is this, again, the sort of thing that Cain was talking about when he described to us the torture he is enduring in Hell as "GITMO"?

For more perspective on what this might be about, let us examine the claims of paranormal researcher Peggy Kane. Anyone who has seen an episode of a modern ghost hunting reality show knows that "EVPs" are messages that can' be heard on either a digital or analog audio recording. People will record themselves talking to disembodied spirits and then play the recording back to hear the spirit's reply, usually whispered and faint, as well as distorted-sounding.

Peggy Kane began practicing this technique many years ago after a long career as a UFO expert. She used it as a way to contact extraterrestrial intelligences that allegedly resided in parallel dimensions. But then she decided to go a step forward. She applied a technique known "reverse speech analysis," perfected by David John Oates. Allegedly, if you reverse a recording of someone talking, it will say something else that will reveal what the person was really thinking as he or she was speaking.

The way it is supposed to work is simple. If the backwards message is "congruent" with the forwards message, it allegedly means that the speaker was being honest at the time. However, frequently the perceived backwards message is something at variance with the initial message. This, practitioners believe, means that analysis of the reversal will reveal the truth that the speaker is trying to hide.

When Peggy Kane applied this technique to the ET EVPs she was recording, it painted a picture of reality that was totally different from what we perceive normally. It was a much more sinister view of our world, as well as the world beyond, and what happens to us when we die. UFO expert Raymond Fowler once asked: "Could it be that death is the ultimate UFO abduction experience?" That is the conclusion that Peggy Kane has come to, and the intentions of our abductors are not nice at all, according to her.

Ms. Kane says that our reality is being controlled from outside forces that do not have our best interests in mind. They are using both our bodies and souls for food, amusement, and scientific experimentation. Their world is what we consider to be the "astral realm" from our perspective over here. But when we leave our bodies to travel over there (which, she says, we do frequently), then it is perceived as a physical world just like our own. There are buildings, streets, factories, stores, and money being exchanged over there just like there is here. But the universe on the other side is ruled by a bloodthirsty race of Reptilians. They walk upright like humans. However, that is where the similarity ends.

According to Kane, the Reptilians keep humans in a three-dimensional prison by the use of some sort of artificial force field called "the Net." The situation is very similar to the plot of the film *The Matrix*, in which human slaves were kept by their robot overlords comatose in little capsules floating in goo. In the film, the captive humans were used as batteries and bled of their energy while they lived their lives in a computer-generated dream-world.

Ms. Kane says that this is kind of what's really happening. She claims that we are constantly being drained of our energy by our hidden masters. Though we are unaware of it, they are constantly sucking our soul essence, both through the emotional vibrations we emit, and also via our blood and other body fluids. The soul essence is called "loosh," allegedly, and pre-adolescent children are the best source.

In order to feed from us, Ms. Kane says that the Reptilians sometimes possess our bodies, the way we think of demon possession. This is called "being seeded." They open portals or "mind gates" into the human psyche that allow them to whisper suggestions to us, which we hear subconsciously. This, she says, results in altering the possessed person's behavior according to the parasite's wishes. This can then create whatever emotional response the parasite wishes to feed from. According to Kane, if a Reptilian inside you really enjoys the emotions you give off when you are fighting with your boyfriend, then he will whisper suggestions to you which instigate these situations.

Kane claims that they also make direct use of our "astral bodies" on the other side. As soon as people die, and their spirit travels to the other side, they are swallowed, just like the worst sinners are depicted being eaten by the Devil in Dante's Inferno. She says that this is taking place even on supposedly "dead" planets in our own solar system. Ms. Kane purports that Mars is a central hub for the trafficking of "astral body parts."

However, that is perhaps not the worst of it. According to Kane, the Reptilians make use of us sexually as well. "Reptilians pull people out of their bodies at night and rape them," she says. "They do it to almost everybody," both male and female. The purpose of this, she believes, is that it is another way of stealing our energy. "Rape is one of the ways they feed," says Peggy. "They call that 'alien honey. '"

Ms. Kane says that many of the Reptilians delight in toying with psychics and channelers who attempt to contact the spiritual dimension. They play the roles of gods, guardian angels, familiar spirits, departed relatives, and whatever else the seeking person wishes to see. They set up situations where the people they contact agree to give them even more loosh, including blood sacrifices, opportunities to possess human bodies, and sexual favors.

Without passing judgment on the veracity of Kane's claims, methods, or referential paradigm, I will say that nothing I have experienced or found in my research really disproves the picture she portrays of reality. A lot of what she has to say rings true, according to my own experience of talking to spirits on the other side, as well as my decades of research into comparative mythology and occult traditions. If what Ms. Kane says is accurate, then so too is that statement made by Mephistopheles to Dr. Faustus: "Why this is hell, nor am I out of it."

Just think about the story of Prometheus having his liver eaten every day by an eagle, a symbol of Zeus, only to have it grow back the next day. If this is what they would do to one of their own, another immortal, imagine what they do to us. Certainly it does seem as if there are invisible entities running the shown that have historically demanded blood sacrifice, from whence they feed on the blood, as well as spiritual energy given in the form of religious rituals, prayers, and meditation.

The events which led up to the unfortunate fate of Prometheus are worth mentioning, for they pertain to the subject of sacrifice. The whole matter began with something called the "Trick at Mecone," where the precedent for the Greek custom of sacrifice was established. At a meeting between gods and men at a mysterious place called "Mecone," Prometheus invited Zeus to choose which portion of the animals killed for meat on Earth would be offered to him in sacrifice.

What Prometheus had done was killed at ox, and created two portions out of the remains. One was the stomach of the ox, stuffed with all of the meat. The other portion was a pile of bones wrapped in glistening fat. Zeus purportedly had not seen Prometheus arrange the portions, and chose the one that looked good on the outside: the bones. Mankind, then, would get to eat the meat from each kill.

Apparently unable to alter the decision once it had been made, Zeus became angry, and punished mankind by removing fire from Earth. Now people could not cook the meat that Prometheus had won for them, nor could they keep themselves warm at night. Prometheus felt sorry for people, and stole fire from Olympus to bring it back to humanity. Then Zeus, in retribution for this, chained Prometheus to the Caucasus Mountains, and sent the eagle after him to peck his liver.

Ancient Greek poets and chroniclers repeatedly wrote that the Gods "starved" and began to die, or fade from existence, whenever belief in religion would wane with the populace. These people clearly suspected that the immortals secretly relied on the efforts of mortals to survive. Similarly, the Mesopotamians described their gods as starving on their holy mountaintop retreat while humanity was drowning in the Deluge. Is this because there was nobody to feed them, both with bloody sacrifices, and with the energy of reverent belief? When Utnapishtim cooked the gods a burnt offering after leaving his ark, they ravenously descended upon it, as God did in the version in *Genesis*.

Let us contemplate again the images of Enki in the Absu. Priests present the god with sacrifices. Then, perhaps, he is taking the energy from that, running it through a divine alchemical process, maybe within his own body, and/or those of others (the "vessels" shown in the images beneath and surrounding Enki's throne). He then returns the energy to the priests in the form of the plant of immortality.

In the Temple in Jerusalem, blood was being poured on the altar. The power of that went towards God, whose "Presence" was inside of the Ark. When the Presence came, it could be seen hovering over the lid of the Ark, seated right between the two cherubim on the top that formed the "Mercy Seat." Perhaps it was the power derived from this blood that was transmuted inside of that mysterious vessel. The output of this was then manifested on top of the Ark in the form of the Presence. This Presence then infused the shewbread, which was eaten by the priests.

Then there is the "hidden Manna" that Jesus promised to give the saved in the New Jerusalem. Is this related to the feast of the meat of Leviathan that Jews believe the pious will eat at the End Times? Is this another type of divine alchemical process? Leviathan can be thought of as the serpent of chaos who encircles creation (thus holding everything within its body, so to speak), and which eats the souls of the dead, like the giant maw that the gates of Hell are frequently depicted as being. In that sense, she had the oldest and largest stomach in the universe, being the ultimate landing place of every soul that dies.

So is it that this beast, having consumed all of this soul essence and gained from it vast energy, is then butchered and served to the chosen few, who get to benefit from ingesting all of that essence into themselves? Is this what brings them immortality, as the symbol of the Ouroborous (an encircled serpent eating its own tail) represents? Is this also the meaning of that other alchemical symbol of eternal life, showing two dragons that form a circle by eating each other's tails?

I think it is true that we are somehow the source of food for the gods, as well as the beasts of burden who hold up the pillars of the universe. We are the slaves who "till the soil" for them, so to speak. At the end, our souls are harvested by the Grim Reaper, who is Saturn with his scythe, cutting down and eating his own children. But it is a symbiotic relationship. Our existence certainly depends on the other side as well.

If man is made in "God's image," it seems to me that part of our role is to act as his eyes, and his imagination, collapsing the trajectories of probability curves as we observe and thus define the reality around us. In other words, I think we are integral to the process of creation, and that is the crushing responsibility that we must bear. That is one way in which we hold aloft the Heavens on our shoulders.

That is why symbols like cornerstones, keystones and foundation stones apply with the matters that we are discussing here. Keystones hold arches together with pillars. That is the role that Adam and Eve are shown playing in the Golden Dawn's diagram of Eden before the Fall. Cornerstones and other foundation stones obviously go on the bottom of edifices, and bear the weight of the entire structure. This is the role formerly played by the realm of the Qlippoth shown beneath Eve's feet in that schematic.

The underworld is the foundation for Earth and everything above it. Therefore, while mankind is shown playing a brutally difficult role in holding the universe together, the weight of it all is ultimately placed upon the world below, just as the weight of the blame for the sin of the world is cast there as well. For Buddhists, the deepest chamber in Hell, reserved for those who have committed unpardonable sins, is called "Avici," and it is said to be cube-shaped.

Throughout history, the greatest sins in society are usually not murder, rape or theft, but blasphemy and heresy. In religions, these are generally considered "unpardonable" and worthy of execution as punishment. Nobody is allowed to talk about what the Matrix might look like from the outside, and you are greatly discouraged from thinking about it. According to the traditions of the Golden Dawn, a glimpse of the truth was had during God's war with Edom:

Then the channels of the Waters were seen and the Foundations of the World were discovered.

In other words, to see how the world really works is itself a world-shattering experience. If everybody had such an experience, the world would not exist.

The cubic foundation stone in the underworld is the city of Enoch that Cain built in Nod. "Enoch" means "inaugurate" or "dedicate." Typically, whenever they erect a new edifice, stonemasons lay a cornerstone to dedicate it. This is the symbolism that applies to the cubic stone down below. Outside of this cube, as Cain has told us in séances, are the prisoners of Hell. This may explain why Eliphas Levi's depiction of Baphomet shows him seated on a cubic stone.

Similar imagery has been used regarding the white cube of the New Jerusalem at the Apocalypse. Sixteenth-century painter Luca Cambiaso depicted God the Father and God the Son sitting in Heaven with their feet resting upon a white cube in his *La Gloria* fresco from the Escorial Palace in Spain.

As I stated before, I see, in all of the scriptures, myths, legends, fairy tales, and esoteric literature that I have examined on this topic, a schema of the universe that involves a black cube beneath a white cube, which both, at the End of Times, come together in some way. In the midst of the white cube, God's throne sits. This is where it is right now, reportedly, right by the Tree of Life in the Supernal Eden, what we in common parlance now refer to as "Heaven." Surrounding this realm, and protecting it, are the four "beasts" or cherubim, and the Flaming Sword, as represented by the "Second Square" in Ageio. In *Revelation* 4:6, St. John describes his vision of it:

...In the midst of the throne, and round about the throne, were four beasts full of eyes before and behind.

Earlier, when Ezekiel had his vision of God's chariot, he too saw the four guardians, and four "wheels," each covered with eyes. Again, this makes sense if we view the universe as a panopticon prison, with God's throne in the center surrounded by his omniscient prison wardens (the cherubim), watching the activities of his prisoners locked outside of the gates of his chamber, where Nod, the underworld, chaos, and Hell are.

Ageio seems to me to be a game about capturing this zone. This is what the message from the parchments found by Bérenger Saunière meant when they said "Destroy this demon guardian at noon." It is about a ritual where you break past the cherubim and the Flaming Sword to get to the Fruit of Life, represented by the words "blue apples." Remember, Baphomet said that these words referred to "BLOOD SACRIFICE."

The zone of Eden, the "Second Square," is, again, the Ark, and the cubic Supernal Altar. It is the "One Box of Things" where the souls, the blood, and the energy of sacrifice is stored. Remember Cain told us that part of the goal of playing Ageio is to "MAKE REAL AGEI," and that the agei is also the same as the "SANGREAL." But we know that "Sangreal," the "Holy Grail," can be broken down into the words "San Greal": royal blood. This refers to the making of the Eucharist on top of the very altar of Heaven.

While I must admit that my understanding of this mystery given to me is not fully understood yet, I think that part of the "game" (the most dangerous game of all) involves filling up the box with agei, or, perhaps, covering the surface of the box with it, as the Eucharist goes on top of an altar. Cain told us that the agei TOKENS- the "BUCKS" - go on top of the "POINTS" where the grid lines intersect.

The other goal of the game is to take the agei for yourself - to "reap all the wealth." To do this, you "GAIN THE AGEI BY SURROUNDING THE SECOND SQUARE ON THE AGEL" If the "Second Square" is the inner cube, that means that, to surround it, you have to "double the cube." In other words, you have to build another altar around that one. Then you get all of the sweet "gum," the ambrosia inside. This, I think, is what Cain was saying is the game that God is playing with the archons of the underworld.

If this is true, then perhaps it sheds new light on some of the most baffling Masonic symbols. There has never been any agreement about what the letter "G" means in the center of the Masonic icon of the square and compass. It has been suggested that it stands for "God" or "geometry." But let us just take the letter "A" to be implied by the shape of the square and compass put together. Add the sound of the letter A to the sound of the letter G and you get the same phonetic sounds that you get when you pronounce the word "agei." The Masonic "G" could be seen as an emblem of the agei formed upon the "Second Square." The latter could itself be implied by the Masonic "square" symbol (based on the "square," a tool used by stonemasons and architects). The presence of the compass tool announces the Masonic plot to "encompass" it- surrounding the Second Square to claim the agei.

On Masonic tracing boards, the symbol of the square and compass, along with the G (or often, in its place, the All-Seeing Eye) is frequently shown in the center of the "Royal Arch," just beneath the keystone, flanked by the two pillars of the temple. This demonstrates the "work" they are involved in, which they blatantly represent as the rebuilding of the Temple in Jerusalem. The Masons are trying to build their own cube around the white cube. They want to form an artificial temple around the real temple, which, as St. John said, is God himself (the New Jerusalem having no temple other than him).

In the Catholic Eucharist rite, once the Holy Spirit is placed inside of the wafer, as I said before, it is put into a vessel called a "tabernacle." If it needs to be transported elsewhere, such as to the home of someone who cannot attend church, then it is placed inside of a small box called a "pyx." The word is Latin, and it is actually the origin of the English word "box." In fact, the term "jack-in-the-box" was originally a derogatory term used by non-Catholics to refer to the host inside of a tabernacle or pyx ("jack" being a slang term for a spirit or a demon).

When ceremonial magicians place a spirit inside of an enclosure, whether it's a magic circle, or a box, or a bottle for a genie, the purpose is always to control it. Similarly, Catholic priests who had been converted to Satanism would try to control the Holy Spirit in the transubstantiated host (the wafer) and use its power as their own. According to Sir James Frazer in *The Golden Bough*, this secret, evil black mass was called "Mass of the Holy Spirit." Recall how Baphomet told us that Saunière got rich by transmuting base metals into gold through the agency of "GOD."

This principal of controlling the power of God by surrounding and capturing him is illustrated in chess. Manly P. Hall, in his *Encyclopedic Outline of Masonic, Hermetic, Qabalistic, and Rosicrucian Symbolical Philosophy*, discussed the esoteric side of the game. He wrote that the pawns represent "the eight parts of the soul," and that the king is "spirit." He remarked:

...The king, being spirit, cannot be captured, but loses the battle when so surrounded that it cannot escape.

Even so, the word "checkmate" is said to come from a mixture of the Persian "shah" ("king") and the Arabic "mat" ("dead"). When the words are put together, the phrase is thought to mean "the king is dead." This implies that he is as good as dead even if you don't actually finish him off as part of the game. In Shatranj, a Persian variant of chess and Chaturanga, the game is over when all of the pieces on one side except for the king are captured. But remember, Cain told us that in Ageio, the white side always wins, and kills the black king anyway, no matter what.

As for our own dark army - the membership of the Ordo Lapsit Exillis and the Dragon Court - most of our guiding lights have passed. Prince Nicholas de Vere von Drakenberg died in February of 2013, seemingly of a heart attack. When the event first occurred, I received a frantic phone call from his secretary, claiming that Nick's fiancé had just called to report that she had found him murdered. The scene was described as that of a struggle. Supposedly, he was lying naked on the kitchen floor, with strange symbols carved into his flesh, surrounded by broken dishes.

Later, the fiancé corrected the record. She said that the part about the bloody symbols on his body was actually just a detail of an ominous premonitory dream about his death that she had experienced a couple of weeks earlier. However, the secretary had already gone on a radio program to announce to the world that De Vere was murdered in a Masonic conspiracy directed by the House of Windsor!

Typical Dragon Court internet drama ensued, with those closest to him all denouncing each other publicly and making bizarre accusations. There are of course, now, dozens of copycat Dragon Courts directed by former members of Nick's group, all claiming to be continuing the tradition that he was steward of. I haven't paid attention to any of them.

Nicholas was aware of the prognostications about him 'and the future of Drakenberg that had come to me under the influence of Baphomet. He knew I had been told via the Ouija board that he was destined to be the Anti-Christ, and that he would somehow gain access to an island where we could establish Drakenberg. He knew that I had channeled information, written in the unpublished *Strange Service* manual, stating that he would be sacrificed at the coronation ceremony, and possessed by the spirit of Baphomet.

He had contacted Dragon Court members in the state of Washington and engaged them in trying to find a suitable location to have this ceremony. Several of these members expressed alarm and concern that he seemed to be outwardly attempting to get someone to willingly murder him as part of a ritual. Of course, they wanted no part of it.

Clearly, De Vere took these "prophecies," as he referred to them, very seriously. While to me, he spoke about them as though they were silly and meaningless, behind my back he was sharing the transcripts and other documents I provided him with other members, trying to get them to agree to work with him to make these predictions come true. But when it came to the topic of ritual human sacrifice, none of his courtiers, as far as I am aware, were interested in participating.

This was actually the fifth major death to occur in connection with the Dragon Court since I became involved in 1999. I mentioned previously that his previous webmaster, who had a falling out with Nick and began using the Court's own website against us, died of his brain tumor shortly after getting involved in an online spat with me and Brian. Within a year of this happening, the next person who took control of the Dragon Court website (a disgruntled former fan of Nicholas de Vere) also died suddenly, of a heart attack. He was in his early fifties. The editor of De Vere's book *The Dragon Legacy* died unexpectedly as well. Most notably, Laurence Gardner, his rival, whom he claimed had plagiarized him, also died.

In March of 2012, I discovered the body of Brian Albert in one of the closets in our home in Vancouver, Washington. He had killed himself with carbon monoxide gas. We had been having marital problems, after ten years of marriage and over twenty years of friendship. It was the most devastating loss and traumatic experience that I have ever had to bear.

I miss him every day. He was irreplaceable in so many ways. Every time I make a major new discovery in my research, I wonder what he would have thought, and about all of the great ideas that he would have contributed. I hope that he is happy now, wherever he is.

Incidentally, I have now been a student of the Invisible College for thirteen years. According to Plutarch's description, I have completed my period of servitude to the headmaster of the school. I have paid my tuition. I am now eligible to decide whether I want to return to the land of the living, or stay and continue my education. Take that to mean what you will.

In closing, I would like to express my profound appreciation for all of the Legionnaires, Quartermasters, and Navigators of the Ordo Lapsit Exillis, as well as to all of the many donors, fans and other contributors who have helped us along the way - even the apostates and the enemies. I am sure we all recall the earnest spirit of selfless giving, and of the daring pursuit of knowledge, in which we each joined this quest together. I am equally sure that this intention will be taken into consideration when our souls are weighed in the balance at the End.

Stipendia enim peccati mors gratia autem Dei vita aeterna in Christo Iesu Domino nostro.

- Romans 6:23

www.ingramcontent.com/pod-product-compliance
Lightning Source LLC
Chambersburg PA
CBHW080913190726
48294CB00009B/2066
* 9 7 8 1 9 6 2 3 1 2 2 0 2 *